CW01512511

TAOISM

THE FUNDAMENTAL BOOKS

R. Medeiros

2021

Taoism
THE FUNDAMENTAL BOOKS

BY

R. MEDEIROS

EDITION
1st

Title:

TAOISM: THE FUNDAMENTAL BOOKS

Authors:

R. Medeiros; Laozi; Liezi; Zhuangzi

This work was edited by:

R. Medeiros

1ˢᵗ edition

Translators:

James Legge; Herbert A. Giles; Lionel Giles

Cover:

R. Medeiros

Acknowledgment:

Dr. Neuza Mazzeo

Contents.

Translators

James Legge (1815 – 1897) was a Scottish sinologist who translated many of Chinese classical texts. He served as a representative of the London Missionary Society in Hong Kong and managed to be the first Professor of Chinese at Oxford University, where he taught for decades.

Herbert Allen Giles (1845 – 1935) was an English sinologist who not only translated many Chinese books, but stablished a Chinese romanisation system after the Mandarin Chinese romanisation system, Giles' system would come to be known as Wade-Giles system. Herbert Giles also served for decades as professor of Chinese at the University of Cambridge.

Lionel Giles (1875 – 1958) was an English sinologist who completely translated The Art of War to English for the first time. Previous translations had serious problems, according Giles, "Omissions were frequent; hard passages were willfully distorted or slurred over. Such offenses are less pardonable. They would not be tolerated in any edition of a Latin or Greek classic, and a similar standard of honesty ought to be insisted upon in translations from Chinese". Lionel Giles was the son of the great Herbert A. Giles.

Introduction

Even if they don't know that they know, Western people are used to some Taoist concepts:

Feng Shui is very popular in the West, and has its origins in Taoism, as a practice to align the Qi of the environment – Qi, which is also a concept present in Taoism that became popular in the West due to Japanese cartoons.

> The goal of feng-shui, or terrestrial divination, is to discover how energy flows in the land and to live in harmony with it. The oldest form of divination in Taoist practice, it cultivates a sensitivity to the land and advocates a philosophy of living with nature, rather than against it.
>
> – Eva Wong, Taoism: An Essential Guide, 1997

The widely known martial art of Tai Chi Chuan was created by the legendary Taoist Zhang Sanfeng in the Middle Ages.

The universally known concept of Yin-Yang is present in Taoist philosophy. In the chapter 42 of Tao Te Ching, for example, we can see a mention of the Yin-Yang:

> All things leave behind them the Obscurity **[yin]** out of which they have come, and go forward to embrace the Brightness **[yang]** into which they have emerged [...]

An interesting thing about Chinese philosophies is the high level of syncretism. Yin-Yang, although present in Chinese philosophy, is a concept also present in other Chinese philosophies. Confucius, for example, absorbs several elements of Taoism, such as wu-wei:

> The sort of effortless ease and unselfconsciousness that characterizes these Daoist accounts also plays a central role in early Confucianism.
>
> – Edward Slingerland, Trying Not to Try, 2014

Although each gives a different guise to the concept – even within the Taoist philosophy, as we will see ahead – the influence of one on the other is clear. Zen Buddhism, for example, which is also well known in the West, has been heavily influenced by Taoism in its religious practice and philosophy.

Taoism itself was influenced by the Chinese shamanism that preceded it, and by other areas that transformed Taoism, hitherto philosophical, into a religion.

The change in Taoism was such that today its tradition is divided into two main branches: philosophical Taoism (Tao Chia) and religious Taoism (Tao Chiao).

Tao Chiao (Daojiao)

The Religious Taoism began its development around 300 CE, or even before if we look through a broader view. Although it tends to be a decentralized religion, without a world-wide known leader like Pope or Dalai Lama, the many branches of the Religious Taoism share beliefs, such as the presence of several types of supernatural beings capable of interacting with humans like deities, ghosts, and ancestral spirits are among them.

Deities are typically benevolent and on the side of righteousness. Ghosts, on the other hand, are dangerous spirits of the departed who must be appeased through offerings, especially during the Chinese Ghost Festival. Ancestors are also spirits of the departed, but they differ from ghosts in that they have descendants who honor them with household rituals.

The millenary tradition of Taoism expanded to many different systems. It goes from Cerimonial Taoism, which aims to honor the sacred powers with ceremonies, to Internal-Alchemical Taoism, Divinational Taoism (which the popular Feng Shui is part of), and even Magical Taoism.

Tao Chia (Daojia)

Or Philosophical taoism. Although it is commonly related to the work of the sages in the classical period of Taoism (20 BCE–600 CE) such as Lao Tzŭ, Lieh Tzŭ, and Chuang Tzŭ, which are the core of Taoism, Tao Chia does not refer to a specific Taoist school, period, or group of sages. Rather, it is related to the philosophical aspects of Taoism such as wu-wei, tzu-jan, te, and tao.

This book specifically brings the three fundamental works of philosophical Taoism: Tao Te Ching, Lieh Tzŭ, and Chuang Tzŭ. These three books will provide all the necessary knowledge to understand Taoist philosophical thought, with the addition of the comments of the great sinologists Hebert A. Giles and his son Lionel in the last two works to help and contextualize the reader.

Western Enlightenment

Although many people in the West are unaware of it, Chinese thought has impacted Western thought through the influence of its philosophers.

The cultural exchange between Europe and Asia has always been remarkable, especially with India and the Near East, it is true, but the cultural impact that Chinese thought had on European thinkers in the 18th century is remarkable. A period that is sometimes called "sinomania".

We can say that the first formal exchange took place with the arrival of the Jesuits in China in the 16th century. The first Jesuit to try to establish a relationship with China was Saint Francis Xavier (1506 – 1552), although he died without being successful in his mission.

But that did not stop the Jesuits from continuing their sacred mission. Some Jesuits were more successful later, their work on China influenced some thinkers like the philosopher Leibniz (1646 – 1716), who maintained a frequent exchange of correspondence with the Jesuits on mission in China. But the advance in the 17th century was still somewhat close to what would come in the next century.

The monarch of France, King Louis XIV, the Sun King (1638 – 1715), sent French Jesuits to China that would have a major impact on European thought, contributing, ironically, to thoughts that would help to dethrone their successors in the near future.

Voltaire, Montesquieu, the Enlightenment Age as a whole saw itself in dialogue with this new knowledge coming from China through the Jesuits, but one of the influences that would have the greatest impact in Europe would be from a name that is little known today: the physiocrat François Quesnay (1694 – 1774).

> "China had a much wider and deeper impact on eighteenth-century Europe through the philosophical and political thought of the philosophes of the Enlightenment. Jesuit reports of the Qing Dynasty, then at the zenith of its dynastic cycle, told of a vast, prosperous Chinese empire run by competitively selected scholar bureaucrats on a secular

basis. Here, it seemed, was an advanced society uncluttered by privileges of birth and ecclesiastical institutions, being instead organized along rational lines. Equally important to the philosophes was the philosophical foundations of Chinese thought: the concept of a general, spontaneous order, found not only in Taoism but also in official Confucianism. Just as China provided a critically important alternative model of society to set against the ancien regime of royalty, clergy and nobility, so the Chinese concept of a spontaneous "natural order" provided a critical ideological weapon and an alternative source of legitimacy to set against the theological buttresses of that regime. In the political sphere, this emerges clearly in those archetypal Enlightenment documents: the French Universal Declaration of the Rights of Man and the American Declaration of Independence with their references to "Nature" and "Nature's God."

The central role of the concept of natural order in the birth of modern economics emerges in the very name of its first school: "Physiocracy" is derived from the Greek "physis" meaning "nature" and "kratis" meaning "power." Some important Physiocratic writings were entitled: Physiocratie, oue constitution naturelle du government le plus avantageux au genre humain [Physiocracy, or the natural constitution of the government most advantageous to mankind] published by Du Pont de Nemours in 1767, Le droit naturel [Natural law] published by Quesnay in 1765 and L'ordre naturel et essentiel des Societes Politiques [The natural and essential order of political societies] published by Mercier de la Riviere in 1767. The Physiocrats believed that civil societies mirror the natural order and are characterized by natural laws which can be studied to provide the foundation for the proper administration of the country. Through the agency of the Physiocrats, Chinese concepts were to be at the root of the development of political economy."

– LESLIE YOUNG, PACIFIC ECONOMIC REVIEW, 1: 2, PP. 137–145, 1996

Physiocrats today are little known, but they have had a huge influence on their time. The French term laissez-faire, now widely known in political theory, originates from the Physiocratic School, the term being coined by the economist Vincent de Gournay (1712–1759) from the reading of the works of François Quesnay:

"The wise ruler knows that, at a certain level of operating, the best policy is in a sense to do nothing, a policy summed up in the central philosophical concept of wu-wei which is translated into French as

> laissez-faire. The historian Basil Guy comments that 'Both lawmaker and law had to recognize the principles of…natural order, and in so doing conform to the Chinese ideal of wu-wei, which has ever inspired their theories of government' (1963:350). It was this principle which also inspired Quesnay […]"

– J.J.CLARKE, ORIENTAL ENLIGHTENMENT, 1997

It is not randomic that the great sociologist Max Weber translated wu-wei as laissez-faire in his book The Religion of China: Confucionism and Taoism (1915).

The idea of natural order and laissez-faire that French physiocrats brought from Chinese philosophy would find shelter in Adam Smith, who cultivated the idea, amalgamated with his theories, and developed it until the elaboration of the concept of the invisible hand.

> "Vincent de Gournay was a precursor to the physiocrats and one of the main thinkers who inspired Adam Smith. […] His favorite phrase was 'Laissez faire, laissez passer,' and he is credited with being the originator of the term laissez-faire. Unlike the French physiocrats who argued for the importance of agriculture, de Gournay regarded the progress of industry and commerce as well as agriculture to all be sources of wealth for the nation. Adam Smith wanted to dedicate The Wealth of Nations to the famous French economist, François Quesnay […]"

– INA BAGHDIANTZ MCCABE, ORIENTALISM IN EARLY MODERN
FRANCE, 2008

From Adam Smith, the influence of these ideas would extend to the whole Europe, from the influence on economists like David Ricardo and F.A. Hayek to political events like the Anti-Corn Law League and the British Free Trade Empire

Wu-wei

The concept of wu-wei, which so influenced certain European thinkers in the Age of Enlightenment, is sometimes misinterpreted if not investigated in depth. Its literal translation is "non-action", and it appears in the Tao Te Ching as, for example:

Chapter 3:

> When there is this abstinence from action **[wu-wei]**, good order is universal.

Chapter 37:

> The Tao in its regular course does nothing (for the sake of doing it) **[wu-wei]**, and so there is nothing which it does not do.

Chapter 43:

> I know hereby what advantage belongs to doing nothing (with a purpose) **[wu-wei]**. There are few in the world who attain to the teaching without words, and the advantage arising from non-action **[wu-wei]**.

Chapter 57:

> Therefore a sage has said, 'I will do nothing (of purpose) **[wu-wei]**, and the people will be transformed of themselves;

And in the Chuang Tzŭ as:

Chapter XI. On Letting Alone:

> By means of inaction **[wu-wei]** he will be able to adapt himself to the natural conditions of existence. And so it is that he who respects the State as his own body is fit to support it, and he who loves the State as his own body, is fit to govern it.
>
> And if I can refrain from injuring my internal economy, and from taxing my powers of sight and hearing, sitting like a corpse while my dragon-power is manifested around, in profound silence while my thunder-voice resounds, the powers of heaven responding to every phase of my will, as under the yielding influence of inaction **[wu-wei]** all things are brought to maturity and thrive,—what leisure then have I to set about governing the world?

This can lead many people to think that wu-wei is literally no action, abscence of action. But, far from it, wu-wei is about acting non-coercively, acting non-forcefully.

Understanding wu-wei is so important that it becomes almost obligatory for commentators of Taoist works to talk about its meaning to better guide their readers:

> One of the most famous ideas of Taoism, and also the source of a lot of misunderstanding, is wu-wei. This word, used in describing the sage

and often translated as nonaction, gives the impression that the Taoist sages "did nothing." This is inaccurate, and could not be used to describe all Taoists. Wu-wei had different meanings for different Taoist philosophers. The wu-wei of the Tao-te ching is different from the wu-wei of Chuang-tzu, which is different again from the wu-wei of Lieh-tzu.

Wu-wei in the Tao-te ching is "going with the principles of the Tao," and the path of the Tao is a benevolent one. Thus, wu-wei in the Tao-te ching is not "doing nothing"; it is not even the noninterference advocated in the Chuang-tzu. In the Tao-te ching, wu-wei means not using force. The sagely ruler who cares for his subjects in a nonintrusive way also practices wu-wei. Far from doing nothing, the Taoist sage of the Tao-te ching is an active member of society and is fit to be a king.

– EVA WONG, TAOISM: AN ESSENTIAL GUIDE, 1997

Not only do Taoist authors – Lao Tzŭ, Chuang Tzŭ... – use the term with a different meaning in their works, as Eva Wong explains above, but other Chinese philosophies also use the term and end up contributing to the misunderstanding:

In order to taste the delicious meal Lao-tzu provided for humanity, we need to understand the core tenet of almost all Chinese philosophical systems. This foundational pillar of Chinese philosophy is found within the classics of Eastern thought, notably the Tao Te Ching, the Analects of Confucius, the Chuang-tzu, attributed to Chuang-tzu, and even the Indian text the Bhagavad Gita.

The core pillar of these classics, in China especially, is believed to originate from Lao-tzu, and it is his essential teaching that is veiled within the mystery of the Chinese word wu-wei, which is the core of Chinese philosophy and a predominant principle in Eastern thought. This word is shrouded in misinterpretation. The main confusion arises from the Confucian translation of wei-wu-wei, which literally means "doing nondoing." This interpretation is built on Confucius's philosophy of trying to install the eternal Tao and its virtue into our character as if it were some external agency. This is the completely opposite perspective to Lao-tzu's teaching of naturalness. Translated into English, wu-wei means "nondoing," "nonaction," or "effortless action." These translations are literally correct and lead us to the intuitive and ultimate psychological experience of wu-wei. This effortless psychological experience means "not forcing" or "allowing," a state of "intelligent spontaneity".

– JASON GREGORY, EFFORTLESS LIVING, 2018

Wu-wei covers every situation in your life. From friendship, love and family relationships, to how a ruler should act. In fact, most of the Tao Te Ching is precisely about government. When the term is used for the latter, wu-wei should be understood as

The political principle of refraining from using political authority to impose control on man's natural condition.

– ROGER AMES, WU-WEI IN "THE ART OF RULERSHIP" CHAPTER OF HUAI NAN TZU: ITS SOURCES AND PHILOSOPHICAL ORIENTA- TION, 1981

The principle of laissez-faire that Westerners are so used to did not derive from wu-wei for nothing, but it should be remembered that, unlike laissez-faire, which is commonly associated only with the political principle, wu-wei goes far beyond politics, it encompasses your relationship with the world as a whole, your relationship with your friend, spouse, parent, child, sibling, work, studies, with the environment, and even with yourself.

Tzu-jan (Ziran)

When it was said that the concept of a spontaneous "natural order" in Chinese philosophy influenced the Physiocrats, the mentioned concept is related to tzu-jan, which is the Chinese for "by itself" and used to refer to something spontaneous, that happens by itself, not by external intervention. In this sense, a natural state.

THE NATURALNESS OF TZU-JAN

To seek refuge from these unnatural systems, we need to understand nature itself. The organic pattern of the individual (li) is our innate nature driven by te, virtue. Nature, then, has no relationship to force, control, or power. The order and pattern of nature is not a forced order, as nature is not bound by external influence or control. The Taoist term for nature is the Chinese tzu-jan, which means that which is spontaneously of itself. When a natural organism is in harmony with all life, it grows of itself spontaneously. Tzu-jan can only arise of itself without ex-ternal compulsion.

– JASON GREGORY, EFFORTLESS LIVING, 2018

Tzu-jan's relationship with wu-wei is therefore quite intimate. It can be understood that tzu-jan is the state that is established by itself spontaneously when wu-wei is practiced. By reading some appearances of tzu-jan in the three main books of Taoism, the concept can be better assimilated:

Tao Te Ching – Chapter 17:

> How irresolute did those earliest rulers appear, showing by their reti-cence the importance which they set upon their words! Their work was done and their undertakings were successful, while the people all said, 'It happened spontaneously **[tzu-jan]**!'

Tao Te Ching – Chapter 23:

> Abstaining from speech marks him who is obeying the spontaneity of his nature **[tzu-jan]**. A violent wind does not last for a whole morn-ing; a sudden rain does not last for the whole day.

Tao Te Ching – Chapter 51:

> All things are produced by the Tao, and nourished by its outflowing operation. They receive their forms according to the nature of each, and are completed according to the circumstances of their condition. There-fore all things without exception honour the Tao, and exalt its outflowing operation.
>
> This honouring of the Tao and exalting of its operation is not the result of any ordination, but always a spontaneous tribute **[tzu-jan]**.

Tao Te Ching – Chapter 64:

> Therefore the sage desires what other men do not desire, and does not prize things difficult to get; he learns what other men do not learn, and turns back to what the multitude of men have passed by. Thus he helps the natural development **[tzu-jan]** of all things, and does not dare to act with an ulterior purpose of his own.

Lieh Tzŭ – Book II – The Yellow Emperor:

> Then the Yellow Emperor sighed heavily and said: 'My fault is want of moderation. The misery I suffer comes from over-attention to my

own self, and the troubles of the Empire from over-regulation in everything.' Thereupon, he threw up all his schemes, abandoned his ancestral palace, dismissed his attendants, removed all the hanging bells, cut down the delicacies of his cuisine, and retired to live at leisure in private apartments attached to the Court. There he fasted in heart, and brought his body under control.

For three months he abstained from personal intervention in government. Then he fell asleep in the daytime, and dreamed that he made a journey to the kingdom of Hua-hsŭ, situated I know not how many tens of thousands of miles distant from the Ch'i State. It was beyond the reach of ship or vehicle or any mortal foot. Only the soul could travel so far.

This kingdom was without head or ruler; it simply went on of itself [tzu-jan]. Its people were without desires or cravings; they simply followed their natural instincts **[tzu-jan]**.

Chuang Tzŭ – Chapter VII. How to Govern:

[…] the Sage replied, "Resolve your mental energy into abstraction, your physical energy into inaction. Allow yourself to fall in with the natural order of phenomena **[tzu-jan]**, without admitting the element of self, —and the empire will be governed."

As Taoism deals with universal issues, many commentators argue about the political consequence of the concept of tzu-jan:

Superficially, this perspective may be incorrectly perceived as "anarchy." But there is a major difference: anarchists' motives are driven by what they oppose. On the other hand, the sages who understand tzu-jan just follow their own nature without any concern for institutional or organizational power, because they are content to let such things run their course. An anarchist is still distracted by external influences. So if the world is thrown into anarchy, then the motive destroys the project. Nature is as it is and can have no motive, nor is it a project to embark upon. Tao can never be induced, as its principle happens spontaneously of itself—tzu-jan. Anarchy is an attempt to induce Tao so as to bring about a real order through an intellectual, artificial decision to abandon the ways of society.

Though anarchy in some sense is a step in the right direction, it is not a suitable method for liberating the world, because it cannot avoid having an agenda. The Russian evolutionary theorist Peter Kropotkin understood this subtle difference between anarchy and tzu-jan. Kropotkin postulated that if we were to leave people alone to follow their own nature, a real social order and true government would emerge out of the current system.

– JASON GREGORY, EFFORTLESS LIVING, 2018

Influenced by Adam Smith, F.A. Hayek is perhaps the intellectual who better developed the concept of spontaneous order in the West – a concept that has been so familiar in the East for a long time. The Austrian economist divides the order into two types: taxis and kosmos, that is, the "made order" that can be referred to as "an exogenous order, an arrangement, a construction, an artificial order", and the "grown order" that can be referred to as "a self-generating or endogenous order, most conveniently described as a spontaneous order in English", that is, the order that grows by itself. What Hayek describes as taxis can be understood as ren zhao (man-made, artificial) in Chinese philosophy, while kosmos is related to tzu-jan.

Te (De)

Generally translated as virtue, Te may have a greater variety of meaning than just what is common sense understood by the term virtue nowadays, depending on the context. The meaning can vary from, in fact, "virtue" to the "strength", the "power", the "manifestation", the "aspect", the "quality" of Tao. Some appearances of Te in Tao Te Ching:

Tao Te Ching – Chapter 10:

> The Tao produces all things and nourishes them; it produces them and does not claim them as its own; it does all, and yet does not boast of it; it presides over all, and yet does not control them. This is what is called 'The mysterious Quality' of the Tao **[Te]**.

Tao Te Ching – Chapter 38:

> Those who possessed in highest degree the attributes of the Tao **[Te]** did not seek to show them **[Te]**, and therefore they possessed them **[Te]** in fullest measure. Those who possessed in a lower degree those attributes **[Te]** sought how not to lose them **[Te]**, and therefore they did not possess them **[Te]** in fullest measure.

Tao Te Ching – Chapter 51:

> All things are produced by the Tao, and nourished by its outflowing operation **[Te]**. They receive their forms according to the nature of

each, and are completed according to the circumstances of their condition. Therefore all things without exception honour the Tao, and exalt its outflowing operation **[Te]**.

In their work to give the philosophical insight of Tao Te Ching, that is how Roger T. Ames and David L. Hall descibre the application of Te in the politics:

> When located within the political realm, de describes the most appropriate relationship between a ruler and the people. In this context, de has a range of meaning that reflects the priority of the situation over agency, thus characterizing both the giving and the getting. That is, de is both the "beneficence" extended to the people in response to their worth, and the "gratitude" expressed by the people in response to the largesse of a worthy ruler. De encompasses both participating agency and its effects. It is the character or the ethos of the polity. On this basis, we might suggest "virtuality" in the archaic sense of the word as "having inherent virtue or power to produce effects" as another possible translation of de.
>
> – ROGER T. AMES AND DAVID L. HALL, DAODEJING: MAKING THIS LIFE SIGNIFICANT, A PHILOSOPHICAL TRANSLATION, 2003

Tao (Dao)

Wu-wei is the action aligned with Tao, tzu-jan is the state in harmony with Tao, Te is the quality of Tao. But after all, what is the central concept of Taoism, Tao? According to Eva Wong:

> The Tao is the source of life of all things. It is nameless, invisible, and ungraspable by normal modes of perception. It is boundless and cannot be exhausted, although all things depend on it for existence. Hidden beneath transition and change, the Tao is the permanent underlying reality. These ideas will become the center of all future Taoist thinking.
>
> Although the Tao is the source of all life, it is not a deity or spirit. This is quite different from the shaman's animistic view of the universe. In the Tao-te ching, the sky, the earth, rivers, and mountains are part of a larger and unified power, known as Tao, which is an impersonal and unnamed force behind the workings of the universe.
>
> However, in the Tao-te ching, this unnamed and unnameable power is not entirely neutral; it is benevolent: "The Celestial Way is to benefit others and not to cause harm" (chapter 81, Tao-te ching); and since

the "Celestial Way follows the Way of the Tao" (chapter 25, Tao-te ching), we can assume that in the Tao-te ching, the Tao is a benevolent force.

– EVA WONG, TAOISM: AN ESSENTIAL GUIDE, 1997

Tao Te Ching:

Probably the most important book in Chinese philosophy alongside Confucian Analects, Tao Te Ching, popularly translated as Book of the Way and Virtue, written around the 6th century BC by Lao Tzǔ, is the fundamental book of of Taoism. Although it has only 81 brief chapters, it ranges from personal relationships to politics. This is the the second most translated book in the world, after the Bible only. The translation presented here is the translation of early sinologist James Legge.

The Book of Lieh Tzǔ:

The third book from Taoism in relevance, behind Tao Te Ching and Chuang Tzǔ only, often highlighted by its practical aspects, Lieh Tzǔ is both entertaining and enlightening, giving the reader positive reflections on life and death. The book is believed to have been compiled around the 4th century BC. The translation presented here is made by the sinologist Lionel Giles, son of the great sinologist Herbert A. Giles, creator of the Wade-Giles system.

Chuang Tzǔ:

The most important Taoist book after Tao Te Ching, Chuang Tzǔ, written around the 3rd century BC, presents us with profound reflections, from our own conscience, as in the case of the butterfly dream, to politics, which is extensively discussed by the author. The translation presented here is made by the sinologist Herbert Allen Giles.

Bibliography

Hebert A. Giles, Chuang Tzǔ: Mystic, Moralist, and Social Reformer (London: Bernard Quaritch, 1889)

James Legge, Tao Te Ching: The Book of the Way and of Virtue (London: Henry Frowde, 1891)

Lionel Giles, Taoist Teachings from the Book of Lieh Tzǔ (New York: E. P. Dutton and Company, 1912)

Max Weber, The Religion of China: Confucionism and Taoism (Glencoe: The Free Press, 1951)

Roger T. Ames, Wu-wei in "The Art of Rulership" Chapter of Huai Nan Tzu: Its Sources and Philosophical Orientation, University of Hawai'i Press Philosophy, East and West, Vol. 31, No. 2 (Apr., 1981), pp. 193-213

Leslie Young, The Tao Of Markets: Sima Qian and the Invisible Hand, Pacific Economic Review, 1: 2, pp. 137–145, 1996

J. J. Clarke, Oriental Enlightenment: The Encounter Between Asian and Western Thought (New York: Routledge, 1997)

F. A. Hayek. Law, Legislation and Liberty: A New Statement of the Liberal Principles of Justice and Political Economy (New York: Routledge, 1998)

Roger T. Ames and David L. Hall, Daodejing: Making This Life Significant, a Philosophical Translation (New York: Bellantine Books, 2003)

Christian Gerlach, Wu-Wei In Europe: A Study of Eurasian Economic Thought, 2004

Ina Baghdiantz McCabe, Orientalism in Early Modern France: Eurasian Trade, Exoticism, and the Ancien Régime (Berg: Oxford, 2008)

Eva Wong, Taoism: An Essential Guide (Boston: Shambhala, 2011)

Edward Slingerland, Trying Not to Try: The Art and Science of Spontaneity (New York: Crown Publishing Group, 2014)

Jason Gregory, Effortless Living: Wu-wei and the Spontaneous State of Natural Harmony (Rochester: Inner Traditions: 2018)

Tao Te Ching

The Book of the Way and of Virtue

Lao Tzŭ

1891

Tao Ching.

1

The Tao that can be described is not the enduring and unchanging Tao. The name that can be named is not the enduring and unchanging name.

(Conceived of as) having no name, it is the Originator of heaven and earth; (conceived of as) having a name, it is the Mother of all things.

Always without desire we must be found,

If its deep mystery we would sound; But if desire always within us be, Its outer fringe is all that we shall see.

Under these two aspects, it is really the same; but as development takes place, it receives the different names. Together we call them the Mystery. Where the Mystery is the deepest is the gate of all that is subtle and wonderful.

2

All in the world know the beauty of the beautiful, and in doing this they have (the idea of) what ugliness is; they all know the skill of the skilful, and in doing this they have (the idea of) what the want of skill is.

So it is that existence and non-existence give birth the one to (the idea of) the other; that difficulty and ease produce the one (the idea of) the other; that length and shortness fashion out the one the figure of the other; that (the ideas of) height and lowness arise from the contrast of the one with the other; that the musical notes and tones become harmonious through the relation of one with another; and that being before and behind give the idea of one following another.

Therefore the sage manages affairs without doing anything, and conveys his instructions without the use of speech.

All things spring up, and there is not one which declines to show itself; they grow, and there is no claim made for their ownership; they go through their processes, and there is no expectation (of a reward for the results). The work is accomplished, and there is no resting in it (as an achievement).

The work is done, but how no one can see; 'Tis this that makes the power not cease to be.

3

Not to value and employ men of superior ability is the way to keep the people from rivalry among themselves; not to prize articles which are difficult to procure is the way to keep them from becoming thieves; not to show them what is likely to excite their desires is the way to keep their minds from disorder.

Therefore the sage, in the exercise of his government, empties their minds, fills their bellies, weakens their wills, and strengthens their bones.

He constantly (tries to) keep them without knowledge and without desire, and where there are those who have knowledge, to keep them from presuming to act (on it). When there is this abstinence from action, good order is universal.

4

The Tao is (like) the emptiness of a vessel; and in our employment of it we must be on our guard against all fulness. How deep and unfathomable it is, as if it were the Honoured Ancestor of all things!

We should blunt our sharp points, and unravel the complications of things; we should attemper our brightness, and bring ourselves into agreement with the obscurity of others. How pure and still the Tao is, as if it would ever so continue!

I do not know whose son it is. It might appear to have been before God.

5

Heaven and earth do not act from (the impulse of) any wish to be benevolent; they deal with all things as the dogs of grass are dealt with. The sages do not act from (any wish to be) benevolent; they deal with the people as the dogs of grass are dealt with.

May not the space between heaven and earth be compared to a bellows?

'Tis emptied, yet it loses not its power;

'Tis moved again, and sends forth air the more. Much speech to swift exhaustion lead we see; Your inner being guard, and keep it free.

6

The valley spirit dies not, aye the same; The female mystery thus do we name.

Its gate, from which at first they issued forth,

Is called the root from which grew heaven and earth. Long and unbroken does its power remain, Used gently, and without the touch of pain.

7

Heaven is long-enduring and earth continues long. The reason why heaven and earth are able to endure and continue thus long is because they do not live of, or for, themselves. This is how they are able to continue and endure.

Therefore the sage puts his own person last, and yet it is found in the foremost place; he treats his person as if it were foreign to him, and yet that person is preserved. Is it not because he has no personal and private ends, that therefore such ends are realised?

8

The highest excellence is like (that of) water. The excellence of water appears in its benefiting all things, and in its occupying, without striving (to the contrary), the low place which all men dislike. Hence (its way) is near to (that of) the Tao.

The excellence of a residence is in (the suitability of) the place; that of the mind is in abysmal stillness; that of associations is in their being with the virtuous; that of government is in its securing good order; that of (the conduct of) affairs is in its ability; and that of (the initiation of) any movement is in its timeliness.

And when (one with the highest excellence) does not wrangle (about his low position), no one finds fault with him.

9

It is better to leave a vessel unfilled, than to attempt to carry it when it is full. If you keep feeling a point that has been sharpened, the point cannot long preserve its sharpness.

When gold and jade fill the hall, their possessor cannot keep them safe. When wealth and honours lead to arrogancy, this brings its evil on itself. When the work is done, and one's name is becoming distinguished, to withdraw into obscurity is the way of Heaven.

10

When the intelligent and animal souls are held together in one embrace, they can be kept from separating. When one gives undivided attention to the (vital) breath, and brings it to the utmost degree of pliancy, he can become as a (tender) babe. When he has cleansed away the most mysterious sights (of his imagination), he can become without a flaw.

In loving the people and ruling the state, cannot he proceed without any (purpose of) action? In the opening and shutting of his gates of heaven, cannot he do so as a female bird? While his intelligence reaches in every direction, cannot he (appear to) be without knowledge?

(The Tao) produces (all things) and nourishes them; it produces them and does not claim them as its own; it does all, and yet does not boast of it; it presides over all, and yet does not control them. This is what is called 'The mysterious Quality' (of the Tao).

11

The thirty spokes unite in the one nave; but it is on the empty space (for the axle), that the use of the wheel depends. Clay is fashioned into vessels; but it is on their empty hollowness, that their use depends. The door and windows are cut out (from the walls) to form an apartment; but it is on the empty space (within), that its use depends. Therefore, what has a (positive) existence serves for profitable adaptation, and what has not that for (actual) usefulness.

12

Colour's five hues from th' eyes their sight will take;

Music's five notes the ears as deaf can make;

The flavours five deprive the mouth of taste;

The chariot course, and the wild hunting waste

Make mad the mind; and objects rare and strange, Sought for, men's conduct will to evil change.

Therefore the sage seeks to satisfy (the craving of) the belly, and not the (insatiable longing of the) eyes. He puts from him the latter, and prefers to seek the former.

13

Favour and disgrace would seem equally to be feared; honour and great calamity, to be regarded as personal conditions (of the same kind).

What is meant by speaking thus of favour and disgrace? Disgrace is being in a low position (after the enjoyment of favour). The getting that (favour) leads to the apprehension (of losing it), and the losing it leads to the fear of (still greater calamity):--this is what is meant by saying that favour and disgrace would seem equally to be feared.

And what is meant by saying that honour and great calamity are to be (similarly) regarded as personal conditions? What makes me liable to great calamity is my having the body (which I call myself); if I had not the body, what great calamity could come to me?

Therefore he who would administer the kingdom, honouring it as he honours his own person, may be employed to govern it, and he who would administer it with the love which he bears to his own person may be entrusted with it.

14

We look at it, and we do not see it, and we name it 'the

Equable.' We listen to it, and we do not hear it, and we name it 'the Inaudible.' We try to grasp it, and do not get hold of it, and we name it 'the Subtle.' With these three qualities, it cannot be made the subject of description; and hence we blend them together and obtain The One.

Its upper part is not bright, and its lower part is not obscure. Ceaseless in its action, it yet cannot be named, and then it again returns and becomes nothing. This is called the Form of the Formless, and the Semblance of the Invisible; this is called the Fleeting and Indeterminable.

We meet it and do not see its Front; we follow it, and do not see its Back. When we can lay hold of the Tao of old to direct the things of the present day, and are able to know it as it was of old in the beginning, this is called (unwinding) the clue of Tao.

15

The skilful masters (of the Tao) in old times, with a subtle and exquisite penetration, comprehended its mysteries, and were deep (also) so as to elude men's knowledge. As they were thus beyond men's knowledge, I will make an effort to describe of what sort they appeared to be.

Shrinking looked they like those who wade through a stream in winter; irresolute like those who are afraid of all around them; grave like a guest (in awe of his host); evanescent like ice that is melting away; unpretentious like wood that has not been fashioned into anything; vacant like a valley, and dull like muddy water.

Who can (make) the muddy water (clear)? Let it be still, and it will gradually become clear. Who can secure the condition of rest? Let movement go on, and the condition of rest will gradually arise.

They who preserve this method of the Tao do not wish to be full (of themselves). It is through their not being full of themselves that they can afford to seem worn and not appear new and complete.

16

The (state of) vacancy should be brought to the utmost degree, and that of stillness guarded with unwearying vigour. All things alike go through their processes of activity, and (then) we see them return (to their original state). When things (in the vegetable world) have displayed their luxuriant growth, we see each of them return to its root. This returning to their root is what we call the state of stillness; and that stillness may be called a reporting that they have fulfilled their appointed end.

The report of that fulfilment is the regular, unchanging rule. To know that unchanging rule is to be intelligent; not to know it leads to wild movements and evil issues. The knowledge of that unchanging rule produces a (grand) capacity and forbearance, and that capacity and forbearance lead to a community (of feeling with all things). From this community of feeling comes a kingliness of character; and he who is king-like goes on to be heaven-like. In that likeness to heaven he possesses the Tao. Possessed of the Tao, he endures long; and to the end of his bodily life, is exempt from all danger of decay.

17

In the highest antiquity, the people did not know that there were their rulers. In the next age they loved them and praised them. In the next they feared them; in the next they despised them. Thus it was that when faith in the Tao was deficient in the rulers a want of faith in them ensued in the people.

How irresolute did those earliest rulers appear, showing by their reticence the importance which they set upon their words! Their work was done and their undertakings were successful, while the people all said, 'It happened spontaneously!'

18

When the Great Tao (Way or Method) ceased to be observed, benevolence and righteousness came into vogue. (Then) appeared wisdom and shrewdness, and there ensued great hypocrisy.

When harmony no longer prevailed throughout the six kinships, filial sons found their manifestation; when the states and clans fell into disorder, loyal ministers appeared.

19

If we could renounce our sageness and discard our wisdom, it would be better for the people a hundredfold. If we could renounce our benevolence and discard our righteousness, the people would again become filial and kindly. If we could renounce our artful contrivances and discard our (scheming for) gain, there would be no thieves nor robbers.

Those three methods (of government)

Thought olden ways in elegance did fail

And made these names their want of worth to veil; But simple views, and courses plain and true Would selfish ends and many lusts eschew.

20

When we renounce learning we have no troubles. The (ready) 'yes,' and (flattering) 'yea;'-Small is the difference they display.

But mark their issues, good and ill;-What space the gulf between shall fill?

What all men fear is indeed to be feared; but how wide and without end is the range of questions (asking to be discussed)!

The multitude of men look satisfied and pleased; as if enjoying a full banquet, as if mounted on a tower in spring. I alone seem listless and still, my desires having as yet given no indication of their presence. I am like an infant which has not yet smiled. I look dejected and forlorn, as if I had no home to go to. The multitude of men all have enough and to spare. I alone seem to have lost everything. My mind is that of a stupid man; I am in a state of chaos.

Ordinary men look bright and intelligent, while I alone seem to be benighted. They look full of discrimination, while I alone am dull and confused. I seem to be carried about as on the sea, drifting as if I had nowhere to rest. All men have their spheres of action, while I alone seem dull and incapable, like a rude borderer. (Thus) I alone am different from other men, but I value the nursing-mother (the Tao).

21

The grandest forms of active force From Tao come, their only source.

Who can of Tao the nature tell?

Our sight it flies, our touch as well.

Eluding sight, eluding touch,

The forms of things all in it crouch;

Eluding touch, eluding sight,

There are their semblances, all right. Profound it is, dark and obscure; Things' essences all there endure.

Those essences the truth enfold Of what, when seen, shall then be told.

Now it is so; 'twas so of old.

Its name--what passes not away;

So, in their beautiful array,

Things form and never know decay.

How know I that it is so with all the beauties of existing things? By this (nature of the Tao).

22

The partial becomes complete; the crooked, straight; the empty, full; the worn out, new. He whose (desires) are few gets them; he whose (desires) are many goes astray.

Therefore the sage holds in his embrace the one thing (of humility), and manifests it to all the world. He is free from self-display, and therefore he shines; from self-assertion, and therefore he is distinguished; from self-boasting, and therefore his merit is acknowledged; from selfcomplacency, and therefore he acquires superiority. It is because he is thus free from striving that therefore no one in the world is able to strive with him.

That saying of the ancients that 'the partial becomes complete' was not vainly spoken:--all real completion is comprehended under it.

23

Abstaining from speech marks him who is obeying the spontaneity of his nature. A violent wind does not last for a whole morning; a sudden rain does not last for the whole day. To whom is it that these two things are owing? To Heaven and Earth. If Heaven and Earth cannot make such spasmodic actings last long, how much less can man!

Therefore when one is making the Tao his business, those who are also pursuing it, agree with him in it, and those who are making the manifestation of its course their object agree with him in that; while even those who are failing in both these things agree with him where they fail.

Hence, those with whom he agrees as to the Tao have the happiness of attaining to it; those with whom he agrees as to its manifestation have the happiness of attaining to it; and those with whom he agrees in their failure have also the happiness of attaining (to the Tao). (But) when there is not faith sufficient (on his part), a want of faith (in him) ensues (on the part of the others).

24

He who stands on his tiptoes does not stand firm; he who stretches his legs does not walk (easily). (So), he who displays himself does not shine; he who asserts his own views is not distinguished; he who vaunts himself does not find his merit acknowledged; he who is self-conceited has no superiority allowed to him. Such conditions, viewed from the standpoint of the Tao, are like remnants of food, or a tumour on the body, which all dislike. Hence those who pursue (the course) of the Tao do not adopt and allow them.

25

There was something undefined and complete, coming into existence before Heaven and Earth. How still it was and formless, standing alone, and undergoing no change, reaching everywhere and in no danger (of being exhausted)! It may be regarded as the Mother of all things.

I do not know its name, and I give it the designation of the Tao (the Way or Course). Making an effort (further) to give it a name I call it The Great.

Great, it passes on (in constant flow). Passing on, it becomes remote. Having become remote, it returns. Therefore the Tao is great; Heaven is great; Earth is great; and the (sage) king is also great. In the universe there are four that are great, and the (sage) king is one of them.

Man takes his law from the Earth; the Earth takes its law from Heaven; Heaven takes its law from the Tao. The law of the Tao is its being what it is.

26

Gravity is the root of lightness; stillness, the ruler of movement.

Therefore a wise prince, marching the whole day, does not go far from his baggage waggons. Although he may have brilliant prospects to look at, he quietly remains (in his proper place), indifferent to them. How should the lord of a myriad chariots carry himself lightly before the kingdom? If he do act lightly, he has lost his root (of gravity); if he proceed to active movement, he will lose his throne.

27

The skilful traveller leaves no traces of his wheels or footsteps; the skilful speaker says nothing that can be found fault with or blamed; the skilful reckoner uses no tallies; the skilful closer needs no bolts or bars, while to open what he has shut will be impossible; the skilful binder uses no strings or knots, while to unloose what he has bound will be impossible. In the same way the sage is always skilful at saving men, and so he does not cast away any man; he is always skilful at saving things, and so he does not cast away anything. This is called 'Hiding the light of his procedure.'

Therefore the man of skill is a master (to be looked up to) by him who has not the skill; and he who has not the skill is the helper of (the reputation of) him who has the skill. If the one did not honour his master, and the other did not rejoice in his helper, an (observer), though intelligent, might greatly err about them. This is called 'The utmost degree of mystery.'

28

Who knows his manhood's strength,

Yet still his female feebleness maintains; As to one channel flow the many drains, All come to him, yea, all beneath the sky. Thus he the constant excellence retains; The simple child again, free from all stains.

Who knows how white attracts,

Yet always keeps himself within black's shade,

The pattern of humility displayed,

Displayed in view of all beneath the sky;

He in the unchanging excellence arrayed, Endless return to man's first state has made.

Who knows how glory shines,

Yet loves disgrace, nor e'er for it is pale;

Behold his presence in a spacious vale,

To which men come from all beneath the sky. The unchanging excellence completes its tale; The simple infant man in him we hail.

The unwrought material, when divided and distributed, forms vessels. The sage, when employed, becomes the Head of all the Officers (of government); and in his greatest regulations he employs no violent measures.

29

If any one should wish to get the kingdom for himself, and to effect this by what he does, I see that he will not succeed. The kingdom is a spirit-like thing, and cannot be got by active doing. He who would so win it destroys it; he who would hold it in his grasp loses it.

The course and nature of things is such that What was in front is now behind; What warmed anon we freezing find. Strength is of weakness oft the spoil; The store in ruins mocks our toil.

Hence the sage puts away excessive effort, extravagance, and easy indulgence.

30

He who would assist a lord of men in harmony with the Tao will not assert his mastery in the kingdom by force of arms. Such a course is sure to meet with its proper return.

Wherever a host is stationed, briars and thorns spring up. In the sequence of great armies there are sure to be bad years.

A skilful (commander) strikes a decisive blow, and stops. He does not dare (by continuing his operations) to assert and complete his mastery. He will strike the blow, but will be on his guard against being vain or boastful or arrogant in consequence of it. He strikes it as a matter of necessity; he strikes it, but not from a wish for mastery.

When things have attained their strong maturity they become old. This may be said to be not in accordance with the Tao: and what is not in accordance with it soon comes to an end.

31

Now arms, however beautiful, are instruments of evil omen, hateful, it may be said, to all creatures. Therefore they who have the Tao do not like to employ them.

The superior man ordinarily considers the left hand the most honourable place, but in time of war the right hand. Those sharp weapons are instruments of evil omen, and not the instruments of the superior man;--he uses them only on the compulsion of necessity. Calm and repose are what he prizes; victory (by force of arms) is to him undesirable. To consider this desirable would be to delight in the slaughter of men; and he who delights in the slaughter of men cannot get his will in the kingdom.

On occasions of festivity to be on the left hand is the prized position; on occasions of mourning, the right hand. The second in command of the army has his place on the left; the general commanding in chief has his on the right;--his place, that is, is assigned to him as in the rites of mourning. He who has killed multitudes of men should weep for them with the bitterest grief; and the victor in battle has his place (rightly) according to those rites.

32

The Tao, considered as unchanging, has no name.

Though in its primordial simplicity it may be small, the whole world dares not deal with (one embodying) it as a minister. If a feudal prince or the king could guard and hold it, all would spontaneously submit themselves to him.

Heaven and Earth (under its guidance) unite together and send down the sweet dew, which, without the directions of men, reaches equally everywhere as of its own accord.

As soon as it proceeds to action, it has a name. When it once has that name, (men) can know to rest in it. When they know to rest in it, they can be free from all risk of failure and error.

The relation of the Tao to all the world is like that of the great rivers and seas to the streams from the valleys.

33

He who knows other men is discerning; he who knows himself is intelligent. He who overcomes others is strong; he who overcomes himself is mighty. He who is satisfied with his lot is rich; he who goes on acting with energy has a (firm) will.

He who does not fail in the requirements of his position, continues long; he who dies and yet does not perish, has longevity.

34

All-pervading is the Great Tao! It may be found on the left hand and on the right.

All things depend on it for their production, which it gives to them, not one refusing obedience to it. When its work is accomplished, it does not claim the name of having done it. It clothes all things as with a garment, and makes no assumption of being their lord;--it may be named in the smallest things. All things return (to their root and disappear), and do not know that it is it which presides over their doing so;--it may be named in the greatest things.

Hence the sage is able (in the same way) to accomplish his great achievements. It is through his not making himself great that he can accomplish them.

35

To him who holds in his hands the Great Image (of the invisible Tao), the whole world repairs. Men resort to him, and receive no hurt, but (find) rest, peace, and the feeling of ease.

Music and dainties will make the passing guest stop (for a time). But though the Tao as it comes from the mouth, seems insipid and has no flavour, though it seems not worth being looked at or listened to, the use of it is inexhaustible.

36

When one is about to take an inspiration, he is sure to make a (previous) expiration; when he is going to weaken another, he will first strengthen him; when he is going to overthrow another, he will first have raised him up; when he is going to despoil another, he will first have made gifts to him:--this is called 'Hiding the light (of his procedure).' The soft overcomes the hard; and the weak the strong.

Fishes should not be taken from the deep; instruments for the profit of a state should not be shown to the people.

37

The Tao in its regular course does nothing (for the sake of doing it), and so there is nothing which it does not do.

If princes and kings were able to maintain it, all things would of themselves be transformed by them.

If this transformation became to me an object of desire, I would express the desire by the nameless simplicity.

Simplicity without a name Is free from all external aim.

With no desire, at rest and still, All things go right as of their will.

Te Ching.

38

———— ◆·■·■·◆ ————

Those who possessed in highest degree the attributes of the Tao did not seek to show them, and therefore they possessed them in fullest measure. Those who possessed in a lower degree those attributes sought how not to lose them, and therefore they did not possess them in fullest measure.

Those who possessed in the highest degree those attributes did nothing with a purpose, and had no need to do anything. Those who possessed them in a lower degree were always doing, and had need to be so doing.

Those who possessed the highest benevolence were always seeking to carry it out, and had no need to be doing so. Those who possessed the highest righteousness were always seeking to carry it out, and had need to be so doing.

Those who possessed the highest sense of propriety were always seeking to show it, and when men did not respond to it, they bared the arm and marched up to them.

Thus it was that when the Tao was lost, its attributes appeared; when its attributes were lost, benevolence appeared; when benevolence was lost, righteousness appeared; and when righteousness was lost, the proprieties appeared.

Now propriety is the attenuated form of leal-heartedness and good faith, and is also the commencement of disorder; swift apprehension is only a flower of the Tao, and is the beginning of stupidity.

Thus it is that the Great man abides by what is solid, and eschews what is flimsy; dwells with the fruit and not with the flower. It is thus that he puts away the one and makes choice of the other.

39

The things which from of old have got the One (the Tao) are--

Heaven which by it is bright and pure;

Earth rendered thereby firm and sure;

Spirits with powers by it supplied;

Valleys kept full throughout their void

All creatures which through it do live Princes and kings who from it get The model which to all they give.

All these are the results of the One (Tao).

If heaven were not thus pure, it soon would rend;

If earth were not thus sure, it would break and bend;

Without these powers, the spirits soon would fail;

If not so filled, the drought would parch each vale;

Without that life, creatures would pass away; Princes and kings, without that moral sway, However grand and high, would all decay.

Thus it is that dignity finds its (firm) root in its (previous) meanness, and what is lofty finds its stability in the lowness

(from which it rises). Hence princes and kings call themselves 'Orphans,' 'Men of small virtue,' and as 'Carriages without a nave.' Is not this an acknowledgment that in their considering themselves mean they see the foundation of their dignity? So it is that in the enumeration of the different parts of a carriage we do not come on what makes it answer the ends of a carriage. They do not wish to show themselves elegant-looking as jade, but (prefer) to be coarse-looking as an (ordinary) stone.

40

The movement of the Tao

By contraries proceeds;

And weakness marks the course Of Tao's mighty deeds.

All things under heaven sprang from It as existing (and named); that existence sprang from It as non-existent (and not named).

41

Scholars of the highest class, when they hear about the Tao, earnestly carry it into practice. Scholars of the middle class, when they have heard about it, seem now to keep it and now to lose it. Scholars of the lowest class, when they have heard about it, laugh greatly at it. If it were not (thus) laughed at, it would not be fit to be the Tao.

Therefore the sentence-makers have thus expressed themselves:--

'The Tao, when brightest seen, seems light to lack; Who progress in it makes, seems drawing back; Its even way is like a rugged track.

Its highest virtue from the vale doth rise; Its greatest beauty seems to offend the eyes; And he has most whose lot the least supplies.

Its firmest virtue seems but poor and low;

Its solid truth seems change to undergo;

Its largest square doth yet no corner show

A vessel great, it is the slowest made;

Loud is its sound, but never word it said;

A semblance great, the shadow of a shade.'

The Tao is hidden, and has no name; but it is the Tao which is skilful at imparting (to all things what they need) and making them complete.

42

The Tao produced One; One produced Two; Two produced Three; Three produced All things. All things leave behind them the Obscurity (out of which they have come), and go forward to embrace the Brightness (into which they have emerged), while they are harmonised by the Breath of Vacancy.

What men dislike is to be orphans, to have little virtue, to be as carriages without naves; and yet these are the designations which kings and princes use for themselves. So it is that some things are increased by being diminished, and others are diminished by being increased.

What other men (thus) teach, I also teach. The violent and strong do not die their natural death. I will make this the basis of my teaching.

43

The softest thing in the world dashes against and overcomes the hardest; that which has no (substantial) existence enters where there is no crevice. I know hereby what advantage belongs to doing nothing (with a purpose).

There are few in the world who attain to the teaching without words, and the advantage arising from non-action.

44

Or fame or life,

Which do you hold more dear?

Or life or wealth,

To which would you adhere?

Keep life and lose those other things; Keep them and lose your life:-- which brings Sorrow and pain more near?

Thus we may see,

Who cleaves to fame

Rejects what is more great; Who loves large stores Gives up the richer state.

Who is content

Needs fear no shame. Who knows to stop Incurs no blame.

From danger free Long live shall he.

45

Who thinks his great achievements poor Shall find his vigour long endure.

Of greatest fulness, deemed a void, Exhaustion ne'er shall stem the tide.

Do thou what's straight still crooked deem; Thy greatest art still stupid seem,

And eloquence a stammering scream.

Constant action overcomes cold; being still overcomes heat. Purity and stillness give the correct law to all under heaven.

46

When the Tao prevails in the world, they send back their swift horses to (draw) the dung-carts. When the Tao is disregarded in the world, the war-horses breed in the border lands.

There is no guilt greater than to sanction ambition; no calamity greater than to be discontented with one's lot; no fault greater than the wish to be getting. Therefore the sufficiency of contentment is an enduring and un-changing sufficiency.

47

Without going outside his door, one understands (all that takes place) under the sky; without looking out from his window, one sees the Tao of Heaven. The farther that one goes out (from himself), the less he knows.

Therefore the sages got their knowledge without travelling; gave their (right) names to things without seeing them; and accomplished their ends without any purpose of doing so.

48

He who devotes himself to learning (seeks) from day to day to increase (his knowledge); he who devotes himself to the Tao (seeks) from day to day to diminish (his doing).

He diminishes it and again diminishes it, till he arrives at doing nothing (on purpose). Having arrived at this point of non-action, there is nothing which he does not do.

He who gets as his own all under heaven does so by giving himself no trouble (with that end). If one take trouble (with that end), he is not equal to getting as his own all under heaven.

49

The sage has no invariable mind of his own; he makes the mind of the people his mind.

To those who are good (to me), I am good; and to those who are not good (to me), I am also good;--and thus (all) get to be good. To those who are sincere (with me), I am sincere; and to those who are not sincere (with me), I am also sincere;--and thus (all) get to be sincere.

The sage has in the world an appearance of indecision, and keeps his mind in a state of indifference to all. The people all keep their eyes and ears directed to him, and he deals with them all as his children.

50

Men come forth and live; they enter (again) and die.

Of every ten three are ministers of life (to themselves); and three are ministers of death.

There are also three in every ten whose aim is to live, but whose movements tend to the land (or place) of death. And for what reason? Because of their excessive endeavours to perpetuate life.

But I have heard that he who is skilful in managing the life entrusted to him for a time travels on the land without having to shun rhinoceros or tiger, and enters a host without having to avoid buff coat or sharp weapon. The rhinoceros finds no place in him into which to thrust its horn, nor the tiger a place in which to fix its claws, nor the weapon a place to admit its point. And for what reason? Because there is in him no place of death.

51

All things are produced by the Tao, and nourished by its outflowing operation. They receive their forms according to the nature of each, and are completed according to the circumstances of their condition. Therefore all things without exception honour the Tao, and exalt its outflowing operation.

This honouring of the Tao and exalting of its operation is not the result of any ordination, but always a spontaneous tribute.

Thus it is that the Tao produces all things, nourishes them, brings them to their full growth, nurses them, completes them, matures them, maintains them, and overspreads them.

It produces them and makes no claim to the possession of them; it carries them through their processes and does not vaunt its ability in doing so; it brings them to maturity and exercises no control over them;--this is called its mysterious operation.

52

(The Tao) which originated all under the sky is to be considered as the mother of them all.

When the mother is found, we know what her children should be. When one knows that he is his mother's child, and proceeds to guard (the qualities of) the mother that belong to him, to the end of his life he will be free from all peril.

Let him keep his mouth closed, and shut up the portals (of his nostrils), and all his life he will be exempt from laborious exertion. Let him keep his mouth open, and (spend his breath) in the promotion of his affairs, and all his life there will be no safety for him.

The perception of what is small is (the secret of clearsightedness; the guarding of what is soft and tender is (the secret of) strength.

Who uses well his light,

Reverting to its (source so) bright,

Will from his body ward all blight,

And hides the unchanging from men's sight.

53

If I were suddenly to become known, and (put into a position to) conduct (a government) according to the Great Tao, what I should be most afraid of would be a boastful display.

The great Tao (or way) is very level and easy; but people love the by-ways.

Their court(-yards and buildings) shall be well kept, but their fields shall be ill-cultivated, and their granaries very empty. They shall wear elegant and ornamented robes, carry a sharp sword at their girdle, pamper themselves in eating and drinking, and have a superabundance of property and wealth;-- such (princes) may be called robbers and boasters. This is contrary to the Tao surely!

54

What (Tao's) skilful planter plants

Can never be uptorn;

What his skilful arms enfold, From him can ne'er be borne. Sons shall bring in lengthening line, Sacrifices to his shrine.

Tao when nursed within one's self,

His vigour will make true; And where the family it rules What riches will accrue!

The neighbourhood where it prevails

In thriving will abound;

And when 'tis seen throughout the state, Good fortune will be found. Employ it the kingdom o'er, And men thrive all around.

In this way the effect will be seen in the person, by the observation of different cases; in the family; in the neighbourhood; in the state; and in the kingdom.

How do I know that this effect is sure to hold thus all under the sky? By this (method of observation).

55

He who has in himself abundantly the attributes (of the Tao) is like an infant. Poisonous insects will not sting him; fierce beasts will not seize him; birds of prey will not strike him. (The infant's) bones are weak and its sinews soft, but yet its grasp is firm. It knows not yet the union of male and female, and yet its virile member may be excited;--showing the perfection of its physical essence. All day long it will cry without its throat becoming hoarse;-- showing the harmony (in its constitution).

To him by whom this harmony is known, (The secret of) the unchanging (Tao) is shown, And in the knowledge wisdom finds its throne.

All life-increasing arts to evil turn;

Where the mind makes the vital breath to burn,

(False) is the strength, (and o'er it we should mourn.)

When things have become strong, they (then) become old, which may be said to be contrary to the Tao. Whatever is contrary to the Tao soon ends.

56

He who knows (the Tao) does not (care to) speak (about it); he who is (ever ready to) speak about it does not know it.

He (who knows it) will keep his mouth shut and close the portals (of his nostrils). He will blunt his sharp points and unravel the complications of things; he will attemper his brightness, and bring himself into agreement with the obscurity (of others). This is called 'the Mysterious Agreement.'

(Such an one) cannot be treated familiarly or distantly; he is beyond all consideration of profit or injury; of nobility or meanness:--he is the noblest man under heaven.

57

A state may be ruled by (measures of) correction; weapons of war may be used with crafty dexterity; (but) the kingdom is made one's own (only) by freedom from action and purpose.

How do I know that it is so? By these facts:--In the kingdom the multiplication of prohibitive enactments increases the poverty of the people; the more implements to add to their profit that the people have, the greater disorder is there in the state and clan; the more acts of crafty dexterity that men possess, the more do strange contrivances appear; the more display there is of legislation, the more thieves and robbers there are.

Therefore a sage has said, 'I will do nothing (of purpose), and the people will be transformed of themselves; I will be fond of keeping still, and the people will of themselves become correct. I will take no trouble about it, and the people will of themselves become rich; I will manifest no ambition, and the people will of themselves attain to the primitive simplicity.'

58

The government that seems the most unwise,

Oft goodness to the people best supplies; That which is meddling, touching everything, Will work but ill, and disappointment bring.

Misery!--happiness is to be found by its side! Happiness!-misery lurks beneath it! Who knows what either will come to in the end?

Shall we then dispense with correction? The (method of) correction shall by a turn become distortion, and the good in it shall by a turn become evil. The delusion of the people (on this point) has indeed subsisted for a long time.

Therefore the sage is (like) a square which cuts no one (with its angles); (like) a corner which injures no one (with its sharpness). He is straightforward, but allows himself no license; he is bright, but does not dazzle.

59

For regulating the human (in our constitution) and rendering the (proper) service to the heavenly, there is nothing like moderation.

It is only by this moderation that there is effected an early return (to man's normal state). That early return is what I call the repeated accumulation of the attributes (of the Tao). With that repeated accumulation of those attributes, there comes the subjugation (of every obstacle to such return). Of this subjugation we know not what shall be the limit; and when one knows not what the limit shall be, he may be the ruler of a state.

He who possesses the mother of the state may continue long. His case is like that (of the plant) of which we say that its roots are deep and its flower stalks firm:--this is the way to secure that its enduring life shall long be seen.

60

Governing a great state is like cooking small fish.

Let the kingdom be governed according to the Tao, and the manes of the departed will not manifest their spiritual energy. It is not that those manes have not that spiritual energy, but it will not be employed to hurt men. It is not that it could not hurt men, but neither does the ruling sage hurt them.

When these two do not injuriously affect each other, their good influences converge in the virtue (of the Tao).

61

What makes a great state is its being (like) a low-lying, down- flowing (stream);--it becomes the centre to which tend (all the small states) under heaven.

(To illustrate from) the case of all females:--the female always overcomes the male by her stillness. Stillness may be considered (a sort of) abasement.

Thus it is that a great state, by condescending to small states, gains them for itself; and that small states, by abasing themselves to a great state, win it over to them. In the one case the abasement leads to gaining adherents, in the other case to procuring favour.

The great state only wishes to unite men together and nourish them; a small state only wishes to be received by, and to serve, the other. Each gets what it desires, but the great state must learn to abase itself.

62

Tao has of all things the most honoured place. No treasures give good men so rich a grace; Bad men it guards, and doth their ill efface.

(Its) admirable words can purchase honour; (its) admirable deeds can raise their performer above others. Even men who are not good are not abandoned by it.

Therefore when the sovereign occupies his place as the Son of Heaven, and he has appointed his three ducal ministers, though (a prince) were to send in a round symbol-of-rank large enough to fill both the hands, and that as the precursor of the team of horses (in the court-yard), such an offering would not be equal to (a lesson of) this Tao, which one might present on his knees.

Why was it that the ancients prized this Tao so much? Was it not because it could be got by seeking for it, and the guilty could escape (from the stain of their guilt) by it? This is the reason why all under heaven consider it the most valuable thing.

63

(It is the way of the Tao) to act without (thinking of) acting; to conduct affairs without (feeling the) trouble of them; to taste without discerning any flavour; to consider what is small as great, and a few as many; and to recompense injury with kindness.

(The master of it) anticipates things that are difficult while they are easy, and does things that would become great while they are small. All difficult things in the world are sure to arise from a previous state in which they were easy, and all great things from one in which they were small. Therefore the sage, while he never does what is great, is able on that account to accomplish the greatest things.

He who lightly promises is sure to keep but little faith; he who is continually thinking things easy is sure to find them difficult. Therefore the sage sees difficulty even in what seems easy, and so never has any difficulties.

64

That which is at rest is easily kept hold of; before a thing has given indications of its presence, it is easy to take measures against it; that which is brittle is easily broken; that which is very small is easily dispersed. Action should be taken before a thing has made its appearance; order should be secured before disorder has begun.

The tree which fills the arms grew from the tiniest sprout; the tower of nine storeys rose from a (small) heap of earth; the journey of a thousand li commenced with a single step.

He who acts (with an ulterior purpose) does harm; he who takes hold of a thing (in the same way) loses his hold. The sage does not act (so), and therefore does no harm; he does not lay hold (so), and therefore does not lose his bold. (But) people in their conduct of affairs are constantly ruining them when they are on the eve of success. If they were careful at the end, as (they should be) at the beginning, they would not so ruin them.

Therefore the sage desires what other men do not desire, and does not prize things difficult to get; he learns what other men do not learn, and turns back to what the multitude of men have passed by. Thus he helps the natural development of all things, and does not dare to act with an ulterior purpose of his own.

65

The ancients who showed their skill in practising the Tao did so, not to enlighten the people, but rather to make them simple and ignorant.

The difficulty in governing the people arises from their having much knowledge. He who (tries to) govern a state by his wisdom is a scourge to it; while he who does not (try to) do so is a blessing.

He who knows these two things finds in them also his model and rule. Ability to know this model and rule constitutes what we call the mysterious excellence (of a governor). Deep and far-reaching is such mysterious excellence, showing indeed its possessor as opposite to others, but leading them to a great conformity to him.

66

That whereby the rivers and seas are able to receive the homage and tribute of all the valley streams, is their skill in being lower than they;--it is thus that they are the kings of them all. So it is that the sage (ruler), wishing to be above men, puts himself by his words below them, and, wishing to be before them, places his person behind them.

In this way though he has his place above them, men do not feel his weight, nor though he has his place before them, do they feel it an injury to them.

Therefore all in the world delight to exalt him and do not weary of him. Because he does not strive, no one finds it possible to strive with him.

67

————◄•▄•▄•◄————

All the world says that, while my Tao is great, it yet appears to be inferior (to other systems of teaching). Now it is just its greatness that makes it seem to be inferior. If it were like any other (system), for long would its smallness have been known!

But I have three precious things which I prize and hold fast. The first is gentleness; the second is economy; and the third is shrinking from taking precedence of others.

With that gentleness I can be bold; with that economy I can be liberal; shrinking from taking precedence of others, I can become a vessel of the highest honour. Now-a-days they give up gentleness and are all for being bold; economy, and are all for being liberal; the hindmost place, and seek only to be foremost;--(of all which the end is) death.

Gentleness is sure to be victorious even in battle, and firmly to maintain its ground. Heaven will save its possessor, by his (very) gentleness protecting him.

68

————◄•▄•▄•◄————

He who in (Tao's) wars has skill

Assumes no martial port;

He who fights with most good will To rage makes no resort.

He who vanquishes yet still

Keeps from his foes apart; He whose hests men most fulfil Yet humbly plies his art.

Thus we say, 'He ne'er contends,

And therein is his might.'

Thus we say, 'Men's wills he bends,

That they with him unite.'

Thus we say, 'Like Heaven's his ends,

No sage of old more bright.'

69

A master of the art of war has said, 'I do not dare to be the host (to commence the war); I prefer to be the guest (to act on the defensive). I do not dare to advance an inch; I prefer to retire a foot.' This is called marshalling the ranks where there are no ranks; baring the arms (to fight) where there are no arms to bare; grasping the weapon where there is no weapon to grasp; advancing against the enemy where there is no enemy.

There is no calamity greater than lightly engaging in war. To do that is near losing (the gentleness) which is so precious. Thus it is that when opposing weapons are (actually) crossed, he who deplores (the situation) conquers.

70

My words are very easy to know, and very easy to practise; but there is no one in the world who is able to know and able to practise them.

There is an originating and all-comprehending (principle) in my words, and an authoritative law for the things (which I enforce). It is because they do not know these, that men do not know me.

They who know me are few, and I am on that account (the more) to be prized. It is thus that the sage wears (a poor garb of) hair cloth, while he carries his (signet of) jade in his bosom.

71

To know and yet (think) we do not know is the highest (attainment); not to know (and yet think) we do know is a disease.

It is simply by being pained at (the thought of) having this disease that we are preserved from it. The sage has not the disease. He knows the pain that would be inseparable from it, and therefore he does not have it.

72

When the people do not fear what they ought to fear, that which is their great dread will come on them.

Let them not thoughtlessly indulge themselves in their ordinary life; let them not act as if weary of what that life depends on.

It is by avoiding such indulgence that such weariness does not arise.

Therefore the sage knows (these things) of himself, but does not parade (his knowledge); loves, but does not (appear to set a) value on, himself. And thus he puts the latter alternative away and makes choice of the former.

73

He whose boldness appears in his daring (to do wrong, in defiance of the laws) is put to death; he whose boldness appears in his not daring (to do so) lives on. Of these two cases the one appears to be advantageous, and the other to be injurious. But

When Heaven's anger smites a man, Who the cause shall truly scan?

On this account the sage feels a difficulty (as to what to do in the former case).

It is the way of Heaven not to strive, and yet it skilfully overcomes; not to speak, and yet it is skilful in (obtaining a reply; does not call, and yet men come to it of themselves. Its demonstrations are quiet, and yet its plans are skilful and effective. The meshes of the net of Heaven are large; far apart, but letting nothing escape.

74

The people do not fear death; to what purpose is it to (try to) frighten them with death? If the people were always in awe of death, and I could always seize those who do wrong, and put them to death, who would dare to do wrong?

There is always One who presides over the infliction death. He who would inflict death in the room of him who so presides over it may be described as hewing wood instead of a great carpenter. Seldom is it that he who undertakes the hewing, instead of the great carpenter, does not cut his own hands!

75

The people suffer from famine because of the multitude of taxes consumed by their superiors. It is through this that they suffer famine.

The people are difficult to govern because of the (excessive) agency of their superiors (in governing them). It is through this that they are difficult to govern.

The people make light of dying because of the greatness of their labours in seeking for the means of living. It is this which makes them think light of dying. Thus it is that to leave the subject of living altogether out of view is better than to set a high value on it.

76

Man at his birth is supple and weak; at his death, firm and strong. (So it is with) all things. Trees and plants, in their early growth, are soft and brittle; at their death, dry and withered.

Thus it is that firmness and strength are the concomitants of death; softness and weakness, the concomitants of life.

Hence he who (relies on) the strength of his forces does not conquer; and a tree which is strong will fill the outstretched arms, (and thereby invites the feller.)

Therefore the place of what is firm and strong is below, and that of what is soft and weak is above.

77

May not the Way (or Tao) of Heaven be compared to the (method of) bending a bow? The (part of the bow) which was high is brought low, and what was low is raised up. (So Heaven) diminishes where there is superabundance, and supplements where there is deficiency.

It is the Way of Heaven to diminish superabundance, and to supplement deficiency. It is not so with the way of man. He takes away from those who have not enough to add to his own superabundance.

Who can take his own superabundance and therewith serve all under heaven? Only he who is in possession of the Tao!

Therefore the (ruling) sage acts without claiming the results as his; he achieves his merit and does not rest (arrogantly) in it:--he does not wish to display his superiority.

78

There is nothing in the world more soft and weak than water, and yet for attacking things that are firm and strong there is nothing that can take precedence of it;--for there is nothing (so effectual) for which it can be changed.

Every one in the world knows that the soft overcomes the hard, and the weak the strong, but no one is able to carry it out in practice.

Therefore a sage has said,

'He who accepts his state's reproach,

Is hailed therefore its altars' lord;

To him who bears men's direful woes They all the name of King accord.'

Words that are strictly true seem to be paradoxical.

79

When a reconciliation is effected (between two parties) after a great animosity, there is sure to be a grudge remaining (in the mind of the one who was wrong). And how can this be beneficial (to the other)?

Therefore (to guard against this), the sage keeps the lefthand portion of the record of the engagement, and does not insist on the (speedy) fulfilment of it by the other party. (So), he who has the attributes (of the Tao) regards (only) the conditions of the engagement, while he who has not those attributes regards only the conditions favourable to himself.

In the Way of Heaven, there is no partiality of love; it is always on the side of the good man.

80

In a little state with a small population, I would so order it, that, though there were individuals with the abilities of ten or a hundred men, there should be no employment of them; I would make the people, while looking on death as a grievous thing, yet not remove elsewhere (to avoid it).

Though they had boats and carriages, they should have no occasion to ride in them; though they had buff coats and sharp weapons, they should have no occasion to don or use them.

I would make the people return to the use of knotted cords (instead of the written characters).

They should think their (coarse) food sweet; their (plain) clothes beautiful; their (poor) dwellings places of rest; and their common (simple) ways sources of enjoyment.

There should be a neighbouring state within sight, and the voices of the fowls and dogs should be heard all the way from it to us, but I would make the people to old age, even to death, not have any intercourse with it.

81

Sincere words are not fine; fine words are not sincere. Those who are skilled (in the Tao) do not dispute (about it); the disputatious are not skilled in it. Those who know (the Tao) are not extensively learned; the extensively learned do not know it.

The sage does not accumulate (for himself). The more that he expends for others, the more does he possess of his own; the more that he gives to others, the more does he have himself.

With all the sharpness of the Way of Heaven, it injures not; with all the doing in the way of the sage he does not strive.

The Book of Lieh Tzŭ

Taoist Teachings

Lieh Tzŭ

1912

Book I – Cosmogony

Our Master Lieh Tzŭ dwelt on a vegetable plot in the Chêng State for forty years, and no man knew him for what he was. The Prince, his Ministers, and all the State officials looked upon him as one of the common herd. A time of dearth fell upon the State, and he was preparing to migrate to Wei, when his disciples said to him: 'Now that our Master is going away without any prospect of returning, we have ventured to approach you, hoping for instruction. Are there no words from the lips of Hu-Ch'iu Tzŭ-lin that you can impart to us? Lieh Tzŭ smiled and said: 'Do you suppose that Hu Tzŭ dealt in words? However, I will try to repeat to you what my Master said on one occasion to Pohun Mou-jên.

> A fellow-disciple. Out of modesty, Lieh Tzŭ does not say that the teaching was imparted directly to himself.

I was standing by and heard his words, which ran as, follows: –

"There is a Creative Principle which is itself uncreated; there is a Principle of Change which is itself unchanging. The Uncreated is able to create life; the Unchanging is able to effect change. That which is produced cannot but continue producing; that which is evolved cannot but continue evolving. Hence there is constant production and constant evolution. The law of constant production and of constant evolution at no time ceases to operate.

> The commentator says: 'That which is once involved in the destiny of living things can never be annihilated.'

So is it with the Yin and the Yang, so is it with the Four Seasons.

> The Yin and the Yang are the Positive and Negative Principles of Nature, alternately predominating in day and night.

The Uncreated we may surmise to be Alone in itself.

> 'The Supreme, the Non-Engendered — how can its reality be proved? We can only suppose that it is mysteriously One, without beginning and without end.'

The Unchanging goes to and fro, and its range is illimitable. We may surmise that it stands Alone, and that its Ways are inexhaustible."

'In the Book of the Yellow Emperor it is written: "The Spirit of the Valley dies not; it may be called the Mysterious Feminine. The issuing-point of the Mysterious Feminine must be regarded as the Root of the Universe. Subsisting to all eternity, it uses its force without effort."

The Book of the Yellow Emperor is no longer extant, but the above passage is now incorporated in the Tao Tê Ching, and attributed to Lao Tzŭ.

'That, then, which engenders all things is itself unengendered; that by which all things are evolved is itself untouched by evolution. Self-engendered and self-evolved, it has in itself the elements of substance, appearance, wisdom, strength, dispersion and cessation. Yet it would be a mistake to call it by any one of these names.

* * *

The Master Lieh Tzŭ said: 'The inspired men of old regarded the Yin and the Yang as controlling the sum total of Heaven and Earth. But that which has substance is engendered from that which is devoid of substance; out of what then were Heaven and Earth engendered?

'They were engendered out of nothing, and came into existence of themselves.'

'Hence we say, there is a great Principle of Change, a great Origin, a great Beginning, a great Primordial Simplicity. In the great Change substance is not yet manifest. In the great Origin lies the beginning of substance. In the great Beginning, lies the beginning of material form.

'After the separation of the Yin and the Yang, when classes of objects assume their forms.'

In the great Simplicity lies the beginning of essential qualities. When substance, form and essential qualities are still indistinguishably blended together it is called Chaos. Chaos means that all things are chaotically intermixed and not yet separated from one another. The purer and lighter elements, tending upwards, made the Heavens; the grosser and heavier elements, tending downwards, made the Earth. Substance, harmoniously proportioned, became Man; and, Heaven and Earth containing thus a spiritual element, all things were evolved and produced.'

* * *

The Master Lieh Tzŭ said: 'The virtue of Heaven and Earth, the powers of the Sage, and the uses of the myriad things in Creation, are not perfect in every direction. It is Heaven's function to produce life and to spread a canopy over it. It is Earth's function to form material bodies and to support them. It is the Sage's function to teach others and to influence them for good. It is the function of created things to conform to their proper nature. That being so, there are things in which Earth may excel, though they lie outside the scope of Heaven; matters in which the Sage has no concern, though they afford free play to others. For it is clear that that which imparts and broods over life cannot form and support material bodies; that which forms and supports material bodies cannot teach and influence for good; one who teaches and influences for good cannot run counter to natural instincts; that which is fixed in suitable environment does not travel outside its own sphere. Therefore the Way of Heaven and Earth will be either of the Yin or of the Yang; the teaching of the Sage will be either of altruism or of righteousness; the quality of created objects will be either soft or hard. All these conform to their proper nature and cannot depart from the province assigned to them.'

* * *

On one hand, there is life, and on the other, there is that which produces life; there is form, and there is that which imparts form; there is sound, and there is that which causes sound; there is colour, and there is that which causes colour; there is taste, and there is that which causes taste.

Things that have been endowed with life die; but that which produces life itself never comes to an end. The origin of form is matter; but that which imparts form has no material existence. The genesis of sound lies in the sense of hearing; but that which causes sound is never audible to the ear. The source of colour is vision; but that which produces colour never manifests itself to the eye. The origin of taste lies in the palate; but that which causes taste is never perceived by that sense. All these phenomena are functions of the principle of Inaction.[8]

> Wu Wei, Inaction, here stands for the inert, unchanging Tao.

To be at will either bright or obscure, soft or hard, short or long, round or square, alive or dead, hot or cold, buoyant or sinking, treble or bass, present or absent, black or white, sweet or bitter, fetid or fragrant — this it is to be devoid of knowledge, yet all-knowing, destitute of power, yet all-powerful.

> Such is Tao.

*   *   *

On his journey to Wei, the Master Lieh Tzŭ took a meal by the roadside. His followers espied an old skull, and pulled aside the undergrowth to show it to him. Turning to his disciple Po Fêng, the Master said: 'That skull and I both know that there is no such thing as absolute life or death.

> 'If we regard ourselves as passing along the road of evolution, then I am alive and he is dead. But looked at from the standpoint of the Absolute, since there is no such principle as life in itself, it follows that there can be no such thing as death.'

This knowledge is better than all your methods of prolonging life, a more potent source of happiness than any other.'

*   *   *

In the Book of the Yellow Emperor it is written: 'When form becomes active it produces not form but shadow; when sound becomes active it produces not sound but echo.'

> This passage does not occur in the Tao Tê Ching.

When Not-Being becomes active, it does not produce Not-Being but Being. Form is something that must come to an end. Heaven and Earth, then, have an end, even as we all have an end. But whether the end is complete we do not know.

> 'When there is conglomeration, form comes into being; when there is dispersion, it comes to an end. That is what we mortals mean by beginning and end. But although for us, in a state of

conglomeration, this condensation into form constitutes a beginning, and its dispersion an end, from the standpoint of dispersion, it is void and calm that constitute the beginning, and
condensation into form the end. Hence there is perpetual alternation in what constitutes beginning and end, and the underly-
ing Truth is that there is neither any beginning nor any end at
all.'

The course of evolution ends where it started, without a beginning; it
finishes up where it began, in Not-Being.

A paradoxical way of stating that there is no beginning and no
end.

That which has life returns again into the Lifeless; that which has form
returns again into the formless. This, that I call the Lifeless, is not the original
Lifelessness. This, that I call the formless, is not the original Formlessness.

'That, which is here termed the Lifeless has formerly possessed
life, and subsequently passed into the extinction of death,
whereas the original Lifelessness from the beginning knows
neither life nor extinction.' We have here again the distinction
between the unchanging life-giving Principle (Tao), which is itself without life, and the living things themselves, which are in
a perpetual flux between life and death.

That which has life must by the law of its being come to an end; and the
end can no more be avoided than the living creature can help having been
born. So that he who hopes to perpetuate his life or to shut out death is
deceived as to his destiny.

The spiritual element in man is allotted to him by Heaven, his corporeal
frame by Earth. The part that belongs to Heaven 'is ethereal and dispersive,
the part that belongs to Earth is dense and tending to conglomeration. When
the spirit parts from the body, each of these elements resumes its true nature.
That is why disembodied spirits are called kuei, which means 'returning', that
is, returning to their true dwelling-place.

'The region of the Great Void.'

The Yellow Emperor said: 'If my spirit returns through the gates whence it came, and my bones go back to the source from which they sprang, where does the Ego continue to exist?'

*   *   *

Between his birth and his latter end, man passes through four chief stages - infancy, adolescence, old age and death. In infancy, the vital force is concentrated, the will is undivided, and the general harmony of the system is perfect. External objects produce no injurious impression, and to the moral nature nothing can be added. In adolescence, the animal passions are wildly exuberant, the heart is filled with rising desires and preoccupations. The man is open to attack by the objects of sense, and thus his moral nature becomes enfeebled. In old age, his desires and preoccupations have lost their keenness, and the bodily frame seeks for repose. External objects no longer hold the first place in his regard. In this state, though not attaining to the perfection of infancy, he is already different from what he was in adolescence. In death, he comes to his rest, and returns to the Absolute.

*   *   *

Confucius was travelling once over Mount T'ai when he caught sight of an aged man roaming in the wilds. He was clothed in a deerskin, girded with a rope, and was singing as he played on a lute. 'My friend,' said Confucius, 'what is it that makes you so happy?' The old man replied: 'I have a great deal to make me happy. God created all things, and of all His creations man is the noblest. It has fallen to my lot to be a man: that is my first ground for happiness. Then, there is a distinction between male and female, the former being rated more highly than the latter. Therefore it is better to be a male; and since I am one, I have a second ground for happiness. Furthermore, some are born who never behold the sun or the moon, and who never emerge from their swaddling-clothes. But I have already walked the earth for the space of ninety years. That is my third ground for happiness. Poverty is the normal lot of the scholar, death the appointed end for all human beings. Abiding in the normal state, and reaching at last the appointed end, what is there that should make me unhappy?; What an excellent thing it is,' cried Confucius, 'to be able to find a source of consolation in oneself!'

*   *   *

Tzŭ Kung was tired of study, and confided his feelings to Confucius, saying: 'I yearn for rest.' Confucius replied: 'In life there is no rest.'

'To toil in anxious planning for the future, to slave in bolstering up the bodily frame — these are the businesses of life.'

'Is rest, then, nowhere to be found? 'Oh yes!' replied Confucius; 'look at all the graves in the wilds, all the vaults, all the tombs, all the funeral urns, and you may know where rest is to be found.' 'Great, indeed, is Death!' exclaimed Tzŭ Kung. 'It gives rest to the noble hearted, and causes the base to cower.' 'You are right,' said Confucius. 'Men feel the joy of life, but do not realize its bitterness. They feel the weariness of old age, but not its peacefulness. They think of the evils of death, but not of the repose which it confers.'

*　　*　　*

Yen Tzŭ said: 'How excellent was the ancients' view of death! — bringing rest to the good and subjection to the wicked. Death is the boundary-line of Virtue.

That is, Death abolishes all artificial and temporary distinctions between good and evil, which only hold good in this world of relativity.

'The ancients spoke of the dead as kuei-jên (men who have returned). But if the dead are men who have returned, the living are men on a journey. Those who are on a journey and think not of returning have cut themselves off from their home. Should any one man cut himself off from his home, he would incur universal reprobation. But all mankind being homeless, there is none to see the error. Imagine one who leaves his native village, separates himself from all his kith and kin, dissipates his patrimony and wanders away to the four corners of the earth, never to return: — what manner of man is this? The world will surely set him down as a profligate and a vagabond. On the other hand, imagine one who clings to respectability and the things of this life, holds cleverness and capacity in high esteem, builds himself up a reputation, and plays the braggart amongst his fellow men without knowing where to stop: — what manner of man, once more, is this? The world will surely look upon him as a gentleman of great wisdom and counsel. Both of these men have lost their way, yet the world will consort with the one, and not with the other. Only the Sage knows with whom to consort and from whom to hold aloof.'

'He consorts with those who regard life and death merely as waking and sleeping, and holds aloof from those who are steeped in forgetfulness of their return.'

*　　*　　*

Yŭ Hsiung said: 'Evolution is never-ending. But who can perceive the secret processes of Heaven and Earth? Thus, things that are diminished here are augmented there; things that are made whole in one place suffer loss in another. Diminution and augmentation, fullness and decay are the constant accompaniments of life and death. They alternate in continuous succession, and we are not conscious of any interval. The whole body of spiritual substance progresses without a pause; the whole body of material substance suffers decay without intermission. But we do not perceive the process of completion, nor do we perceive the process of decay. Man, likewise, from birth to old age becomes something different every day in face and form, in wisdom and in conduct. His skin, his nails and his hair are continually growing and continually perishing. In infancy and childhood there is no stopping nor respite from change. Though imperceptible while it is going on, it may be verified afterwards if we wait.'

*　　*　　*

There was once a man in the Ch'i State who was so afraid the universe would collapse and fall to pieces, leaving his body without a lodgement, that he could neither sleep nor eat. Another man, pitying his distress, went to enlighten him. 'Heaven,' he said, 'is nothing more than an accumulation of ether, and there is no place where ether is not. Processes of contraction and expansion, inspiration and expiration are continually taking place up in the heavens. Why then should you be afraid of a collapse?' The man said: 'It is true that Heaven is an accumulation of ether; but the sun, the moon, and the stars — will they not fall down upon us? His informant replied: 'Sun, moon and stars are likewise only bright lights within this mass of ether. Even supposing they were to fall, they could not possibly harm us by their impact.' 'But what if the earth should fall to pieces? 'The earth,' replied the other, 'is merely an agglomeration of matter, which fills and blocks up the four corners of space. There is no part of it where matter is not. All day long there is constant treading and tramping on the surface of the earth. Why then should you be afraid of its falling to pieces? Thereupon the man was relieved of his fears and rejoiced exceedingly. And his instructor was also joyful and easy in mind. But Ch'ang Lu Tzŭ laughed at them both, saying: 'Rainbows, clouds and mist, wind and rain, the four seasons — these are perfected forms of accumulated ether, and go to make up the heavens. Mountains and cliffs, rivers and seas, metals and rocks, fire and timber — these are perfected forms of agglomerated matter, and constitute the earth. Knowing these facts, who can say that they will never be destroyed? Heaven and earth form only a small speck in the midst of the Void, but they are the greatest things in the sum of Being. This much is certain: even as their nature is hard to fathom, hard to understand, so they will be slow to pass away, slow to come to an end. He who fears lest they should suddenly fall to pieces is assuredly very far from the truth. He, on the other hand, who says that they will never be destroyed has also not reached the right solution. Heaven and earth must of necessity pass away, but neither will revert to destruction apart from the other.

The speaker means that though there is no immediate danger of a collapse, it is certain that our universe must obey the natural law of disintegration, and at some distant date disappear altogether. But the process of decay will be so gradual as to be imperceptible.

Who, having to face the day of disruption, would not be alarmed?

The Master Lieh Tzŭ heard of the discussion, and smiling said: 'He who maintains that Heaven and earth are destructible, and he who upholds the contrary, are both equally at fault. Whether they are destructible or not is something we can never know, though in both cases it will be the same for all alike. The living and the dead, the going and the coming, know nothing of each other's state. Whether destruction awaits the world or no, why should I trouble my head about it?

*   *   *

Mr Kuo of the Ch'i State was very rich, while Mr Hsiang of the Sung State was very poor. The latter travelled from Sung to Ch'i and asked the other for the secret of his prosperity. Mr Kuo told him. 'It is because I am a good thief,' he said. 'The first year I began to be a thief, I had just enough. The second year, I had ample. The third year, I reaped a great harvest. And, in course of time, I found myself the owner of whole villages and districts.' Mr Hsiang was overjoyed; he understood the word 'thief' in its literal sense, but he did not understand the true way of becoming a thief. Accordingly, he climbed over walls and broke into houses, grabbing everything he could see or lay hands upon. But before very long his thefts brought him into trouble, and he was stripped even of what he had previously possessed. Thinking that Mr Kuo had basely deceived him, Hsiang went to him with a bitter complaint. 'Tell me,' said Mr Kuo, 'how did you set about being a thief?' On learning from Mr Hsiang what had happened, he cried out: 'Alas and alack! You have been brought to this pass because you went the wrong way to work. Now let me put you on the right track. We all know that Heaven has its seasons, and that earth has its riches. Well, the things that I steal are the riches of Heaven and earth, each in their season — the fertilizing rain-water from the clouds, and the natural products of mountain and meadow-land. Thus I grow my grain and ripen my crops, build my walls and construct my tenements. From the dry land I steal winged and four-footed game, from the rivers I steal fish and turtles. There is nothing that I do not steal. For corn and grain, clay and wood, birds and beasts, fishes and turtles are all products of Nature. How can I claim them as mine?[20]

It will be observed that Lieh Tzŭ anticipates here, in a somewhat different sense, Proudhon's famous paradox: 'La propriété c'est le vol.' [Property is theft.]

'Yet, stealing in this way from Nature, I bring on myself no retribution. But gold, jade, and precious stones, stores of grain, silk stuffs, and other kinds of property, are things accumulated by men, not bestowed upon us by Nature. So who can complain if he gets into trouble by stealing them?

Mr Hsiang, in a state of great perplexity, and fearing to be led astray a second time by Mr Kuo, went off to consult Tung Kuo, a man of learning. Tung Kuo said to him: 'Are you not already a thief in respect of your own body? You are stealing the harmony of the Yin and the Yang in order to keep alive and to maintain your bodily form. How much more, then, are you a thief with regard to external possessions! Assuredly, Heaven and earth cannot be dissociated from the myriad objects of Nature. To claim any one of these as your own betokens confusion of thought. Mr Kuo's thefts are carried out in a spirit of justice, and therefore bring no retribution. But your thefts were carried out in a spirit of self-seeking and therefore landed you in trouble. Those who take possession of property, whether public or private, are thieves.

By 'taking possession of public property', as we have seen, Lieh Tzŭ means utilizing the products of Nature open to all — rain and the like.

Those who abstain from taking property, public or private, are also thieves.

'For no one can help possessing a body, and no one can help acquiring some property or other which cannot be got rid of with the best will in the world. Such thefts are unconscious thefts.'

The great principle of Heaven and earth is to treat public property as such and private property as such. Knowing this principle, which of us is a thief, and at the same time which of us is not a thief?'

The object of this anecdote is to impress us with the unreality of mundane distinctions. Lieh Tzŭ is not much interested in the social aspect of the question. He is not an advocate of communism, nor does he rebel against the common-sense view that theft is a crime which must be punished. With him, everything is intended to lead up to the metaphysical standpoint.

Book II – The Yellow Emperor

━━◆◗◆◗◆━━

The Yellow Emperor sat for fifteen years on the throne, and rejoiced that the Empire looked up to him as its head. He was careful of his physical well-being, sought pleasures for his ears and eyes, and gratified his senses of smell and taste. Nevertheless, he grew melancholy in spirit, his complexion became sallow, and his sensations became dull and confused. Then, for a further period of fifteen years, he grieved that the Empire was in disorder; he summoned up all his intelligence, exhausted his resources of wisdom and strength in trying to rule the people. But, in spite of all, his face remained haggard and pale, and his sensations dull and confused.

'The practice of enlightened virtue will not succeed in establishing good government, but only disorganize the spiritual faculties.'

Then the Yellow Emperor sighed heavily and said: 'My fault is want of moderation. The misery I suffer comes from over-attention to my own self, and the troubles of the Empire from over-regulation in everything.' Thereupon, he threw up all his schemes, abandoned his ancestral palace, dismissed his attendants, removed all the hanging bells, cut down the delicacies of his cuisine, and retired to live at leisure in private apartments attached to the Court. There he fasted in heart, and brought his body under control.

Fasting in heart means freeing oneself from earthly desires, after which, says the commentator, the body will naturally be under control. Actual abstention from food or other forms of bodily mortification are not intended. See Musings of a Chinese Mystic, p. 71.

For three months he abstained from personal intervention in government. Then he fell asleep in the daytime, and dreamed that he made a journey to the kingdom of Hua-hsŭ, situated I know not how many tens of thousands of miles distant from the Ch'i State. It was beyond the reach of ship or vehicle or any mortal foot. Only the soul could travel so far.

In sleep, the hun or spiritual part of the soul is supposed by the Chinese, to quit the body.

This kingdom was without head or ruler; it simply went on of itself. Its people were without desires or cravings; they simply followed their natural instincts. They felt neither joy in life nor abhorrence of death; thus they came to no untimely ends. They felt neither attachment to self nor indifference to others; thus they were exempt from love and hatred alike. They knew neither aversion from one course nor inclination to another; hence profit and loss existed not among them. All were equally untouched by the emotions of love and sympathy, of jealousy and fear. Water had no power to drown them, nor fire to burn; cuts and blows caused them neither injury nor pain, scratching or tickling could not make them itch. They bestrode the air as though treading on solid earth; they were cradled in space as though resting in a bed. Clouds and mist obstructed not their vision, thunder-peals could not stun their ears, physical beauty disturbed not their hearts, mountains and valleys hindered not their steps. They moved about like gods.

When the Yellow Emperor awoke from his dream, he summoned his three Ministers and told them what he had seen. 'For three months,' he said, 'I have been living a life of leisure, fasting in heart, subduing my body, and casting about in my mind for the true method of nourishing my own life and regulating the lives of others. But I failed to discover the secret.

> 'It is wrong to nourish one's own life, wrong to regulate those of others. No attempt to do this by the light of intelligence can be successful.'

Worn out, I fell asleep and dreamed this dream. Now I know that the Perfect Way is not to be sought through the senses. This Way I know and hold within me, yet I cannot impart it to you.'

> 'If the Way cannot be sought through the senses, it cannot be communicated through the senses.'

For twenty-eight years after this, there was great orderliness in the Empire, nearly equalling that in the kingdom of Huahsŭ. And when the Emperor ascended on high, the people bewailed him for two hundred years without intermission.

*   *   *

Lieh Tzŭ had Lao Shang for his teacher, and Po Kao Tzŭ for his friend. When he had fully mastered the system of these two philosophers, he rode home again on the wings of the wind.[6]

Cf. Chuang Tzŭ, ch. 1: 'There was Lieh Tzŭ again. He could ride upon the wind, and travel whithersoever he wished, staying away as long as fifteen days.'

Yin Shêng heard of this, and became his disciple. He dwelt with Lieh Tzŭ for many months without visiting his own home. While he was with him, he begged to be initiated into his secret arts. Ten times he asked, and each time received no answer. Becoming impatient Yin Shêng announced his departure, but Lieh Tzŭ still gave no sign. So Yin Shêng went away, but after many months his mind was still unsettled, so he returned and became his follower once more. Lieh Tzŭ said to him: 'Why this incessant going and coming?' Yin Shêng replied: 'Some time ago, I sought instruction from you, Sir, but you would not tell me anything. That made me vexed with you. But now I have got rid of that feeling, and so I have come again.' Lieh Tzŭ said: 'Formerly, I used to think you were a man of penetration, and have you now fallen so low? Sit down, and I will tell you what I learned from my Master. After I had served him, and enjoyed the friendship of Po Kao, for the space of three years, my mind did not venture to reflect on right and my wrong, my lips did not venture to speak of profit and loss. Then, for the first time, my Master bestowed one glance upon me — and that was all.

'To be in reality entertaining the ideas of profit and loss, though without venturing to utter them, is a case of hiding one's resentment and harbouring secret passions; hence a mere glance was vouchsafed.'

'At the end of five years a change had taken place; my mind was reflecting on right and wrong, and my lips were speaking of profit and loss. Then, for the first time, my Master relaxed his countenance and smiled.

'Right and wrong, profit and loss, are the fixed principles prevailing in the world of sense. To let the mind reflect on what it will, to let the lips utter what they please, and not grudgingly bottle it up in one's breast, so that the internal and the external may become as one, is still not so good as passing beyond the bounds of self and abstaining from all manifestation. This first step, however, pleased the Master and caused him to give a smile.'

'At the end of seven years, there was another change. I let my mind reflect on what it would, but it no longer occupied itself with right and wrong. I let my lips utter whatsoever they pleased, but they no longer spoke of profit and loss. Then, at last, my Master led me in to sit on the mat beside him.

> 'The question is, how to bring the mind into a state of calm, in which there is no thinking or mental activity; how to keep the lips silent, with only natural inhalation and exhalation going on. If you give yourself up to mental perfection, right and wrong will cease to exist; if the lips follow their natural law they know not profit or loss. Their ways agreeing, Master and friend sat side by side with him on the same seat. That was only as it should be.'

'At the end of nine years my mind gave free rein to its reflections, my mouth free passage to its speech. Of right and wrong, profit and loss, I had no knowledge, either as touching myself or others. I knew neither that the Master was my instructor, nor that the other man was my friend. Internal and External were blended into Unity. After that, there was no distinction between eye and ear, ear and nose, nose and mouth: all were the same. My mind was frozen, my body in dissolution, my flesh and bones all melted together. I was wholly unconscious of what my body was resting on, or what was under my feet. I was borne this way and that on the wind, like dry chaff or leaves falling from a tree. In fact, I knew not whether the wind was riding on me or I on the wind. Now, you have not spent one whole season in your teacher's house, and yet you have lost patience two or three times already. Why, at this rate, the atmosphere will never support an atom of your body, and even the earth will be unequal to the weight of one of your limbs!

> The only way to etherealize the body being to purge the mind of its passions.

How can you expect to walk in the void or to be charioted on the wind?'

Hearing this, Yin Shêng was deeply ashamed. He could hardly trust himself to breathe, and it was long ere he ventured to utter another word.

* * *

Mr Fan had a son named Tzŭ Hua, who succeeded in achieving great fame as an exponent of the black art, and the whole kingdom bowed down before him. He was in high favour with the Prince of Chin, taking no office but standing on a par with the three Ministers of State. Any one on whom he turned a partial eye was marked out for distinction; while those of whom he spoke unfavourably were forthwith banished. People thronged his hall in the same way as they went to Court. Tzŭ Hua used to encourage his followers to contend amongst themselves, so that the clever ones were always bullying the slow-witted, and the strong riding rough-shod over the weak. Though this resulted in blows and wounds being dealt before his eyes, he was not in the habit of troubling about it. Day and night, this sort of thing served as an amusement, and practically became a custom in the State.

One day, Ho Shêng and Tzŭ Po, two of Fan's leading disciples, set off on a journey and, after traversing a stretch of wild country, they put up for the night in the hut of an old peasant named Shang Ch'iu Wai. During the night, the two travellers conversed together, speaking of Tzŭ Hua's reputation and influence, his power over life and death, and how he could make the rich man poor and the poor man rich. Now, Shang Ch'iu Wai was living on the border of starvation. He had crept round under the window and overheard this conversation. Accordingly, he borrowed some provisions and, shouldering his basket, set off for Tzŭ Hua's establishment. This man's followers, however, were a worldly set, who wore silken garments and rode in high carriages and stalked about with their noses in the air.

Seeing that Shang Ch'iu Wai was a weak old man, with a weather-beaten face and clothes of no particular cut, they one and all despised him. Soon he became a regular target for their insults and ridicule, being hustled about and slapped on the back and what not. Shang Ch'iu K'ai, however, never showed the least annoyance, and at last the disciples, having exhausted their wit on him in this way, grew tired of the fun. So, by way of a jest, they took the old man with them to the top of a cliff, and the word was passed round that whosoever dared to throw himself over would be rewarded with a hundred ounces of silver. There was an eager response, and Shang Ch'iu K'ai, in perfect good faith, was the first to leap over the edge. And lo! he was wafted down to earth like a bird on the wing, not a bone or muscle of his body being hurt. Mr Fan's disciples, regarding this as a lucky chance, were merely surprised, but not yet moved to great wonder. Then they pointed to a bend in the foaming river below, saying: 'There is a precious pearl at the bottom of that river, which can be had for the diving.' Ch'iu K'ai again acted on their suggestion and plunged in. And when he came out, sure enough he held a pearl in his hand.

Then, at last, the whole company began to suspect the truth, and Tzŭ Hua gave orders that an array of costly viands and silken raiment should be prepared; then suddenly a great fire was kindled round the pile. 'If you can walk through the midst of these flames,' he said, 'you are welcome to keep what you can get of these embroidered stuffs, be it much or little, as a reward.' Without moving a muscle of his face, Shang Ch'iu K'ai walked straight into the fire, and came back again with his garments unsoiled and his body unsinged.

Mr Fan and his disciples now realized that he was in possession of Tao, and all began to make their apologies, saying: 'We did not know, Sir, that you had Tao, and were only playing a trick on you. We insulted you, not knowing that you were a divine man. You have exposed our stupidity, our deafness and out blindness. May we venture to ask what the Great Secret is?' 'Secret I have none,' replied Shang Ch'iu K'ai. 'Even in my own mind I have no clue as to the real cause. Nevertheless, there is one point in it all which I must try to explain to you. A short time ago, Sir, two disciples of yours came and put up for the night in my hut. I heard them extolling Mr Fan's powers — how he could dispense life and death at his will, and how he was able to make the rich man poor and the poor man rich. I believed this implicitly, and as the distance was not very great I came hither. Having arrived, I unreservedly accepted as true all the statements made by your disciples, and was only afraid lest the opportunity might never come of putting them triumphantly to the proof I knew not what part of space my body occupied, nor yet where danger lurked. My mind was simply One, and material objects thus offered no resistance. That is all. But now, having discovered that your disciples were deceiving me, my inner man is thrown into a state of doubt and perplexity, while outwardly my senses of sight and hearing re-assert themselves. When I reflect that I have just had a providential escape from being drowned and burned to death, my heart within me freezes with horror, and my limbs tremble with fear. I shall never again have the courage to go near water or fire.'

From that time forth, when Mr Fan's disciples happened to meet a beggar or a poor horse-doctor on the road, so far from jeering at him, they would actually dismount and offer him a humble salute.

Tsai Wo heard this story, and told it to Confucius. 'Is this so strange to you?' was the reply. 'The man of perfect faith can extend his influence to inanimate things and disembodied spirits; he can move heaven and earth, and fly to the six cardinal points without encountering any hindrance.

Compare the familiar passage in the Bible (Matt. xvii. 20).

[He replied, "Because you have so little faith. Truly I tell you, if you have faith as small as a mustard seed, you can say to this mountain, 'Move from here to there,' and it will move. Nothing will be impossible for you."]

His powers are not confined to walking in perilous places and passing through water and fire. If Shang Ch'iu K'ai, who put his faith in falsehoods, found no obstacle in external matter, how much more certainly will that be so when both parties are equally sincere! Young man, bear this in mind.'

In Shang Ch'iu K'ai's case, though he himself was sincere, his Master Fan Tzŭ Hua was merely an impostor.

---

* * *

The Keeper of Animals under King Hsüan, of the Chou dynasty, had an assistant named Liang Yang, who was skilled in the management of wild birds and beasts. When he fed them in their park-enclosure, all the animals showed themselves tame and tractable, although they comprised tigers, wolves, eagles and ospreys. Male and female freely propagated their kind, and their numbers multiplied.

The difficulty of getting wild animals to breed in captivity is well known to naturalists.

The different species lived promiscuously together, yet they never clawed nor bit one another.

The King was afraid lest this man's secret should die with him, and commanded him to impart it to the Keeper. So Liang Yang appeared before the Keeper and said: 'I am only a humble servant, and have really nothing to impart. I fear his Majesty thinks I am hiding something from you. With regard to my method of feeding tigers, all I have to say is this: when yielded to, they are pleased; when opposed, they are angry. Such is the natural disposition of all living creatures. But neither their pleasure nor their anger is manifested without a cause. Both are really excited by opposition.

> Anger directly, pleasure indirectly, owing to the natural reaction when the opposition is overcome.

'In feeding tigers, then, I avoid giving them either live animals or whole carcasses, lest in the former case the act of killing, in the latter the act of tearing them to pieces, should excite them to fury. Again, I time their periods of hunger and repletion, and I gain a full understanding of the causes of their anger. Tigers are of a different species from man, but, like him, they respond to those who coax them with food, and consequently the act of killing their victims tends to provoke them. This being so, I should not think of opposing them and thus provoking their anger; neither do I humour them and thus cause them to feel pleased. For this feeling of pleasure will in time be succeeded by anger, just as anger must invariably be succeeded by pleasure. Neither of these states hits the proper mean. Hence it is my aim to be neither antagonistic nor compliant, so that the animals regard me as one of themselves. Thus it happens that they walk about the park without regretting the tall forests and the broad marshes, and rest in the enclosure without yearning for the lonely mountains and the dark valleys. Such are the principles which have led to the results you see.'

∗   ∗   ∗

There was once a man, a sailor by profession, who was very fond of sea-gulls. Every morning he went into the sea and swam about in their midst, at which times a hundred gulls and more would constantly flock about him.

> 'Creatures are not shy of those whom they feel to be in mental and bodily harmony with themselves.'

One day his father said to him: 'I am told that sea-gulls swim about with you in the water. I wish you would catch one or two for me to make pets of.' On the following day, the sailor went down to the sea as usual, but the gulls only wheeled about in the air and would not alight.

> 'There was disturbance in his mind, accompanied by a change in his outward demeanour; thus the birds became conscious of

the fact that he was a human being. How could their instinct be deceived?'

* * *

Chao Hsiang Tzŭ led out a company of a hundred thousand men to hunt in the Central Mountains. Lighting the dry undergrowth, they set fire to the whole forest, and the glow of the flames was visible for a hundred miles around.

Suddenly a man appeared, emerging from a rocky cliff,

> That is to say, passing miraculously out of the actual stone itself.

and was seen to hover in the air amidst the flames and the smoke. Everybody took him for a disembodied spirit. When the fire had passed, he walked quietly out, and showed no trace of having been through the ordeal. Hsiang Tzŭ marvelled thereat, and detained him for the purpose of careful examination. In bodily form he was undoubtedly a man, possessing the seven channels of sense, besides which his breathing and his voice also proclaimed him a man. So the prince inquired what secret power it was that enabled him to dwell in rock and to walk through fire. 'What do you mean by rock?' replied the man; 'what do you mean by fire?' Hsiang Tzŭ said: 'What you just now came out of is rock; what you just now walked through is fire.' 'I know nothing of them,' replied the man.

> 'It was this extreme feat of unconsciousness that enabled him to perform the above feats.'

The incident came to the ears of Marquis Wên of the Wei State, who spoke to Tzŭ Hsia about it, saying: 'What an extraordinary man this must be!' 'From what I have heard the Master say,' replied Tzŭ Hsia, 'the man who achieves harmony with Tao enters into close unison with external objects, and none of them has the power to harm or hinder him. Passing through solid metal or stone, walking in the midst of fire or on the surface of water — all these things become possible to him.' 'Why, my friend,' asked the Marquis, 'cannot you do all this? 'I have not yet succeeded,' said Tzŭ Hsia, 'in cleansing my heart of impurities and discarding Wisdom. I can only find leisure to discuss the matter in tentative fashion.' 'And why,' pursued the Marquis, 'does not the Master himself perform these feats?' 'The Master,' replied Tzǔ' Hsia, 'is able to do these things, but he is also able to refrain from doing them.' Which answer hugely delighted the Marquis.

*   *   *

There may be similarity in understanding without similarity in outward form. There may also be similarity in form without similarity in understanding. The Sage embraces similarity of understanding and pays no regard to similarity of form. The world in general is attracted by similarity of form, but remains indifferent to similarity of understanding. Those creatures that resemble them in shape they love and consort with; those that differ from them in shape they fear and keep at a distance. The creature that has a skeleton seven feet long,

---

The Chinese foot at that time being considerably shorter than ours.

---

hands differently shaped from the feet, hair on its head, and an even set of teeth in its jaws, and walks erect, is called a man. But it does not follow that a man may not have the mind of a brute. Even though this be the case, other men will still recognize him as one of their own species in virtue of his outward form. Creatures which have wings on the back or horns on the head, serrated teeth or extensile talons, which fly overhead or run on all fours, are called birds and beasts. But it does not follow that a bird or a beast may not have the mind of a man. Yet, even if this be so, it is nevertheless assigned to another species because of the difference in form.

P'ao Hsi, Nǔ Kua, Shên Nung and Hsia Hou had serpents' bodies, human faces, ox-heads and tigers' snouts. Thus, their forms were not human, yet their virtue was of the saintliest. Chieh of the Hsia dynasty, Chou of the Yin, Huan of the Lu State, and Mu of the Ch'u State, were in all external respects, as facial appearance and possession of the seven channels of sense, like unto other men; yet they had the minds of savage brutes. Howbeit, in seeking perfect understanding, men attend to the outward form alone, which will not bring them near to it.

When the Yellow Emperor fought with Yen Ti on the field of P'an-ch'ŭan, his vanguard was composed of bears, wolves, panthers, lynxes and tigers, while his ensign-bearers were eagles, ospreys, falcons and kites. This was forcible impressment of animals into the service of man. The Emperor Yao entrusted K'uei with the regulation of music.

> K'uei was a composite being, half beast, half man, of irreproachable virtue. His son, on the other hand, is said to have had 'the heart of a pig'. He was insatiably gluttonous, covetous and quarrelsome.

When the latter tapped the musical stone in varying cadence, all the animals danced to the sound of the music. When the Shao in its nine variations was heard on the flute, the phœnix itself flew down to assist. This was the attraction of animals by the power of music. In what, then, do the minds of birds and beasts differ from the minds of men? Their shapes and the sounds they utter are different from ours, and they know no way of communicating with us. But the wisdom and penetration of the Sage are unlimited: that is why he is able to lead then, to do his bidding. The intelligence of animals is innate, even as that of man. Their common desire is for self-preservation, but they do not borrow their knowledge from men. There is pairing between the male and the female, and mutual attachment between the mother and her young. They shun the open plain and keep to the mountainous parts; they flee the cold and make for warmth; when they settle, they gather in flocks; when they travel, they preserve a fixed order. The young ones are stationed in the middle, the stronger ones place themselves on the outside. They show one another the way to the drinking-places, and call to their fellows when there is food. In the earliest ages, they dwelt and moved about in company with man. It was not until the age of emperors and kings that they began to be afraid and broke away into scattered bands. And now, in this final period, they habitually hide and keep out of man's way so as to avoid injury at his hands. At the present day, the Chieh-shih in the far east can in many cases interpret the language of the six domestic animals, although they have probably but an imperfect understanding of it.

In remote antiquity, there were men of divine enlightenment who were perfectly acquainted with the feelings and habits of all living things, and thoroughly understood the languages of the various species. They brought them together, trained them, and admitted them to their society, exactly like human being... These sages declared that, in mind and understanding, there was no wide gulf between any of the living species endowed with blood and breath.

And therefore, knowing that this was so, they omitted nothing from their course of training and instruction.

*   *   *

Hui Yang went to visit Prince K'ang of the Sung State. The Prince, however, stamped his foot, rasped his throat, and said angrily: 'The things I like are courage and strength. I am not fond of your good and virtuous people. What can a stranger like you have to teach me? 'I have a secret,' replied Hui Yang, 'whereby my opponent, however brave or strong, can be prevented from harming me either by thrust or by blow. Would not your Highness care to know that secret?' 'Capital!' exclaimed K'ang; 'that is certainly something I should like to hear about.' Hui Yang went on: 'To render ineffectual the stabs and blows of one's opponent is indeed to cover him with shame. But my secret is one which will make your opponent, however brave or strong, afraid to stab or to strike at all! His being afraid, however, does not always imply that he has not the will to do so. Now, my secret method operates so that even the will is absent. Not having the will to harm, however, does not necessarily connote the desire to love and to do good. But my secret is one whereby every man, woman and child in the Empire shall be inspired with the friendly desire to love and do good to one another! This is something that transcends all social distinctions, and is much better than the mere possession of courage and strength. Has your Highness no mind to acquire such a secret as this?' 'Nay,' said the Prince, 'I am anxious to learn it. What is the secret, pray?' 'Nothing else,' replied Hui Yang, 'than the teachings of Confucius and Mo Tzŭ.

A famous philosopher who flourished about 400 B.C. and propounded, chiefly on utilitarian grounds, the doctrine of 'universal love'.

[Mo Tzŭ is said to have the philosophy more aligned to the later philosophy of Jesus Christ among the ancient Chinese sages.]

Neither of these two men possessed any land, and yet they were princes; they held no official rank, and yet they were leaders. All the inhabitants of the Empire, old and young, used to crane their necks and stand on tiptoe to catch a glimpse of them. For it was their object to bring peace and happiness to all. Now, your Highness is lord of ten thousand chariots.

> A conventional way of saying that Sung was a feudal State of
> the first class.

If you are sincere in your purpose, all the people within the four borders
of your realm will reap the benefit, and the fame of your virtue will far exceed
that of Confucius or of Mo Tzŭ.'

> They not having enjoyed the advantage of ruling over a large
> State.

The Prince of Sung found himself at loss for an answer, and Hui Yang
quickly withdrew. Then the Prince turned to his courtiers and said: 'A forcible argument! This stranger has carried me away by his eloquence.'

Book III – Dreams

In the time of King Mu of Chou, there was a magician who came from a kingdom in the far west. He could pass through fire and water, penetrate metal and stone, overturn mountains and make rivers flow backwards, transplant whole towns and cities, ride on thin air without falling, encounter solid bodies without being obstructed. There was no end to the countless variety of changes and transformations which he could effect; and, besides changing the external form, he could also spirit away men's internal cares.

King Mu revered him as a god, and served him like a prince. He set aside for his use a spacious suite of apartments, regaled him with the daintiest of food, and selected a number of singing-girls for his express gratification. The magician, however, condemned the King's palace as mean, the cooking as rancid, and the concubines as too ugly to live with. So King Mu had a new building erected to please him. It was built entirely of bricks and wood, and gorgeously decorated in red and white, no skill being spared in its construction. The five royal treasuries were empty by the time that the new pavilion was complete. It stood six thousand feet high, over-topping Mount Chung-nan, and it was called Touch-the-sky Pavilion. Then the King proceeded to fill it with maidens, selected from Chêng and Wei, of the most exquisite and delicate beauty. They were anointed with fragrant perfumes, adorned with moth-eyebrows, provided with jewelled hairpins and earrings, and arrayed in the finest silks, with costly satin trains. Their faces were powdered, and their eyebrows pencilled, their girdles were studded with precious stones. All manner of sweet-scented plants filled the palace with their odours, and ravishing music of the olden time was played to the honoured guest. Every month he was presented with fresh and costly raiment; every morning he had set before him some new and delicious food.

The magician could not well refuse to take up his abode in this palace of delight. But he had not dwelt there very long before he invited the King to accompany him on a jaunt. So the King clutched the magician's sleeve, and soared up with him higher and higher into the sky, until at last they stopped, and lo! they had reached the magician's own palace. This palace was built with beams of gold and silver, and incrusted with pearls and jade. It towered high above the region of clouds and rain, and the foundations whereon it rested were unknown. It appeared like a stupendous cloud-mass to the view.

The sights and sounds it offered to eye and ear, the scents and flavours which abounded there, were such as exist not within mortal ken. The King verily believed that he was in the Halls of Paradise, tenanted by God Himself, and that he was listening to the mighty music of the spheres. He gazed at his own palace on the earth below, and it seemed to him no better than a rude pile of clods and brushwood.

It seemed to the King as if his stay in this place lasted for several decades, during which he gave no thought to his own kingdom. Then the magician invited him to make another journey, and in the new region they came to, neither sun nor moon could be seen in the heavens above, nor any rivers or seas below. The King's eyes were dazed by the quality of the light, and he lost the power of vision; his ears were stunned by the sounds that assailed them, and he lost the faculty of hearing. The framework of his bones and his internal organs were thrown out of gear and refused to function. His thoughts were in a whirl, his intellect became clouded, and he begged the magician to take him back again.

> 'This was the region of the Great Void, where all is dim and blurred, assuredly not meant to be traversed by the ordinary man. The dizziness of brain and eye was the effect produced by the Absolute.'

Thereupon, the magician gave him a shove, and the King experienced a sensation of falling through space...

When he awoke to consciousness, he found himself sitting on his throne just as before, with the self-same attendants round him. He looked at the wine in front of him, and saw that it was still full of sediment; he looked at the viands, and found that they had not yet lost their freshness. He asked where he had come from, and his attendants told him that he had only been sitting quietly there. This threw King Mu into a reverie, and it was three months before he was himself again. Then he made further inquiry, and asked the magician to explain what had happened. 'Your Majesty and I,' replied the magician, 'were only wandering about in the spirit, and, of course, our bodies never moved at all. What essential difference is there between that sky-palace we dwelt in and your Majesty's palace on earth, between the spaces we travelled through and your Majesty's own park?

> Looked at from the standpoint of the Absolute, both palaces
> were unreal.

During your retirement from public affairs, you have been in a perpetual
state of doubt as to the reality of your experience. But in a universe where
changes are everlasting in progress, and fast and slow are purely relative con-
ceptions, how can the Ideal ever be fully attained?'

> The sky-palace was only some degrees finer than the King's,
> just as the King's palace was only some degrees finer than the
> hovel of a peasant. To strive for something that shall satisfy
> man's desires and aspirations once and for all is only labour
> lost. The story continues with an account of the King's marvel-
> lous journey to the West. But though he drained the cup of
> pleasure to the dregs, the upshot of it all was that he never truly
> attained to Tao. We may seek the moral in a saying of Lao Tzu:
> 'Without going out of doors, one may know the whole world;
> without looking out of window, one may see the Way of
> Heaven. The farther one travels, the less one may know.'

*   *   *

Lao Ch'êng Tzŭ went to learn magic from the venerable Yin Wên. After
a period of three years, having obtained no communication, he humbly asked
permission to go home. Yin Wên bowed, and led him into the inner apartment. There, having dismissed his attendants, he spoke to him as follows:
'Long ago, when Lao Tzŭ was setting out on his journey to the West, he
addressed me and said: "All that has the breath of life, all that possesses
bodily form, is mere illusion. The point at which creation begins, the change
effected by the Dual Principles — these are called respectively Life and
Death. That which underlies the manifold workings of Destiny is called Evolution; that which produces and transforms bodily substance is called Illusion. The ingenuity of the Creative Power is mysterious, and its operations
are profound. In truth, it is inexhaustible and eternal.

> The 'Creative Power', of course, is Tao; but how widely the
> conception of Tao, differs from that of a personal God may be
> seen from the commentator's note: 'How should the Creative
> Power possess a conscious mind? It is its spontaneity that con-
> stitutes the mystery. Spirit and matter eagerly come together

and coalesce into perceptible forms. Following the path of evolution they proceed on their way, and before long relapse into nothingness.'

The ingenuity of that which causes material form is patent to the eye, and its operations are superficial. Therefore it arises anon, and anon it vanishes." Only one who knows that Life is really Illusion, and that Death is really Evolution, can begin to learn magic from me. You and I are both illusions. What need, then, to make a study of the subject?'

> 'If a person wishes to make a study of illusion, in spite of the fact that his own body is an illusion, we are reduced to the absurdity of an illusion studying an illusion.'

Lao Ch'êng Tzŭ returned home, and for three months pondered deeply over the words of the Venerable Yin Wên. Subsequently, he had the power of appearing or disappearing at will; he could reverse the order of the four seasons, produce thunderstorms in winter and ice in summer, make flying things creep and creeping things fly. But to the end of his days he never published the secret of his art, so that it was not handed down to after generations.

*   *   *

The Master Lieh Tzŭ said: 'A dream is something that comes into contact with the mind; an external event is something that impinges on the body. Hence our feelings by day and our dreams by night are the result of contacts made by mind or body. It follows that if we can concentrate the mind in abstraction, our feelings and our dreams will vanish of themselves. Those who rely on their waking perceptions will not argue about them. Those who put faith in dreams do not understand the processes of change in the external world.

> This refers to a previous passage, omitted in the present selection. Contrary to the received opinion of his own day, Lieh Tzu held that dreams were not just arbitrary manifestations portending future events, but the effects of regular antecedent causes, without any further significance. They are produced by certain processes of the mind, and if these processes can be checked (as Lieh Tzu believes they can) by means of abstraction, dreaming will also cease.

"The pure men of old passed their waking existence in self-oblivion, and slept without dreams." How can this be dismissed as an empty phrase?'

*   *   *

Mr Yin of Chou was the owner of a large estate who harried his servants unmercifully, and gave them no rest from morning to night. There was one old servant in particular whose physical strength had quite left him, yet his master worked him all the harder. All day long he was groaning as he went about his work, and when night came he was reeling with fatigue and would sleep like a log. His spirit was then free to wander at will, and every night he dreamt that he was a king, enthroned in authority over the multitude, and controlling the affairs of the whole State. He took his Pleasure in palaces and belvederes, following his own fancy in everything, and his happiness was beyond compare. But when he awoke, he was servant once more. To some one who condoled with him on his hard lot the old man replied: 'Human life may last a hundred years, and the whole of it is equally divided into nights and days. In the daytime I am only a slave, it is true, and my misery cannot be gainsaid. But by night I am a king, and my happiness is beyond compare. So what have I to grumble at?'

Now, Mr Yin's mind was full of worldly cares, and he was always thinking with anxious solicitude about the affairs of his estate. Thus he was wearing out mind and body alike, and at night he also used to fall asleep utterly exhausted. Every night he dreamt that he was another man's servant, running about on menial business; of every description, and subjected to every possible kind of abuse and ill-treatment. He would mutter and groan in his sleep, and obtained no relief until morning came. This state of things at last resulted in a serious illness, and Mr Yin besought the advice of a friend. 'Your station in life,' his friend said, 'is a distinguished one, and you have wealth and property in abundance. In these respects you are far above the average. If at night you dream that you are a servant and exchange ease for affliction, that is only the proper balance in human destiny. What you want is that your dreams should be as pleasant as your waking moments. But that is beyond your power to compass.' On hearing what his friend said, Mr Yin lightened his servant's toil, and allowed his own mental worry to abate; whereupon his malady began to decrease in proportion.

*   *   *

A man was gathering fuel in the Cheng State when he fell in with a deer that had been startled from its usual haunts. He gave chase, and succeeded in killing it. He was overjoyed at his good luck; but, for fear of discovery, he hastily concealed the carcass in a dry ditch, and covered it up with brush-wood. Afterwards, he forgot the spot where he had hidden the deer, and finally became convinced that the whole affair was only a dream. He told the story to people he met as he went along; and one of those who heard it, following the indications given, went and found the deer. On reaching home with his booty, this man made the following statement to his wife: 'Once upon a time,' he said, 'a wood-cutter dreamt that he had got a deer, but couldn't remember the place where he had put it. Now I have found the deer, so it appears that his dream was a true dream.' 'On the contrary,' said his wife, 'it is you who must have dreamt that you met a wood-cutter who had caught a deer. Here you have a deer, true enough. But where is the wood-cutter? it is evidently your dream that has come true.' 'I have certainly got a deer,' replied her husband; 'so what does it matter to us whether it was his dream or mine?'

Meanwhile, the wood-cutter had gone home, not at all disgusted at having lost the deer.

For he thought the whole thing must have been a dream.

But the same night, he saw in a dream the place where he had really hidden it, and he also dreamt of the man who had taken it. So, the next morning, in accordance with his dream, he went to seek him out in order to recover the deer. A quarrel ensued, and the matter was finally brought before the magistrate, who gave judgment in these terms: 'You,' he said to the wood-cutter, 'began by really killing a deer, but wrongly thought it was a dream. Then you really dreamt that you had got the deer, but wrongly took the dream to be a reality. The other man really took your deer, which he is now disputing with you.

His wife, on the other hand, declares that he saw both man and deer in a dream, so that nobody can be said to have killed the deer at all. Meanwhile, here is the deer itself in court, and you had better divide it between you.'

The case was reported to the Prince of the Chêng State, who said: 'Why, the magistrate must have dreamt the whole thing himself!' The question was referred to the Prime Minister, but the latter confessed himself unable to disentangle the part that was a dream from that part that was not a dream. 'If you want to distinguish between waking and dreaming,' he said, 'only the Yellow Emperor or Confucius could help you. But both these sages are dead, and there is nobody now alive who can draw any such distinction.

Of course, it is implied that there is no real distinction between the two.

So the best thing you can do is to uphold the magistrate's decision.'

*   *   *

Yang-li Hua-tzŭ, of the Sung State, was afflicted in middle age by loss of memory. Anything he received in the morning he had forgotten by the evening, anything he gave away in the evening he had forgotten the next morning. Out-of-doors, he forgot to walk; indoors, he forgot to sit down. At any given moment, he had no recollection of what had just taken place; and a little later on, he could not even recollect what had happened then. All his family were perfectly disgusted with him. Fortune-tellers were summoned, but their divinations proved unsuccessful; Wizards were sought out, but their exorcisms were ineffectual; physicians were called in, but their remedies were of no avail. At last, a learned professor from the Lu State volunteered his services, declaring that he could effect a cure. Hua-Tzŭ's wife and family immediately offered him half their estate if only he would tell them how to set to work. The professor replied: 'This is a case which cannot be dealt with by means of auspices and diagrams; the evil cannot be removed by prayers and incantations, nor successfully combated by drugs and potions. What I shall try to do is to influence his mind and turn the current of his thoughts; in that way a cure is likely to be brought about.'

Accordingly, the experiment was begun. The professor exposed his patient to cold, so that he was forced to beg for clothes; subjected him to hunger, so that he was fain to ask for food; left him in darkness, so that he was obliged to search for light. Soon, he was able to report progress to the sons of the house, saying gleefully: 'The disease can be checked. But the methods I shall employ have been handed down as a secret in my family, and cannot be made known to the public. All attendants must, therefore, be kept out of the way, and I must be shut up alone with my patient.' The professor was allowed to have his way, and for the space of seven days no one knew what was going on in the sick man's chamber. Then, one fine morning, the treatment came to an end, and, wonderful to relate, the disease of so many years' standing had entirely disappeared!

No sooner had Hua-Tzŭ regained his senses, however, than he flew into a great rage, drove his wife out of doors, beat his sons, and, snatching up a spear, hotly pursued the professor through the town. On being arrested and asked to explain his conduct, this is what he said: 'Lately when I was steeped in forgetfulness, my senses were so benumbed that I was quite unconscious of the existence of the outer world. But now I have been brought suddenly to a perception of the events of half a lifetime. Preservation and destruction, gain and loss, sorrow and joy, love and hate have begun to throw out their myriad tentacles to invade my peace; and these emotions will, I fear, continue to keep my mind in the state of turmoil that I now experience. Oh! if I could but recapture a short moment of that blessed oblivion!'

> 'If this is the sentiment of a man whose mental infirmity bears some resemblance to the Highest Principle (Tao), how much stronger will be on entering the realm of the Absolute itself!'

*   *   *

There was once a man who, though born in Yen, was brought up in Ch'u, and it was only in his old age that he returned to his native country.

> Yen was the northernmost State of ancient China, while Ch'u was bounded by the left bank of the Yangtsze.

On the way thither, as they were passing through the Chin State, a fellow-traveller played a practical joke on him. Pointing to the city he said: 'Here is the capital of the Yen State'; whereupon the old man flushed with excitement. Pointing out a certain shrine, he told him that it was his own village altar, and the old man heaved a deep sigh. Then he showed him a house, and said: 'This is where your ancestors lived'; and the tears welled up in his eyes. Finally, a mound was pointed out to him as the tomb where his ancestors lay buried, whereupon the old man could control himself no longer, and wept aloud. But his fellow-traveller burst into roars of laughter. 'I have been hoaxing you,' he cried; 'this is only the Chin State.' His victim was greatly mortified; and when he arrived at his journey's end, and really did see before him the city and altars of Yen, with the actual abode and tombs of his ancestors. his emotion was much less acute.

Book IV – Confucius

A high official from Shang paid a visit to Confucius 'You are a sage, are you not?' he inquired. 'A sage!' replied Confucius. 'How could I venture to think so? I am only a man with a wide range of learning and information.' The Minister then asked: 'Were the Three Kings sages?'

> The Three Kings, in this particular passage, are probably T'ang, surnamed 'The Completer' or 'The Successful', who founded the Shang dynasty, 1766 B.C., and the two founders of the Chou dynasty, Wên and Wu. The word shêng, here translated 'sage', implies a man inspired by Heaven.

'The Three Kings,' replied Confucius, 'were great in the exercise of wisdom and courage. I do not know, however, that they were sages.' 'What of the Five Emperors? Were they not sages?'

> Shao Hao, Chuan Hsü, Yao, Shun, and the Great Yü. The last-named came to the throne in 2205 B.C.

'The Five Emperors excelled in the exercise of altruism and righteousness. I do not know that they were sages.' 'And the Three Sovereigns: surely they were sages?'

> The Three Sovereigns always denote the legendary rulers Fu Hsi, Shên Nung and the Yellow Emperor.

'The Three Sovereigns excelled in the virtues that were suited to their age. But whether they were sages or no I really cannot say.'

> 'The wide learning of Confucius, the warlike prowess of T'ang and Wu, the humility and self-abnegation of Yao, and Shun, the rude simplicity of Fu Hsi and Shên Nung, simply represent the ordinary activities of the sage who accommodates himself to the necessities of the world he lives in. They are not the qualities which make them sages. Those qualities are truly such as neither word nor deed can adequately express.'

'Why, who is there, then,' cried the Minister, much astonished, 'that is really a sage?' The expression of Confucius' countenance changed, and he replied after a pause: 'Among the people of the West a true sage dwells. He governs not, yet there is no disorder. He speaks not, yet he is naturally trusted. He makes no reforms, yet right conduct is spontaneous and universal. So great and incomprehensible is he that the people can find no name to call him by. I suspect that this man is a sage, but whether in truth he is a sage or is not a sage I do not know.'

The early Jesuit missionaries saw in the above an allusion to Jesus Christ. But (apart from other considerations) it is almost certain that the present work had taken definite shape before the Christian era. On the other hand, it is quite possible that the Sage whom Lieh Tzŭ had in mind was Śākyamuni Buddha.

The Minister from Shang meditated awhile in silence. Then he said to himself: 'Confucius is making a fool of me!'

*   *   *

When the Master Lieh Tzŭ took up his abode in Nan-kuo the number of those who settled down with him was past reckoning, though one were to count them day by day. Lieh Tzŭ, however, continued to live in retirement, and every morning would hold discussions with them, the fame of which spread far and wide.

Nan-kuo Tzŭ was his next-door neighbour, but for twenty years no visit passed between them, and when they met in the street they made as though they had not seen each other.

'There was a mysterious harmony between their doctrines, and therefore they arrived at old age without having had any mutual intercourse.' Nan-kuo Tzu means simply 'the Philosopher of Nan-kuo'.

Lieh Tzŭ's disciples felt convinced that there was enmity between their Master and Nan-kuo Tzŭ; and at last, one who had come from the Ch'u State spoke to Lieh Tzŭ about it, saying: 'How comes it, Sir, that you and Nan-kuo Tzŭ are enemies?' 'Nan-kuo Tzŭ,' replied the Master, 'has the appearance of fullness, but his mind is a blank.

By no means a term of disparagement, in the mouth of a Taoist.

His ears do not hear, his eyes do not see, his mouth does not speak, his mind is devoid of knowledge, his body free from agitation. What would be the object of visiting him?

However, we will try, and you shall accompany me thither to see.' Accordingly, forty of the disciples went with him to call on Nan-kuo Tzŭ, who turned out to be a repulsive-looking creature with whom they could make no contact.

Taoist writers seem to delight in attributing ugliness and deformity to their sages, no doubt as a sort of foil or set-off to their inward grandeur.

He only gazed blankly at Lieh Tzŭ. Mind and body seemed not to belong together, and his guests could find no means of approach.

'The soul had subjugated the body. The mind being void of sense-impressions, the countenance remained motionless. Hence it seemed as if there were no co-operation between the two. How could they respond to external stimuli?'

Suddenly, Nan-kuo Tzŭ singled out the hindermost row of Lieh Tzŭ's disciples, and began to talk to them quite pleasantly and simply, though in the tone of a superior.

'Fraternizing with the hindmost row, he recognized no distinctions of rank or standing; meeting a sympathetic influence, and responding thereto, he did not allow his mind to be occupied with the external.'

The disciples were astonished at this, and when they got home again, all wore a puzzled expression. Their Master Lieh Tzŭ said to them: 'He who has reached the stage of thought is silent. He who has attained to perfect knowledge is also silent. He who uses silence in lieu of speech really does speak. He who for knowledge substitutes blankness of mind really does know. Without words and speaking not, without knowledge and knowing not, he really speaks and really knows. Saying nothing and knowing nothing, there is in reality nothing that he does not say, nothing that he does not know. This is how the matter stands, and there is nothing further to be said. Why are you thus astonished without cause?'

*   *   *

Lung Shu said to Wên Chih:

> 'Wên Chih lived in the time of the Six States, and acted as physician to Prince Wei of Ch'i (378-333 B.C.]. Another account says that he was an able physician of the Sung State in the "Spring and Autumn" period, and that he cured Prince Wen of Ch'i by making him angry, whereupon his sickness vanished.'

'You are the master of cunning arts. I have a disease. Can you cure it, Sir?' 'I am at your service,' replied Wên Chih. 'But please let me know first the symptoms of your disease.' 'I hold it no honour,' said Lung Shu, 'to be praised in my native village, nor do I consider it a disgrace to he decried in my native State. Gain excites in me no joy, and loss no sorrow. I look upon life in the same light as death, upon riches in the same light as poverty, upon my fellow-men as so many swine, and upon myself as I look upon my fellow-men. I dwell in my home as though it were a mere caravanserai, and regard my native district with no more feeling than I would a barbarian State. Afflicted as I am in these various ways, honours and rewards fail to rouse me, pains and penalties to overawe me, good or bad fortune to influence me, joy or grief to move me. Thus I am incapable of serving my sovereign, of associating with my friends and kinsmen, of directing my wife and children, or of controlling my servants and retainers.

> 'Men are controlled by external influences in so far as their minds are open to impressions of good and evil, and their bodies are sensitive to injury or the reverse. But one who is able to discern a connecting unity in the most multiform diversity will surely, in his survey of the universe, be unconscious of the differences between positive and negative.'

What disease is this, and what remedy is there that will cure it?'

Wên Chih replied by asking Lung Shu to stand with his back to the light, while he himself faced the light and looked at him intently. 'Ah!' said he after a while, 'I see that a good square inch of your heart is hollow. You are within an ace of being a true sage. Six of the orifices in your heart are open and clear, and only the seventh is blocked up.

'It was an ancient belief that the sage had seven orifices in his heart' (the seat of the understanding).

This, however, is doubtless due to the fact that you are mistaking for a disease that which is really divine enlightenment. It is a case in which my shallow art is of no avail.'

*　　　*　　　*

Pu-tsê, in the Cheng State, was rich in wise men, and Tungli in men of administrative talent. Among the vassals of Putsê was a certain Po Fêng Tzŭ, who happened to travel through Tung-li and had a meeting with Têng Hsi.

A noted sophist of the sixth century B.C.

The latter cast a glance at his followers, and asked them, with a smile: 'Would you like to see me have some sport with this stranger?' They understood what he would be at, and assented. Têng Hsi then turned to Po Fêng Tzŭ. 'Are you acquainted with the true theory of Sustentation?' he inquired. 'To receive sustenance from others, through inability to support oneself, places one in the category of dogs and swine. It is man's prerogative to give sustenance to other creatures, and to use them for his own purposes. That you and your fellows are provided with abundant food and comfortable clothing is due to us administrators. Young and old, you herd together, and are penned up like cattle destined for the shambles: in what respect are you to be distinguished from dogs and swine?'

Po Fêng Tzŭ made no reply, but one of his company, disregarding the rules of precedence, stepped forward and said: 'Has your Excellency never heard of the variety of craftsmen in Ch'i and Lu? Some are skilled potters and carpenters, others are clever workers in metal and leather; there are good musicians, trained scribes and accountants, military experts and men learned in the ritual of ancestor-worship. All kinds of talent are there fully represented. But without proper organization, these craftsmen cannot be usefully employed. But those who organize them lack knowledge, those who employ them lack technical ability, and therefore they make use of those who have both knowledge and ability.

'Whoso possesses skill and knowledge of any particular kind is incapable of helping his prince in the direction of affairs.'

So it is really we who may be said to employ the Government administrators. What is it, then, that you are boasting about?'

Têng Hsi could think of nothing to say in reply. He glanced round at his disciples and retreated.

Book V – The Questions of T'ang

T'ang of Yin questioned Hsia Ko, saying: 'In the beginnings of antiquity, did individual things exist?'

> 'He suspected that there was only Chaos, and nothing more.

'If things did not exist then,' replied Hsia Ko, 'how could they be in existence now? Or will the men of future ages be right in denying the existence of things at the present time?'

'Things in that case,' pursued T'ang, 'have no before nor after?'

Hsia Ko replied: 'To the beginning and end of things there is no precise limit. Beginning may be end, and end may be beginning. How can we conceive of any fixed period to either?

> 'That which we call an end at the present moment may be the beginning of a new thing, and that which we call a beginning may, contrariwise, be the end of something. End and beginning succeed one another until at last they cannot be distinguished.'

But when it comes to something outside matter in space, or anterior to events in time, our knowledge fails us.'

'Then upwards and downwards and in every direction space is a finite quantity?'

Ko replied: 'I do not know.'

> 'It was not so much that he did not know as that it is unknowable.'

T'ang asked the question again with more insistence, and Ko said: 'If there is nothing in space, then it is infinite; if there is something, then that something must have limits.

How can I tell which is true? But beyond infinity there must again exist non-infinity, and within the unlimited again that which is not unlimited.

> Lieh Tzu means that in this universe of relativity there must be contraries, even to a negative. We are only brought back, however, to our starting-point, for, as the commentator points out, that which is not infinite and not unlimited really stands for that which is finite and limited.

It is this consideration — that infinity must be succeeded by non-infinity, and the unlimited by the not-unlimited — that enables me to apprehend the infinity and unlimited extent of space, but does not allow me to conceive of its being finite and limited.'

*   *   *

T'ang continued his inquiries, saying: 'What is there beyond the Four Seas?'

> That is, the inhabited world as known to the Chinese.

Ko replied: 'Just what there is here in the province of Ch'i.' 'How can you prove that?' asked T'ang.

'When travelling eastwards,' said Ko, 'I came to the land of Ying, where the inhabitants were nowise different from those in this part of the country. I inquired about the countries east of Ying, and found that they, too, were similar to their neighbour. Travelling westwards, I came to Pin, where the inhabitants were similar to our own countrymen. I inquired about the countries west of Pin, and found that they were again similar to Pin. That is how I know that the regions within the Four Seas, the Four Wildernesses and the Four Uttermost Ends of the Earth are nowise different from the country we ourselves inhabit.

Thus, the lesser is always enclosed by a greater, without ever reaching an end. Heaven and earth, which enclose the myriad objects of creation, are themselves enclosed in some outer shell.

> 'That which contains heaven and earth is the Great Void.'

Enclosing heaven and earth and the myriad objects within them, this outer shell is infinite and immeasurable. How do we know but that there is some mightier universe in existence outside our own? That is a question to which we can give no answer.

'Heaven and earth, then, are themselves only material objects, and therefore imperfect. Hence it is that Kua of old fashioned many-coloured blocks of stone to repair the defective parts.

> 'Nü Kua, being a divine man, was able to refine and extract the essence of the five constituents of matter!

He cut off the legs of the Ao and used them to support the four corners of the heavens.

> This Chinese 'Atlas' was a gigantic sea-turtle.

Later on, Kung Kung fought with Chuan Hsǔ for the throne, and, blundering in his rage against Mount Pu-chou, he snapped the pillar which connects Heaven and earth.

> At the north-western corner.

That is why Heaven dips downwards to the north-west, so that sun, moon and stars travel towards that quarter. The earth, on the other hand, is now not large enough to fill up the south-east, so that all rivers and streams roll in that direction.'

> An ingenious theory to account for the apparent westward revolution of the heavenly bodies, as also for the easterly trend of the great Chinese rivers.

*   *   *

The two mountains T'ai-hsing and Wang-wu, which cover an area of 700 square li, and rise to an enormous altitude, originally stood in the south of the Chi district and north of Ho-yang. The Simpleton of the North Mountain, an old man of ninety, dwelt opposite these mountains, and was vexed in spirit because their northern flanks blocked the way to travellers, who had to go all the way round. So he called his family together, and broached a plan. 'Let us,' he said, 'put forth our utmost strength to clear away this obstacle, and cut right through the mountains until we come to Han-yin. What say you?' They all assented except his wife, who made objections and said: 'My goodman has not the strength to sweep away a dunghill, let alone two such mountains as T'ai-hsing and Wang-wu. Besides, where will you put all the earth and stones that you dig up?' The others replied that they would throw them on the promontory of P'o-hai. So the old man, followed by his son and grandson, sallied forth with their pickaxes, and the three of them began hewing away at the rocks, and cutting up the soil, and carting it away in baskets to the promontory of P'o-hai. A widowed woman who lived near had a little boy who, though he was only just shedding his milk teeth, came skipping along to give them what help he could. Engrossed in their toil, they never went home except once at the turn of the season.

The Wise Old Man of the River-bend burst out laughing and urged them to stop. 'Great indeed is your witlessness!' he said. 'With the poor remaining strength of your declining years you will not succeed in removing a hair's breadth of the mountain, much less the whole vast mass of rock and soil.' With a sigh, the Simpleton of the North Mountain replied: 'Surely it is you who are narrow-minded and unreasonable. You are not to be compared with the widow's son, despite his puny strength. Though I myself must die, I shall leave a son behind me, and through him a grandson. That grandson will beget sons in his turn, and those soils will also have sons and grandsons. With all this posterity, my line will not die out, while on the other hand the mountain will receive no increment or addition. Why then should I despair of levelling it to the ground at last?' The Wise Old Man of the River-bend had nothing to say in reply.

One of the serpent-brandishing deities heard of the undertaking and, fearing that it might never be finished, went and told God Almighty, who was touched by the old man's simple faith, and commanded the two sons of K'ua O to transport the mountains, one to the extreme north-east, the other to the southern comer of Yung.

> In the south-west. That is, as far apart as possible. K'ua O was apparently a god of strength.

Ever since then, the region lying between Chi in the north and Han in the south has been an unbroken plain.

> Roughly, the modern province of Honan.

*   *   *

Kung-hu of Lu and Ch'i-ying of Chao both fell ill at the same time, and called in the aid of the great Pien-ch'iao.

A famous physician of the fifth century B.C.

Pien-ch'iao cured them both, and when they were well again he told them that the malady they had been suffering from was one that attacked the internal organs from without, and for that reason was curable by the application of vegetable and mineral drugs. 'But,' he added, 'each of you is also the victim of a congenital disease, which has grown along with the body itself. Would you like me now to grapple with this?' They said, 'Yes'; but asked to hear his diagnosis first.

Pien-ch'iao turned to Kung-hu. 'Your mental powers,' he said, 'are strong, but your willpower is weak. Hence, though fruitful in plans, you are lacking in decision. Ch'i-ying's mental powers, on the other hand, are weak, while his willpower is strong. Hence there is want of forethought, and he is placed at a disadvantage by the narrowness of his aim. Now, if I can effect an exchange of hearts between you, the good will be equally balanced in both.'

That is, Kung-hu, who has the weaker character, will get weaker brainpower to match, while Ch'i-ying, with the stronger will, receives a stronger mind to direct it. Though it may be that Ch'i-ying has the best of the bargain, each man, under the new arrangement, will at any rate be perfectly well balanced. The heart, as we have seen, was regarded as the seat of the mental faculties.

So saying, Pien-ch'iao administered to each of them a potion of medicated wine, which threw them into a deathlike trance lasting three days.

A striking proof of the knowledge and practical application of anaesthesia at a very early date.

Then, making an incision in their breasts, he took out each man's heart and placed it in the other's body, poulticing the wounds with herbs of marvellous efficacy.

When the two men regained consciousness, they looked exactly the same as before; and, taking their leave, they returned home. Only it was Kung-hu who went to Ch'iying's house, where Ch'i-ying's wife and children naturally did not recognize him, while Ch'i-ying went to Kung-hu's house and was not recognized either. This led to a lawsuit between the two families, and Pien-ch'iao was called in as arbitrator. On his explaining how the matter stood, peace was once more restored.

*   *   *

King Mu of Chou made a tour of inspection in the west. He crossed the K'un-lun range, but turned back before he reached the Yen mountains.

'The place where the sun sets.'

On his return journey, before arriving in China, a certain artificer was presented to him, by name Yen Shih. King Mu received him in audience, and asked what he could do. 'I will do anything,' replied Yen Shih, 'that your Majesty may please to command. But there is a piece of work, already finished, that I should like to submit first to your Majesty's inspection.' 'Bring it with you to-morrow.' said the King, 'and we will look at it together.' So Yen Shih called again the next day, and was duly admitted to the royal presence. 'Who is that man accompanying you?' asked the King. 'That, Sire, is my own handiwork. He can sing and he can act.' The King stared at the figure in astonishment. It walked with rapid strides, moving its head up and down, so that any one would have taken it for a live human being. The artificer touched its chin, and it began singing, perfectly in tune. He touched its hand, and it started posturing, keeping perfect time. It went through any number of movements that fancy might happen to dictate. The King, looking on with his favourite concubine and the other inmates of his harem, could hardly persuade himself that it was not real.

As the performance was drawing to an end, the automaton winked his eye and made sundry advances to the ladies in attendance on the King. This, however, threw the King into a passion, and he would have put Yen Shih to death on the spot had not the latter, in mortal terror, instantly pulled the automaton to pieces to let him see what it really was. And lo! it turned out to be merely a conglomeration of leather, wood, glue and paint, variously coloured white, black, red and blue. Examining it closely, the King found all the internal organs complete — liver, gall, heart, lungs, spleen, kidneys, stomach and intestines — and, over these, again, muscles and bones and limbs with their joints, skin and teeth and hair, all of them artificial. Not a part but was fashioned with the utmost nicety and skill; and when it was put together again, the figure presented the same appearance as when first brought in. The King tried the effect of taking away the heart, and found that the mouth would no longer utter a sound; he took away the liver, and the eyes could no longer see; he took away the kidneys, and the legs lost their power of locomotion.

Now the King was delighted. Drawing a deep breath, he exclaimed: 'Can it be that human skill is really on a par with that of the Creator?' And forthwith he gave an order for two extra chariots, in which he took home with him the artificer and his handiwork.

Now, Pan Shu, with his cloud-scaling ladder, and Mo Ti, with his flying kite, thought that they had reached the limits of human achievement.

> 'Pan Shu made a cloud-ladder by which he could mount to the sky and assail the heights of heaven; Mo Ti made a wooden kite which would fly for three days without coming down.'

But when Yen Shih's wonderful piece of work had been brought to their knowledge, the two philosophers never again ventured to boast of their mechanical skill, and ceased to busy themselves so frequently with the square and compasses.

*   *   *

Hei Luan of Wei had a secret grudge against Ch'iu Pingchang, for which he slew him; and Lai Tan, the son of Ch'iu Ping-chang, plotted vengeance against his father's enemy. Lai Tan's spirit was very fierce, but his body was very slight. You could count the grains of rice that he ate, and he was at the mercy of every gust of wind. For all the anger in his heart, he was not strong enough to take his revenge in open fight, and he was ashamed to seek help from others. So he swore that, sword in hand, he would cut Hei Luan's throat unawares. This Hei Luan was the most ferocious character of his day, and in brute strength he was a match for a hundred men. His bones and sinews, skin and flesh were cast in superhuman mould. He would stretch out his neck to the blade or bare his breast to the arrow, but the sharp steel would bend or break, and his body show no scar from the Impact. Trusting to his native strength, he looked disdainfully upon Lai Tan as a mere fledgling.

Lai Tan had a friend Shên T'o, who said to him: 'You have a bitter feud against Hei Luan, and Hei Luan treats you with sovereign contempt. What is your plan of action?' Shedding tears, Lai Tan besought his friend's counsel. 'Well,' said Shên T'o, 'I am told that K'ung Chou of Wei has inherited, through an ancestor, a sword formerly possessed by the Yin Emperors, of such magical power that a mere boy wielding it can put to flight the embattled hosts of an entire army. Why not sue for the loan of this sword?' Acting on this advice, Lai Tan betook himself to Wei and had an interview with K'ung Chou. Following the usage of supplicants, he first went through the ceremony of handing over his wife and children, and then stated his request. 'I have three swords,' replied K'ung Chou, 'but with none of them can you kill a man. You may choose which you like. First, however, let me describe their qualities. The first sword is called "Light-absorber". It is invisible to the eye, and when you swing it you cannot tell that there is anything there. Things struck by it retain an unbroken surface, and it will pass through a man's body without his knowing it. The second is called "Shadow-receiver". If you face north and examine it at the point of dawn, when darkness melts into light, or in the evening, when day gives way to dusk, it appears misty and dim, as though there were something there, the shape of which is not discernible. Things struck by it give out a low sound, and it passes through men's bodies without causing them any pain. The third is called "Night-tempered", because in broad daylight you only see its outline and not the brightness of its blade, while at night you see not the sword itself but the dazzling light which it emits.

'Alluding to its reflecting power.'

The objects which it strikes are cleft through with a sibilant sound, but the line of cleavage closes up immediately. Pain is felt, but no blood remains on the blade. 'These three precious heirlooms have been handed down for thirteen generations, but have never been in actual use. They lie stored away in a box, the seals of which have never been broken.' 'In spite of what you tell me,' said Lai Tan, 'I should like to borrow the third sword.' K'ung Chou then returned his wife and children to him, and they fasted together for seven days. On the seventh day, in the dusk of evening, he knelt down and presented the third sword to Lai Tan, who received it with two low obeisances and went home again.

'He chose the third of the swords because it could be both handled and seen.'

Grasping his new weapon, Lai Tan now sought out his enemy, and found him lying in a drunken stupor at his window. He cut clean through his body in three places between the neck and the navel, but Hei Luan was quite unconscious of it. Thinking he was dead, Lai Tan made off as fast as he could, and happening to meet Hei Luan's son at the door, he struck at him three times with his sword. But it was like hitting the empty air. Hei Luan's son laughed and said: 'Why are you motioning to me in that silly way with your hand?'

It will be remembered that the sword was invisible in daylight.

Realizing at last that the sword had no power to kill a man, Lai Tan heaved a sigh and returned home.

When Hei Luan recovered from the effects of his debauch, he was angry with his wife: 'What do you mean by letting me lie exposed to a draught?' he growled; 'it has given me a sore throat and aching pains in the small of my back.' 'Why,' said his son, 'I am also feeling a pain in my body, and a stiffness in my limbs. Lai Tan, you know, was here a little time ago and, meeting me at the door, made three gestures, which seem somehow to have been the cause of it. How he hates us, to be sure!'

Thus, the improper use of divine weapons only leads to discomfiture. In this allegory, Lieh Tzŭ is satirizing the blood-feud, which must have been a terrible feature of the lawless times in which he lived. The powerlessness of the magic sword to kill may symbolically represent the essential futility of the vendetta which perpetuates itself from father to son.

Book VI – Effort and Destiny

Effort said to Destiny:

I have purposely avoided the familiar modern terms, Fate and Free will, which might seem to furnish the best equivalent to li and ming. Li is the ordinary word for 'strength' or 'force,' and here indicates human effort exerted in some definite direction (the German 'streben') as opposed to the blind and unconscious workings of Nature or Tao.

'Your achievements are not equal to mine.' 'Pray what do you achieve in the working of things,' replied Destiny, 'that you would compare yourself with me?' 'Why,' said Effort, 'the length of man's life, his measure of success, his rank, and his wealth, are all things which I have the power to determine.' To this, Destiny made reply: 'P'êng Tsu's wisdom did not exceed that of Yao and Shun, yet he lived to the age of eight hundred. Yen Yŭan's ability was not inferior to that of the average man, yet he died at the early age of thirty-two. The virtue of Confucius was not less than that of the feudal princes, yet he was reduced to sore straits between Ch'ên and Ts'ai.

See The Sayings of Confucius, p. 115.

The conduct of Chou, of the Yin dynasty, did not surpass that of the Three Men of Virtue, yet he occupied a kingly throne.

Wei Tzu, Chi Tzu and Pi Kan were all relatives of Chou Hsin, by whose orders the last-named was disembowelled.

Chi Cha would not accept the overlordship of Wu, while T'ien Hêng usurped sole power in Ch'i. Po I and Shu. Ch'i starved to death at Shou-yang, while Chi Shih waxed rich at Chan-ch'in. If these results were compassed by your efforts, how is it that you allotted long life to P'êng Tsu and an untimely death to Yen Yŭan; that you awarded discomfiture to the sage and success to the impious, humiliation to the wise man and high honours to the fool, poverty to the good and wealth to the wicked?' 'If, as you say,' re-joined Effort, 'I have really no control over events, is it not, then, owing to your management that things turn out as they do?' Destiny replied: 'The very name "Destiny"

Something already immutably fixed.

---

shows that there can be no question of management in the case. When the way is straight, I push on; when it is crooked, I put up with it. Old age and early death, failure and success, high rank and humble station, riches and poverty — all these come naturally and of themselves. How can I know anything about them?

'Being what it is, without knowing why — that is the meaning of Destiny. What room is there for management here?'

---

*   *   *

Yang Chu had a friend called Chi Liang, who fell ill. In seven days' time his illness had become very grave; medical aid was summoned, and his sons stood weeping round his bed. Chi Liang said to Yang Chu: 'Such excess of emotion shows my children to be degenerate. Will you kindly sing them something which will enlighten their minds?' Yang Chu then chanted the following words:

'How can men be aware of things outside God's ken? Over misfortune man has no control, and can look for no help from God. Have doctors and wizards this knowledge that you and I have not?'

The sons, however, did not understand, and finally called in three physicians, Dr Chiao, Dr Yŭ and Dr Lu. They all diagnosed his complaint; and Dr Chiao delivered his opinion first: 'The hot and cold elements of your body,' he said to Chi Liang, 'are not in harmonious accord, and the impermeable and infundibular parts are mutually disproportionate. The origin of your malady is traceable to disordered appetites, and to the dissipation of your vital essence through worry and care. Neither God nor devil is to blame. Although the illness is grave, it is amenable to treatment.' Chi Liang said: 'You are only one of the common ruck,' and speedily got rid of him. Then Dr Yŭ came forward and said: 'You were born with too little nervous force, and were too freely fed with mother's milk. Your illness is not one that has developed in a matter of twenty-four hours; the causes which have led up to it are of gradual growth. It is incurable.' Chi Liang replied: 'You are a good

105

doctor,' and told them to give him some food. Lastly, Dr Lu said: 'Your illness is attributable neither to God, nor to man, nor to the agency of spirits. It was already foreordained in the mind of Providence when you were endowed with this bodily form at birth. What possible good can herbs and drugs do you?' 'You are a heaven-born physician indeed!' cried Chi Liang; and he sent him away laden with presents.

Not long after, his illness disappeared of itself.

*   *   *

Duke Ching of Ch'i was travelling across the northern flank of the Ox-mountain in the direction of the capital. Gazing at the view before him, he burst into a flood of tears, exclaiming: 'What a lovely scene! How verdant and luxuriantly wooded! To think that some day I must die and leave my kingdom, passing away like running water! If only there were no such things as death, nothing should induce me to stir from this spot.' Two of the Ministers in attendance on the Duke, taking their cue from him, also began to weep, saying: 'We, who are dependent on your Highness's bounty, whose food is of an inferior sort, who have to ride on broken-down hacks or in creaking carts — even we do not want to die. How much less our sovereign liege!'

Yen Tzŭ, meanwhile, was standing by, with a broad smile on his face. The Duke wiped away his tears and, looking at him, said: 'To-day I am stricken with grief on my journey, and both K'ung and Chŭ mingle their tears with mine. How is it that you alone can smile? Yen Tzŭ replied: 'If the worthy ruler were to remain in perpetual possession of his realm, Duke T'ai and Duke Huan would still be exercising their sway. If the bold ruler were to remain in perpetual possession, Duke Chuang and Duke Ling would still be ruling the land. But if all these rulers were now in possession, where would your Highness be? Why, standing in the furrowed fields, clad in coir cape and hat!

The ordinary garb of a Chinese peasant in wet weather.

Condemned to a hard life on earth, you would have had no time, I warrant, for brooding over death. Again, how did you yourself come to occupy this throne? By a series of successive reigns and removals, until at last your turn came. And are you alone going to weep and lament over this order of things? That is pure selfishness. it was the sight of these two objects — a self-centred prince and his fawning attendants — that set me quietly laughing to myself just now.'

Duke Ching felt much ashamed. Raising his goblet, he filled himself one cup, and his obsequious courtiers two cups of wine apiece.

*   *   *

There was once a man, Tung-mên Wu of Wei, who when his son died testified no grief. His house-steward said to him: 'The love you bore your son could hardly be equalled by that of any other parent. Why, then, do you not mourn for him now that he is dead?' 'There was a time,' replied Tung-mên Wu, 'when I had no son, yet I never had occasion to grieve on that account. Now that my son is dead, I am only in the same condition as I was before my son was born. What reason have I, then, to mourn?

> There is a story of Plutarch consoling his wife in exactly similar terms after the death of their daughter.

The husbandman takes his measures according to the season, the trader occupies himself with gain, the craftsman strives to master his art, the official pursues power. Here we have the operation of human forces.

> Or 'effort'. See Book VII.

But the husbandman has seasons of rain and seasons of drought, the trader meets with gains and losses, the craftsman experiences both failure and success, the official finds opportunities or the reverse. Here we see the working of Destiny.

Book VII – Causality

In the course of Lieh Tzŭ's instruction by Hu-ch'iu Tzŭ-lin, the latter said to him: 'You must familiarize yourself with the theory of consequents before you can talk of regulating conduct.' Lieh Tzŭ said: 'Will you explain what you mean by the theory of consequents?' 'Look at your shadow,' said his Master, 'and then you will know.' Lieh turned and looked at his shadow. When his body was bent, the shadow was crooked; when his body was upright, the shadow was straight. Thus it appeared that the attributes of straightness and crookedness were not inherent in the shadow, but corresponded to certain positions of the body. Likewise, contraction and extension are not inherent in the subject, but take place in obedience to external causes. Holding this theory of consequents is to be at home in the antecedent.

> The Law of Causality is the foundation of all science.

Kuan Yin spoke to the Master Lieh Tzŭ, saying: 'If speech is sweet, the echo will be sweet; if speech is harsh, the echo will be harsh. If the body is long, the shadow will be long; if the body is short, the shadow will be short. Reputation is like an echo, personal experiences like a shadow.

'Hence the saying: "Heed your words, and they will meet with harmonious response; heed your actions, and they will find agreeable accord." Therefore, the Sage observes the origin in order to know the issue, scrutinizes the past in order to know the future. Such is the principle whereby he attains foreknowledge.

'The standard of conduct lies with one's own self; the testing of it lies with other men. We are impelled to love those who love us, and to hate those who hate us. T'ang and Wu loved the Empire, and therefore each became King. Chieh and Chou hated the Empire, and therefore they perished. Here we have the test applied. He who does not follow Tao when standard and test are both clear may be likened to one who, when leaving a house, does not go by the door, Or, when travelling abroad, does not keep to the straight road. To seek profit in this way is surely impossible.

> 'No one has ever profited himself by opposing natural law.'

'You may consider the virtues of Shên Nung and Yu Yen, you may examine the books of Yŭ, Hsia, Shang and Chou, you may weigh the utterances of great teachers and sages, but you will find no instance of preservation or destruction, fullness or decay, which has not obeyed this supreme Law.'

Of Causality.

---

* * *

Lieh Tzŭ learned archery and, when he was able to hit the target, he asked the opinion of Kuan Yin Tzŭ on his shooting. 'Do you know why you hit the target?' said Kuan

Yin Tzŭ. 'No, I do not,' was the reply. 'Then you are not good enough yet,' re-joined Kuan Yin Tzŭ. Lieh Tzŭ withdrew and practised for three years after which he again presented himself. Kuan Yin Tzŭ asked, as before: 'Do you know why you hit the target?' 'Yes,' said Lieh Tzŭ, 'I do.' 'In that case, all is well. Hold that knowledge fast, and do not let it slip.'

'Mental and bodily equilibrium are to be sought within oneself. Once you know the causal process which makes you hit the target, you will be able to determine the operation of Destiny beforehand, and when you let fly you will make no mistake.'

The above principle does not apply only to shooting, but also to the government of a State and to personal conduct. Therefore the Sage investigates not the mere facts of preservation and destruction, but rather the causes which bring them about.

* * *

Lieh Tzŭ said: 'Those who excel in beauty become vain; those who excel in strength become violent. To such, it is useless to speak of Tao. He who is not yet turning grey will surely err if he but speak of Tao; how much less can he put it into practice!

'No man will confide in one who shows himself aggressive.

And he in whom no man confides will remain solitary and without support.

'The arrogant and the aggressive will accept no confidences, even if they are made. Their mental attitude to others is one of distrust, and they keep their ears and eyes blocked. Who can render them assistance?'

'The wise man puts his trust in others: thus he reaches fullness of years without decay, perfection of Wisdom without bewilderment. In the government of a State, then, the hardest thing is to recognize the worth of others, not to rely upon one's own.'

'If you succeed in recognizing worth, then the wise will think out plans for you, and the able will act for you. By never rejecting talent from outside, you will find the State easy to govern.'

*   *   *

There was once a man in Sung who carved a mulberry leaf out of jade for his prince. It took three years to complete, and it imitated Nature so exquisitely in its down, its glossiness, and its general configuration from tip to stem, that, if placed in a heap of real mulberry leaves, it could not be distinguished from them. This man was subsequently pensioned by the Sung State as a reward for his skill. Lieh Tzŭ, hearing of it, said: 'If it took the Creator three years to make a single leaf, there would be very few trees with leaves on them. The Sage will rely not so much on human science and skill as on the operations of Tao.'

*   *   *

The Master Lieh Tzŭ was very poor, and his face wore a hungry look. A certain stranger spoke about it to Tzŭ Yang, of Cheng. 'Lieh Yŭ-k'ou,' said he, 'is a scholar in possession of Tao. Yet here he is, living in destitution, within your Excellency's dominion. It surely cannot be that you have no liking for scholars?' Tzŭ Yang forthwith directed that an official allowance of grain should be sent to him. Lieh Tzŭ came out to receive the messengers, made two low bows and declined the gift, whereupon the messengers went away, and Lieh Tzŭ re-entered the house. There he was confronted by his Wife, who beat her breast and cried aloud: 'I have always understood that the wife and family of a man of Tao live a life of ease and pleasure. Yet now, when his Honour sends you a present of food, on account of your starved appearance, you refuse to accept it! I suppose you will call that "destiny"!' The Master Lieh Tzŭ smiled and replied: 'The Minister did not know about me himself. His present of grain was made on the suggestion of another. If it had been a question of punishing me, that too would have been done at some one else's prompting. That is the reason why I did not accept the gift.'

Later on, the masses rose in actual rebellion against Tzǔ Yang, and slew him.

It is implied that Lieh Tzǔ's independence of spirit saved his life, inasmuch as a pensioner would have shared the fate of his patron.

---

*   *   *

Mr Shih of Lu had two sons, one of whom was a scholar and the other a soldier. The former found in his accomplishments the means of ingratiating himself with the Marquis of Ch'i, who engaged him as tutor to the young princes. The other brother proceeded to Ch'u, and won favour with the King of that State by his military talents. The King was so well pleased that he installed him at the head of his troops. Thus both of them succeeded in enriching their family and shedding lustre on their kinsfolk.

Now, a certain Mr Mêng, the neighbour of Mr Shih, also had two sons who followed the self-same professions but were straitened by poverty. Envying the affluence of the Shih family, Mr Mêng called at his neighbour's house, and wanted to know the secret of their rapid rise in the world. The two brothers readily gave him the desired information, whereupon the eldest son immediately set off for Ch'in, hoping that his cultural attainments would recommend him to the King of that State. But the King said: 'At the present moment all the feudal princes are struggling to outbid one another in power, and the great essential is to keep up a large army. If I tried to govern my State on the lines of benevolence and righteousness, ruin and annihilation would be the outcome! So saying, he had the unfortunate man castrated, and turned him away.

The second son, meanwhile, had gone to Wei, hoping that his military knowledge would stand him in good stead. But the Marquis of Wei said to himself — 'Mine is a weak State hedged in by powerful ones.

Wei was bounded by Chin and Ch'i on the north, Lu on the east, and Chêng on the south.

111

My method of preserving tranquillity is to show subservience to the larger States and to conciliate the lesser ones. If I were to rely on armed force, I could only expect utter destruction. I must not allow this man to depart unscathed, or he may find his way to some other State and be a terrible thorn in my side.' So, without more ado, he cut off his feet and sent him back to Lu.

On their return, the whole family fell to beating their breasts in despair, and uttered imprecations on Mr Shih. Mr Shih, however, said: 'Success consists in hitting off the right moment, while missing it means failure. Your method was identical with ours, only the result was different. That is not due to any flaw in the action itself, but simply because it was not well timed. Nothing, in the ordering of this world, is either at all times right or at all times wrong. What formerly passed current may nowadays be rejected; what is now rejected may by and by come into use again. The fact that a thing is in use or in disuse forms no criterion whatever of right or wrong. There is no fixed rule for seizing opportunities, hitting off the right moment, or adapting oneself to circumstances; it is all a matter of native wit. If you are deficient in that, you may possess the learning of a Confucius or the strategical gifts of a Lǔ Shang, and yet you will remain poor wherever you go.

The Mêng family were now in a more resigned frame of mind, and their indignation had subsided. 'Yes, you are right,' they said; 'please say no more about it.'

*   *   *

Duke Wên of Chin put an army into the field with the intention of attacking the Duke of Wei, whereat Tzǔ Ch'u threw his head back and laughed aloud. On being asked the reason of his behaviour, he replied: 'I was thinking of the experience of a neighbour of mine, who was escorting his wife on a visit to her own family. On the way, he came across a woman tending silkworms, who attracted him greatly, and he fell into conversation with her. Happening to look up, what should he see but his own wife also receiving the attentions of an admirer! It was the recollection of this incident that made me laugh.'

The Duke saw the point, and forthwith turned home with his army. Before he got back, an invading force had already crossed his northern frontier!

'As you behave to others, so others will behave to you. He who rides roughshod towards the accomplishment of his own desires, in the belief that it will not occur to others to do the like, will in all probability find himself circumstanced as above.'

*   *   *

In the Chin State, which was infested with robbers, there lived a certain Ch'i Yung, who was able to tell a robber by his face; by examining the expression of his eyes he could read his inmost thoughts. The Marquis of Chin employed him in the inspection of hundreds and thousands of robbers, and he never missed a single one. The Marquis expressed his delight to Wên Tzŭ of Chao, saying: 'I have a man who, singlehanded, is ridding my whole State of robbers. He saves me the necessity of employing a whole staff of police.' Wên Tzŭ replied: 'If your Highness relies on a detective for catching robbers, you will never get rid of them. And what is more, Ch'i Yung is certain sooner or later to meet with a violent end.'

Meanwhile, a band of robbers were plotting together. 'Ch'i Yung,' they said, 'is the enemy who is trying to exterminate us.' So one day they stole upon him in a body and murdered him. When the Marquis of Chin heard the news, he was greatly alarmed and immediately sent for Wên Tzŭ. 'Your prophecy has come true,' he said; 'Ch'i Yung is dead. What means can I adopt for catching robbers now?' 'In Chou,' replied Wên Tzŭ, 'we have a proverb: "Search not the ocean-depths for fish: calamity comes upon those who pry into hidden mysteries." If you want to be quit of robbers, the best thing your Highness can do is to promote the worthy to office. Let them instruct and enlighten their sovereign on the one hand, and reform the masses below them on the other. if once the people acquire a sense of shame, you will not find them turning into robbers.' The Marquis then appointed Sui Hui to be Prime Minister, and all the robbers fled to the Ch'in State.

A shrewd thrust at the brigand State which eventually swallowed up all the rest. The commentator says: 'Apply cleverness to ferret out wrongdoing, and the cunning rogue will escape. Using the gift of intuition to expose crime only excites hatred in the wicked. That "sagacity is an evil" is no empty saying.'

*   *   *

Duke Mu of Ch'in said to Po Lo:

A famous judge of horses, of whom Chuang Tzŭ speaks with scant respect. See Musings of a Chinese Mystic, p. 66.

'You are now advanced in years. Is there any member of your family whom I could employ to look for horses in your stead?' Po Lo replied: 'A good horse can be picked out by its general build and appearance. But the superlative horse — one that raises no dust and leaves no tracks — is something evanescent and fleeting, elusive as thin air. The talent of my sons lies on a lower plane altogether: they can tell a good horse when they see one, but they cannot tell a superlative horse. I have a friend, however, one Chiu-fang Kao, a hawker of fuel and vegetables, who in things appertaining to horses is nowise my inferior. Pray see him.'

Duke Mu did so, and subsequently despatched him on the quest for a steed. Three months later, he returned with the news that he had found one. 'It is now in Sha-ch'iu,' he added. 'What kind of a horse is it?' asked the Duke. 'Oh, it is a dun-coloured mare,' was the reply. However, on some one being sent to fetch it, the animal turned out to be a coal-black stallion! Much displeased, the Duke sent for Po Lo. 'That friend of yours,' he said, 'whom I commissioned to look for a horse, has made a nice mess of it. Why, he cannot even distinguish a beast's colour or sex! What on earth can he know about horses?' Po Lo heaved a sigh of satisfaction. 'Has he really got as far as that?' he cried. 'Ah, then he is worth a thousand of me put together. There is no comparison between us. What Kao keeps in view is the spiritual mechanism. In making sure of the essential, he forgets the homely details; intent on the inward qualities, he loses sight of the external. He sees what he wants to see, and not what he does not want to see. He looks at the things he ought to look at, and neglects those that need not be looked at. So clever a judge of horses is Kao, that he has it in him to judge something better than horses.'

When the horse arrived, it turned out indeed to be a superlative horse.

*   *   *

Mr Yŭ was a wealthy man of the Liang State.

Another name for the Wei State in the fourth century B.C.

His household was rolling in riches, and his hoards of money and silk and other valuables were quite incalculable. It was his custom to have banquets served, to the accompaniment of music, in a high upper hall overlooking the main road; there he and his friends would sit drinking their wine and amusing themselves with bouts of gambling.

One day, a party of young gallants happened to pass along the road. In the chamber above, play was going on as usual, and a lucky throw of the dice, which resulted in the capture of both fishes, evoked a loud burst of merriment from the players.

The game here alluded to was played on a board with a 'river' in the middle.

Precisely at that moment, it happened that a kite which was sailing overhead dropped the carcass of a rat in the midst of the company outside. The young men held an angry consultation on the spot: 'This Mr Yŭ,' they said, 'has been enjoying his wealth for many a long day, and has always treated his neighbours in the most arrogant spirit. And now, although we have never offended him, he insults us with this dead rat. If such an outrage goes unavenged, the world will look upon us as a set of poltroons. Let us summon up our utmost resolution, and combine with one accord to wipe him and his family out of existence!' The whole party signified their agreement, and when the evening of the day appointed had come, they collected, fully armed for the attack, and exterminated every member of the family.

'Pride and extravagance lead to calamity and ruin in more ways than one. Mr. Yŭ's family was destroyed, although in this particular instance he had no thought of insulting others; nevertheless, the catastrophe was due to an habitual lack of modesty and courtesy in his conduct.'

---

*   *   *

In the east of China there was a man named Yŭan Ching Mu, who set off on a journey but was overcome by hunger on the way. A certain robber from Hu-fu, of the name of Ch'iu, saw him lying there, and fetched a bowl of ricegruel in order to feed him. After swallowing three mouthfuls, Yŭan Ching Mu opened his eyes and murmured, 'Who are you?' 'I am a native of Hu-fu, and my name is Ch'iu.' 'Oh misery!' cried Yŭan Ching Mu, 'are not you the robber Ch'iu? What are you feeding me for? I am an honest man and cannot eat your food.' So saying, he clutched the ground with both hands, and began retching and coughing in order to bring it up again. Not succeeding, however, he fell flat on his face and expired.

Now the man from Hu-fu was a robber, no doubt, but the food he brought was not affected thereby. Because a man is a robber, to refuse to eat the food he offers you, on the ground that it is tainted with crime, is to have lost all power of discriminating between the normal and the real.

*　　　*　　　*

Yang Chu's younger brother, named Pu, went out one day wearing a suit of white clothes. It came on to rain, so that he had to change and came back dressed in a suit of black. His dog failed to recognize him in this garb, and rushed out at him, barking. This made Yang Pu angry, and he was going to give the dog a beating, when Yang Chu said: 'Do not beat him. You are no wiser than he. For, suppose your dog went away white and came home black, do you mean to tell me that you would not think it strange?'

*　　　*　　　*

Yang Chu said: 'You may do good without thinking about fame, but fame will follow in its wake. Fame makes no tryst with gain, but gain will come all the same. Gain makes no tryst with strife, but strife will certainly ensue. Therefore the superior man is very cautious about doing good.'

*　　　*　　　*

The good people of Han-tan were in the habit, every New Year's day, of presenting their Governor, Chien Tzŭ, with a number of live pigeons. This pleased the Governor very much, and he liberally rewarded the donors. To a stranger who asked the meaning of the custom, Chien Tzŭ explained that the release of living creatures on New Year's day was the sign of a benevolent disposition. 'But,' re-joined the stranger, 'the people, being aware of your Excellency's whim, no doubt exert themselves to catch as many pigeons as possible, and large numbers must get killed in the process. If you really wish to let the birds live, the best way would be to prohibit the people from capturing them at all. If they have to be caught first in order to be released, the kindness does not compensate for the cruelty.' Chien Tzŭ acknowledged that he was right.

*　　　*　　　*

Mr T'ien, of the Ch'i State, was holding an ancestral banquet in his hall, to which a thousand guests were bidden. As he sat in their midst, many came up to him with presents of fish and game. Eyeing them approvingly, he exclaimed with unction: 'How generous is Almighty God to man! He makes the five kinds of grain to grow, and creates the finny and the feathered tribes, especially for our benefit.' All Mr T'ien's guests applauded this sentiment to the echo; but the twelve-year-old son of a Mr Pao, regardless of seniority, came forward and said: 'You are wrong, my lord. All the living creatures of the universe stand in the same category as ourselves, and one is of no greater intrinsic value than another. It is only by reason of size, strength or cunning that some particular species gains the mastery, or that one preys upon another. None of them are produced in order to subserve the uses of others. Man catches and eats those that are fit for food, but how can it be maintained that God creates these expressly for man's use? Mosquitoes and gnats suck man's blood, and tigers and wolves devour his flesh; but we do not therefore assert that God created man expressly for the benefit of mosquitoes and gnats, or to provide food for tigers and wolves.'

In reading these words, penned before the beginning of our era, it is curious to reflect that only about fifty years ago Christian teleology used solemnly to preach this very doctrine of 'design', until Darwin arose and swept it away for ever.

---

*   *   *

A man, having lost his axe, suspected his neighbour's son of having taken it. Certain peculiarities in his gait, his countenance and his speech, marked him out as the thief. In his actions, his movements, and in fact his whole demeanour, it was plainly written that he and no other had stolen the axe. By and by, however, while digging in a dell, the owner came across the missing implement. The next day, when he saw his neighbour's son again, he found no trace of guilt in his movements, his actions, or his general demeanour.

'The man in whose mind suspicion is at work will let himself be carried away by utterly distorted fancies, until at last he sees white as black, and detects squareness in a circle.'

---

*   *   *

There was once a man in the Ch'i State who had a burning lust for gold. Rising early one morning, he dressed and put on his hat and went down to the marketplace, where he proceeded to seize and carry off the gold from a moneychanger's shop.

An ordinary thief would have gone at night, and probably naked, after smearing his body with oil.

He was arrested by the police, who were puzzled to know why he had committed the theft at a time when every body was about. 'When I was taking the gold,' he replied, 'I did not see anybody at all; what I saw was the gold, and nothing but the gold.'

Chuang Tzŭ

Mystic, Moralist, and Social Reformer

Chuang Tzŭ

1889

Inner Chapters.

────◆•◼•◼•◆────

CHAPTER I. TRANSCENDENTAL BLISS.

Argument:

—Space infinite—Time infinite—Relativity of magnitudes, physical and moral—The magnitude absolute—Usefulness as a test of value—The usefulness of the useless.

IN the northern ocean there is a fish, called the Leviathan, many thousand *li* in size. This leviathan changes into a bird, called the Rukh, whose back is many thousand *li* in breadth. With a mighty effort it rises, and its wings obscure the sky like clouds.

At the equinox, this bird prepares to start for the Southern Ocean, the Celestial Lake. And in the *Record of Marvels* we read that when the rukh flies southwards, the water is smitten for a space of three thousand *li* around, while the bird itself mounts upon a typhoon to a height of ninety thousand *li*, for a flight of six months' duration.

Just so are the motes in a sunbeam, blown aloft by God. For whether the blue of the sky is its real colour, or only the result of distance without end, the effect to the bird looking down would be just the same as to the motes.

If there is not sufficient depth, water will not float large ships. Upset a cupful into a small hole, and a mustard-seed will be your boat. Try to float the cup, and it will stick, from the disproportion between water and vessel.

So, with air. If there is not a sufficient depth, it cannot support large birds. And for this bird a depth of ninety thousand *li* is necessary; and then, with nothing save the clear sky above, and no obstacle in the way, it starts upon its journey to the south.

A cicada laughed, and said to a young dove, "Now, when I fly with all my might, 'tis as much as I can do to get from tree to tree. And sometimes I do not reach, but fall to the ground midway. What then can be the use of going up ninety thousand *li* in order to start for the south?"

He who goes to Mang-ts'ang, taking three meals with him, comes back with his stomach as full as when he started. But he who travels a hundred *li* must grind flour enough for a night's halt. And he who travels a thousand *li* must supply himself with provisions for three months. Those two little creatures, —what should they know? Small knowledge has not the compass of great knowledge any more than a short year has the length of a long year.

How can we tell that this is so? The mushroom of a morning knows not the alternation of day and night. The chrysalis knows not the alternation of spring and autumn. Theirs are short years.

But in the State of Ch'u there is a tortoise whose spring and autumn are each of five hundred years' duration. And in former days there was a large tree which had a spring and autumn each of eight thousand years' duration. Yet, P'êng Tsu is still, alas! an object of envy to all.

It was on this very subject that the Emperor T'ang spoke to Chi, as follows: —"At the barren north there is a great sea, the Celestial Lake. In it there is a fish, several thousand *li* in breadth, and I know not how many in length. It is called the Leviathan. There is also a bird, called the Rukh, with a back like Mount T'ai, and wings like clouds across the sky. Upon a typhoon it soars up to a height of ninety thousand *li*, beyond the clouds and atmosphere, with only the clear sky above it. And then it directs its flight towards the south pole.

"A quail laughed, and said: Pray, what may that creature be going to do? I rise but a few yards in the air, and settle again after flying around among the reeds. That is the most I can manage. Now, wherever can this creature be going to?"

Such, indeed, is the difference between small and great. Take, for instance, a man who creditably fills some small office, or who is a pattern of virtue in his neighbourhood, or who influences his prince to right government of the State, —his opinion of himself will be much the same as that quail's. The philosopher Yung laughs at such a one. He, if the whole world flattered him, would not be affected thereby, nor if the whole world blamed him would he lose his faith in himself. For Yung can distinguish between the intrinsic and the extrinsic, between honour and shame, — and such men are rare in their generation. But even he has not established himself.

There was Lieh Tzŭ again.

He could ride upon the wind, and travel whithersoever he wished, staying away as long as fifteen days. Among mortals who attain happiness, such a man is rare. Yet although Lieh Tzŭ was able to dispense with walking, he was still dependent upon something.

But had he been charioted upon the eternal fitness of Heaven and Earth, driving before him the elements as his team while roaming through the realms of For-Ever,—upon what, then, would he have had to depend?

Thus, it has been said, "The perfect man ignores *self*; the divine man ignores *action*; the true Sage ignores *reputation*."

The Emperor Yao wished to abdicate in favour of Hsü Yu, saying, "If, when the sun and moon are shining, you persist in lighting a torch, is not that a misapplication of fire? If, when the rainy season is at its height, you still continue to water the ground, is not this a waste of labour? Now, sir, do you assume the reins of government, and the empire will be at peace. I am but a dead body, conscious of my own deficiency. I beg you will ascend the throne."

"Ever since you, sire, have directed the administration," replied Hsü Yu, "the empire has enjoyed tranquillity. Supposing, therefore, that I were to take your place now, should I gain any reputation thereby? Besides, reputation is but the shadow of reality; and should I trouble myself about the shadow? The tit, building its nest in the mighty forest, occupies but a single twig. The tapir slakes its thirst from the river, but drinks enough only to fill its belly. To you, sire, belongs the reputation: the empire has no need for me. If a cook is unable to dress his funeral sacrifices, the boy who impersonates the corpse may not step over the wines and meats and do it for him."

Chien Wu said to Lien Shu, "I heard Chieh Yü utter something unjustifiably extravagant and without either rhyme or reason.

I was greatly startled at what he said, for it seemed to me boundless as the Milky Way, though very improbable and removed from the experiences of mortals."

"What was it?" asked Lien Shu.

"He declared," replied Chien Wu, "that on the Miao-ku-shê mountain there lives a divine man whose flesh is like ice or snow, whose demeanour is that of a virgin, who eats no fruit of the earth, but lives on air and dew, and who, riding on clouds with flying dragons for his team, roams beyond the limits of mortality. This being is absolutely inert. Yet he wards off corruption from all things, and causes the crops to thrive. Now I call that nonsense, and do not believe it."

"Well," answered Lien Shu, "you don't ask a blind man's opinion of a picture, nor do you invite a deaf man to a concert. And blindness and deafness are not physical only. There is blindness and deafness of the mind, diseases from which I fear you yourself are suffering. The good influence of that man fills all creation. Yet because a paltry generation cries for reform, you would have him condescend to the details of an empire!

"Objective existences cannot harm him. In a flood which reached to the sky, he would not be drowned. In a drought, though metals ran liquid and mountains were scorched up, he would not be hot. Out of his very dust and siftings you might fashion two such men as Yao and Shun. And you would have him occupy himself with objectives!"

A man of the Sung State carried some sacrificial caps into the Yüeh State, for sale. But the men of Yüeh used to cut off their hair and paint their bodies, so that they had no use for such things. And so, when the Emperor Yao, the ruler of all under heaven and pacificator of all within the shores of ocean, paid a visit to the four sages of the Miao-ku-shê mountain, on returning to his capital at Fên-yang, the empire existed for him no more.

Hui Tzǔ said to Chuang Tzǔ, "The Prince of Wei gave me a seed of a large-sized kind of gourd. I planted it, and it bore a fruit as big as a five-bushel measure. Now had I used this for holding liquids, it would have been too heavy to lift; and had I cut it in half for ladles, the ladles would have been ill adapted for such purpose. It was uselessly large, so I broke it up."

"Sir," replied Chuang Tzǔ, "it was rather you who did not know how to use large things. There was a man of Sung who had a recipe for salve for chapped hands, his family having been silk-washers for generations. Well, a stranger who had heard of it, came and offered him 100 *oz*. of silver for this recipe; whereupon he called together his clansmen and said, 'We have never made much money by silkwashing. Now, we can make 100 *oz*. in a single day. Let the stranger have the recipe.'

"So the stranger got it, and went and informed the Prince of Wu who was just then at war with the Yüeh State.

126

Accordingly, the Prince used it in a naval battle fought at the beginning of winter with the Yüeh State, the result being that the latter was totally defeated.

The stranger was rewarded with territory and a title. Thus, while the efficacy of the salve to cure chapped hands was in both cases the same, its application was different. Here, it secured a title; there, a capacity for washing silk.

"Now as to your five-bushel gourd, why did you not make a boat of it, and float about over river and lake? You could not then have complained of its not holding anything! But I fear you are rather woolly inside."

Hui Tzŭ said to Chuang Tzŭ, "Sir, I have a large tree, of a worthless kind. Its trunk is so irregular and knotty that it cannot be measured out for planks; while its branches are so twisted as to admit of no geometrical subdivision whatever. It stands by the roadside, but no carpenter will look at it. And your words, sir, are like that tree; — big and useless, not wanted by anybody."

"Sir," rejoined Chuang Tzŭ, "have you never seen a wild cat, crouching down in wait for its prey? Right and left it springs from bough to bough, high and low alike, — until perchance it gets caught in a trap or dies in a snare. On the other hand, there is the yak with its great huge body. It is big enough in all conscience, but it cannot catch mice.

"Now if you have a big tree and are at a loss what to do with it, why not plant it in the domain of non-existence, whither you might betake yourself to inaction by its side, to blissful repose beneath its shade?

There it would be safe from the axe and from all other injury; for being of no use to others, itself would be free from harm."

CHAPTER II. THE IDENTITY OF CONTRARIES.

Argument:

—Contraries spring from our subjective individuality—Identity of subjective and objective—The centre where all distinctions are merged in ONE—How to reach this point—Speech an obstacle—The negative state —Light out of darkness—Illustrations.

T ZŬ CH'I of Nan-kuo sat leaning on a table. Looking up to heaven, he sighed and became absent, as though soul and body had parted.

Yen Ch'êng Tzŭ Yu, who was standing by him, exclaimed, "What are you thinking about that your body should become thus like dry wood, your mind like dead ashes? Surely the man now leaning on the table is not he who was here just now."

"My friend," replied Tzŭ Ch'i, "your question is apposite. *To-day I have buried myself*... Do you understand? ... Ah! perhaps you only know the music of Man, and not that of Earth. Or even if you have heard the music of Earth, you have not heard the music of Heaven."

"Pray explain," said Tzŭ Yu.

"The breath of the universe," continued Tzŭ Ch'i, "is called wind. At times, it is inactive. But when active, every aperture resounds to the blast. Have you never listened to its growing roar?

"Caves and dells of hill and forest, hollows in huge trees of many a span in girth;—these are like nostrils, like mouths, like ears, like beam-sockets, like goblets, like mortars, like ditches, like bogs. And the wind goes rushing through them, sniffing, snoring, singing, soughing, puffing, purling, whistling, whirring, now shrilly treble, now deeply bass, now soft, now loud; until, with a lull, silence reigns supreme. Have you never witnessed among the trees such a disturbance as this?"

"Well, then," enquired Tzŭ Yu, "since the music of earth consists of nothing more than holes, and the music of man of pipes and flutes, —of what consists the music of Heaven?"

"The effect of the wind upon these various apertures," replied Tzŭ Ch'i, "is not uniform. But what is it that gives to each the individuality, to all the potentiality, of sound?

"Great knowledge embraces the whole: small knowledge, a part only. Great speech is universal: small speech is particular.

"For whether when the mind is locked in sleep or whether when in waking hours the body is released, we are subject to daily mental perturbations,—indecision, want of penetration, concealment, fretting fear, and trembling terror. Now like a javelin the mind flies forth, the arbiter of right and wrong.

Now like a solemn covenanter it remains firm, the guardian of rights secured.

Then, as under autumn and winter's blight, comes gradual decay, a passing away, like the flow of water, never to return. Finally, the block when all is choked up like an old drain, —the failing mind which shall not see light again.

"Joy and anger, sorrow and happiness, caution and remorse, come upon us by turns, with ever-changing mood. They come like music from hollowness, like mushrooms from damp. Daily and nightly they alternate within us, but we cannot tell whence they spring. Can we then hope in a moment to lay our finger upon their very Cause?

"But for these emotions *I* should not be. But for *me*, they would have no scope. So far, we can go; but we do not know what it is that brings them into play. 'Twould seem to be a *soul;* but the clue to its existence is wanting. That such a Power operates, is credible enough, though we cannot see its form. It has functions without form.

"Take the human body with all its manifold divisions. Which part of it does a man love best? Does he not cherish all equally, or has he a preference? Do not all equally serve him? And do these servitors then govern themselves, or are they subdivided into rulers and subjects? Surely there is some soul which sways them all.

"But whether or not we ascertain what are the functions of this soul, it matters but little to the soul itself. For coming into existence with this mortal coil of mine, with the exhaustion of this mortal coil its mandate will also be exhausted. To be harassed by the wear and tear of life, and to pass rapidly through it without possibility of arresting one's course, —is not this pitiful indeed? To labour without ceasing, and then, without living to enjoy the fruit, worn out, to depart, suddenly, one knows not whither, —is not that a just cause for grief?

"What advantage is there in what men call not dying? The body decomposes, and the mind goes with it. This is our real cause for sorrow. Can the world be so dull as not to see this? Or is it I alone who am dull, and others not so?

"If we are to be guided by the criteria of our own minds, who shall be without a guide?

What need to know of the alternations of passion, when the mind thus affords scope to itself? —verily even the minds of fools! Whereas, for a mind without criteria to admit the idea of contraries, is like saying, *I went to Yüeh today, and got there yesterday.*

Or, like placing nowhere somewhere, —topography which even the Great Yü would fail to understand; how much more I?

"Speech is not mere breath. It is differentiated by meaning. Take away that, and you cannot say whether it is speech or not. Can you even distinguish it from the chirping of young birds?

"But how can TAO be so obscured that we speak of it as true and false? And how can speech be so obscured that it admits the idea of contraries? How can TAO go away and yet not remain?

How can speech exist and yet be impossible?

"TAO is obscured by our want of grasp. Speech is obscured by the gloss of this world.

Hence the affirmatives and negatives of the Confucian and Mihist schools, each denying what the other affirmed and affirming what the other denied. But he who would reconcile affirmative with negative and negative with affirmative, must do so by the light of nature.

"There is nothing which is not objective: there is nothing which is not subjective. But it is impossible to start from the objective. Only from subjective knowledge is it possible to proceed to objective knowledge. Hence it has been said,

'The objective emanates from the subjective; the subjective is consequent upon the objective. This is the *Alternation Theory*.' Nevertheless, when one is born, the other dies. When one is possible, the other is impossible. When one is affirmative the other is negative. Which being the case, the true sage rejects all distinctions of this and that. He takes his refuge in GOD, and places himself in subjective relation with all things.

"And inasmuch as the subjective is also objective, and the objective also subjective, and as the contraries under each are indistinguishably blended, does it not become impossible for us to say whether subjective and objective really exist at all?

"When subjective and objective are both without their correlates, that is the very axis of TAO. And when that axis passes through the centre at which all Infinities converge, positive and negative alike blend into an infinite ONE. Hence it has been said that there is nothing like the light of nature.

"To take a finger in illustration of a finger not being a finger is not so good as to take something which is not a finger. To take a horse in illustration of a horse not being a horse is not so good as to take something which is not a horse.

"So, with the universe and all that in it is. These things are but fingers and horses in this sense. The possible is possible: the impossible is impossible. TAO operates, and given results follow. Things receive names and are what they are. They achieve this by their natural affinity for what they are and their natural antagonism to what they are not. For all things have their own particular constitutions and potentialities. Nothing can exist without these.

"Therefore, it is that, viewed from the standpoint of TAO, a beam and a pillar are identical.

So are ugliness and beauty, greatness, wickedness, perverseness, and strangeness. Separation is the same as construction: construction is the same as destruction. Nothing is subject either to construction or to destruction, for these conditions are brought together into ONE.

"Only the truly intelligent understand this principle of the identity of all things. They do not view things as apprehended by themselves, subjectively; but transfer themselves into the position of the things viewed.

And viewing them thus they are able to comprehend them, nay, to master them; —and he who can master them is near. So it is that to place oneself in subjective relation with externals, without consciousness of their objectivity, —this is TAO. But to wear out one's intellect in an obstinate adherence to the individuality of things, not recognising the fact that all things are O_{NE}, —this is called *Three in the Morning.*"

"What is *Three in the Morning?*" asked Tzŭ Yu.

"A keeper of monkeys," replied Tzŭ Ch'i, "said with regard to their rations of chestnuts that each monkey was to have three in the morning and four at night. But at this the monkeys were very angry, so the keeper said they might have four in the morning and three at night, with which arrangement they were all well pleased. The actual number of the chestnuts remained the same, but there was an adaptation to the likes and dislikes of those concerned. Such is the principle of putting oneself into subjective relation with externals.

"Wherefore the true Sage, while regarding contraries as identical, adapts himself to the laws of Heaven. This is called following two courses at once.

"The knowledge of the men of old had a limit. It extended back to a period when matter did not exist. That was the extreme point to which their knowledge reached.

"The second period was that of matter, but of matter unconditioned.

"The third epoch saw matter conditioned, but contraries were still unknown. When these appeared, TAO began to decline. And with the decline of TAO, individual bias arose.

"Have then these states of falling and rising real existences? Surely they are but as the falling and rising of Chao Wên's music, —the consequences of his playing.

Chao Wên played the guitar. Shih K'uang wielded the *bâton.*

Hui Tzŭ argued. Herein these three men excelled, and in the practice of such arts they passed their lives.

"Hui Tzŭ's particular views being very different from those of the world in general, he was correspondingly anxious to enlighten people. But he did not enlighten them as he should have done, and consequently, ended in the obscurity of the 'hard and white.'

Subsequently, his son searched his works for some clue, but never succeeded in establishing the principle. And indeed, if such were possible to be established, then even I am established; but if not, then neither I nor anything in the universe is established!

"Therefore, what the true Sage aims at is the light which comes out of darkness. He does not view things as apprehended by himself, subjectively, but transfers himself into the position of the things viewed. This is called using the light.

"There remains, however, Speech. Is that to be enrolled under either category of contraries, or not? Whether it is so enrolled or not, it will in any case belong to one or the other, and thus be as though it had an objective existence. At any rate, I should like to hear some speech which belongs to neither category.

"If there was a beginning, then there was a time before that beginning. And a time before the time which was before the time of that beginning.

"If there is existence, there must have been non-existence. And if there was a time when nothing existed, then there must have been a time before that—when even nothing did not exist. Suddenly, when nothing came into existence, could one really say whether it belonged to the category of existence or of non-existence? Even the very words I have just now uttered, —I cannot say whether they have really been uttered or not.

"There is nothing under the canopy of heaven greater than the tip of an autumn spikelet. A vast mountain is a small thing. Neither is there any age greater than that of a child cut off in infancy. P'êng Tsu himself died young. The universe and I came into being together; and I, and everything therein, are ONE.

"If then all things are ONE, what room is there for Speech? On the other hand, since I can utter these words, how can Speech not exist?

"If it does exist, we have ONE and Speech=two; and two and one=three. From which point onwards even the best mathematicians will fail to reach:

how much more then will ordinary people fail?

"Hence, if from nothing you can proceed to something, and subsequently reach three, it follows that it would be still more easy if you were to start from something. To avoid such progression, you must put yourself into subjective relation with the external.

"Before conditions existed, TAO was. Before definitions existed. Speech was. Subjectively, we are conscious of certain delimitations which are, —

Right	and	Left
Relationship	and	Obligation
Division	and	Discrimination
Emulation	and	Contention

These are called the *Eight Predicables*.

For the true Sage, beyond the limits of an external world, they exist, but are not recognised. By the true Sage, within the limits of an external world, they are recognised, but are not assigned. And so with regard to the wisdom of the ancients, as embodied in the canon of *Spring and Autumn*, the true Sage assigns, but does not justify by argument. And thus, classifying he does not classify; arguing, he does not argue."

"How can that be?" asked Tzŭ Yu.

"The true Sage," answered Tzŭ Ch'i, "keeps his knowledge within him, while men in general set forth theirs in argument, in order to convince each other. And therefore, it is said that in argument he does not manifest himself.

"Perfect TAO does not declare itself. Nor does perfect argument express itself in words. Nor does, perfect charity show itself in act. Nor is perfect honesty absolutely incorruptible. Nor is perfect courage absolutely unyielding.

"For the Tao which shines forth is not TAO. Speech which argues falls short of its aim. Charity which has fixed points loses its scope. Honesty which is absolute is wanting in credit. Courage which is absolute misses its object. These five are, as it were, round, with a strong bias towards squareness. Therefore, that knowledge which stops at what it does not know, is the highest knowledge.

"Who knows the argument which can be argued without words? —the TAO which does not declare itself as TAO? He who knows this may be said to be of GOD. To be able to pour in without making full, and pour out without making empty, in ignorance of the power by which such results are accomplished, —this is accounted *Light*."

Of old, the Emperor Yao said to Shun, "I would smite the Tsungs, and the Kueis, and the Hsu-aos. Ever since I have been on the throne, I have had this desire. What do you think?"

"These three States," replied Shun, "are paltry out-of-theway places. Why can you not shake off this desire? Once upon a time, ten suns came out together, and all things were illuminated thereby. How much more then should virtue excel suns?"

Yeh Ch'üeh asked Wang I, saying, "Do you know for certain that all things are subjectively the same?"

"How can I know?" answered Wang I. "Do you know what you do not know?"

"How can I know?" replied Yeh Ch'üeh. "But can then nothing be known?"

"How can I know?" said Wang I. "Nevertheless, I will try to tell you. How can it be known that what I call knowing is not really not knowing, and that what I call not knowing is not really knowing? Now I would ask you this. If a man sleeps in a damp place, he gets lumbago and dies. But how about an eel? And living up in a tree is precarious and trying to the nerves; —but how about monkeys? Of the man, the eel, and the monkey, whose habitat is the right one, absolutely? Human beings feed on flesh, deer on grass, centipedes on snakes, owls and crows on mice. Of these four, whose is the right taste, absolutely? Monkey mates with monkey, the buck with the doe; eels consort with fishes, while men admire Mao Ch'iang and Li Chi, at the sight of whom fishes plunge deep down in the water, birds soar high in the air, and deer hurry away.

Yet who shall say which is the correct standard of beauty? In my opinion, the standard of human virtue, and of positive and negative, is so obscured that it is impossible to actually know it as such."

"If you then," asked Yeh Ch'üeh, "do not know what is bad for you, is the Perfect Man equally without this knowledge?"

"The Perfect Man," answered Wang I, "is a spiritual being. Were the ocean itself scorched up; he would not feel hot.
Were the Milky Way frozen hard, he would not feel cold.

Were the mountains to be riven with thunder, and the great deep to be thrown up by storm, he would not tremble. In such case, he would mount upon the clouds of heaven, and driving the sun and the moon before him, would pass beyond the limits of this external world, where death and life have no more victory over man;—how much less what is bad for him?"

Chü Ch'iao addressed Chang Wu Tzŭ as follows: —"I heard Confucius say, 'The true sage pays no heed to mundane affairs. He neither seeks gain nor avoids injury. He asks nothing at the hands of man. He adheres, without questioning, to TAO. Without speaking, he can speak; and he can speak and yet say nothing. And so, he roams beyond the limits of this dusty world. These,' added Confucius, 'are wild words.'

Now to me they are the skilful embodiment of TAO. What, Sir, is your opinion?"

"Points upon which the Yellow Emperor doubted," replied Chang Wu Tzŭ, "how should Confucius know?

You are going too fast. You see your egg, and expect to hear it crow. You look at your cross-bow, and expect to have broiled duck before you. I will say a few words to you at random, and do you listen at random.

"How does the Sage seat himself by the sun and moon, and hold the universe in his grasp? He blends everything into one harmonious whole, rejecting the confusion of this and that. Rank and precedence, which the vulgar prize, the Sage stolidly ignores. The revolutions of ten thousand years leave his Unity unscathed. The universe itself may pass away, but he will flourish still.

"How do I know that love of life is not a delusion after all? How do I know but that he who dreads to die is not as a child who has lost the way and cannot find his home?

"The lady Li Chi was the daughter of Ai Fêng.

When the Duke of Chin first got her, she wept until the bosom of her dress was drenched with tears. But when she came to the royal residence, and lived with the Duke, and ate rich food, she repented of having wept. How then do I know but that the dead repent of having previously clung to life?

"Those who dream of the banquet, wake to lamentation and sorrow. Those who dream of lamentation and sorrow wake to join the hunt. While they dream, they do not know that they dream. Some will even interpret the very dream they are dreaming; and only when they awake do, they know it was a dream. By and by comes the Great Awakening, and then we find out that this life is really a great dream. Fools think they are awake now, and flatter themselves they know if they are really princes or peasants. Confucius and you are both dreams; and I who say you are dreams, —I am but a dream myself. This is a paradox. Tomorrow a sage may arise to explain it; but that tomorrow will not be until ten thousand generations have gone by.

"Granting that you and I argue. If you beat me, and not I you, are you necessarily right and I wrong? Or if I beat you and not you me, am I necessarily right and you wrong? Or are we both partly right and partly wrong? Or are we both wholly right and wholly wrong? You and I cannot know this, and consequently the world will be in ignorance of the truth.

"Who shall I employ as arbiter between us? If I employ someone who takes your view, he will side with you. How can such a one arbitrates between us? If I employ someone who takes my view, he will side with me. How can such a one arbitrates between us? And if I employ someone who either differs from, or agrees with, both of us, he will be equally unable to decide between us. Since then you, and I, and man, cannot decide, must we not depend upon Another?

Such dependence is as though it were not dependence. We are embraced in the obliterating unity of God. There is perfect adaptation to whatever may eventuate; and so, we complete our allotted span.

"But what is it to be embraced in the obliterating unity of God? It is this. With reference to positive and negative, to that which is so and that which is not so,—if the positive is really positive, it must necessarily be different from its negative: there is no room for argument. And if that which is so really is so, it must necessarily be different from that which is not so: there is no room for argument.

"Take no heed of time, nor of right and wrong. But passing into the realm of the Infinite, take your final rest therein."

The Penumbra said to the Umbra, "At one moment you move: at another you are at rest. At one moment you sit down: at another you get up. Why this instability of purpose?" "I depend," replied the Umbra, "upon something which causes me to do as I do; and that something depends in turn upon something else which causes it to do as it does. My dependence is like that of a snake's scales or of a cicada's wings.

How can I tell why I do one thing, or why I do not do another?"

Once upon a time, I, Chuang Tzŭ, dreamt I was a butterfly, fluttering hither and thither, to all intents and purposes a butterfly. I was conscious only of following my fancies as a butterfly, and was unconscious of my individuality as a man. Suddenly, I awaked, and there I lay, myself again. Now I do not know whether I was then a man dreaming I was a butterfly, or whether I am now a butterfly dreaming I am a man. Between a man and a butterfly there is necessarily a barrier. The transition is called *Metempsychosis.*

CHAPTER III. NOURISHMENT OF THE SOUL.

Argument:

—Life too short—Wisdom unattainable—Accommodation to circumstances—Liberty paramount—Death a release—The soul immortal.

MY life has a limit, but my knowledge is without limit. To drive the limited in search of the limitless, is fatal; and the knowledge of those who do this is fatally lost.

In striving for others, avoid fame. In striving for self, avoid disgrace. Pursue a middle course. Thus, you will keep a sound body, and a sound mind, fulfil your duties, and work out your allotted span.

Prince Hui's cook was cutting up a bullock. Every blow of his hand, every heave of his shoulders, every tread of his foot, every thrust of his knee, every *whshh* of rent flesh, every *chhk* of the chopper, was in perfect harmony,—rhythmical like the dance of the Mulberry Grove, simultaneous like the chords of the Ching Shou.

"Well done!" cried the Prince. "Yours is skill indeed."

"Sire," replied the cook; "I have always devoted myself to TAO. It is better than skill. When I first began to cut up bullocks, I saw before me simply *whole* bullocks. After three years' practice, I saw no more whole animals.

And now I work with my mind and not with my eye. When my senses bid me stop, but my mind urges me on, I fall back upon eternal principles. I follow such openings or cavities as there may be, according to the natural constitution of the animal. I do not attempt to cut through joints: still less through large bones.

"A good cook changes his chopper once a year, —because he cuts. An ordinary cook, once a month, —because he hacks. But I have had this chopper nineteen years, and although I have cut up many thousand bullocks, its edge is as if fresh from the whetstone. For at the joints there are always interstices, and the edge of a chopper being without thickness, it remains only to insert that which is without thickness into such an interstice.

By these means the interstice will be enlarged, and the blade will find plenty of room. It is thus that I have kept my chopper for nineteen years as though fresh from the whetstone.

"Nevertheless, when I come upon a hard part where the blade meets with a difficulty, I am all caution. I fix my eye on it. I stay my hand, and gently apply my blade, until with a *hwah* the part yields like earth crumbling to the ground. Then I take out my chopper, and stand up, and look around, and pause, until with an air of triumph I wipe my chopper and put it carefully away."

"Bravo!" cried the Prince. "From the words of this cook I have learnt how to take care of my life."

When Hsien, of the Kung-wên family, beheld a certain official, he was horrified, and said, "Who is that man? How came he to lose a foot? Is this the work of God, or of man?

"Why, of course," continued Hsien, "it is the work of God, and not of man. When God brought this man into the world, he wanted him to be unlike other men. Men always have two feet. From this it is clear that God and not man made him as he is.

"Now, wild fowl get a peck once in ten steps, a drink once in a hundred. Yet they do not want to be fed in a cage. For although they would thus be able to command food, they would not be free."

When Lao Tzŭ died, Ch'in Shih went to mourn. He uttered three yells and departed.

A disciple asked him saying, "Were you not our Master's friend?"

"I was," replied Ch'in Shih.

"And if so, do you consider that a sufficient expression of grief at his loss?" added the disciple.

"I do," said Ch'in Shih. "I had believed him to be the man of all men, but now I know that he was not. When I went in to mourn, I found old persons weeping as if for their children, young ones wailing as if for their mothers. And for him to have gained the attachment of those people in this way, he too must have uttered words which should not have been spoken, and dropped tears which should not have been shed, thus violating eternal principles, increasing the sum of human emotion, and forgetting the source from which his own life was received. The ancients called such emotions the trammels of mortality. The Master came, because it was his time to be born; he went, because it was his time to die. For those who accept the phenomenon of birth and death in this sense, lamentation and sorrow have no place. The ancients spoke of death as of God cutting down a man suspended in the air. The fuel is consumed, but the fire may be transmitted, and we know not that it comes to an end."

CHAPTER IV. MAN AMONG MEN.

Argument:

> —Man must fall in with his mortal environment — His virtue should be passive, not active—He should *be* rather than *do*—Talents a hindrance —But of petty uselessness great usefulness is achieved.

YEN HUI went to take leave of Confucius.

"Whither are you bound?" asked the Master.

"I am going to the State of Wei," was the reply.

"And what do you propose to do there?" continued Confucius.

"I hear," answered Yen Hui, "that the Prince of Wei is of mature age, but of an unmanageable disposition. He behaves as if the State were of no account and will not see his own faults. Consequently, the people perish; and their corpses lie about like so much undergrowth in a marsh. They are at extremities. And I have heard you, Sir, say that if a State is well governed it may be neglected; but that if it is badly governed, then we should visit it.

The science of medicine embraces many various diseases. I would test my knowledge in this sense, that perchance I may do some good to that State."

"Alas!" cried Confucius, "you will only succeed in bringing evil upon yourself. For TAO must not be distributed. If it is, it will lose its unity. If it loses its unity, it will be uncertain; and so cause mental disturbance, —from which there is no escape.

"The sages of old first got TAO for themselves, and then got it for others. Before you possess this yourself, what leisure have you to attend to the doings of wicked men? Besides, do you know what Virtue results in and where Wisdom ends? Virtue results in a desire for fame; Wisdom ends in contentions. In the struggle for fame men crush each other, while their wisdom but provokes rivalry. Both are baleful instruments, and may not be incautiously used.

"Besides, those who, before influencing by their own solid virtue and unimpeachable sincerity, and before reaching the heart by the example of their own disregard for name and fame, go and preach charity and duty to one's neighbour to wicked men,—only make these men hate them for their very goodness' sake. Such persons are called *evil speakers*. And those who speak evil of others are apt to be evil spoken of themselves. That, alas! will be your end.

"On the other hand, if the Prince loves the good and hates the bad, what object will you have in inviting him to change his ways? Before you have opened your mouth to preach, the Prince himself will have seized the opportunity to wrest the victory from you. Your eye will fall, your expression fade, your words will stick, your face will change, and your heart will die within you. It will be as though you took fire to quell fire, water to quell water, which is popularly known as 'pouring oil on the flames.' And if you begin with concessions, there will be no end to them. Neglect this sound advice, and you will be the victim of that violent man.

"Of old, Chieh murdered Kuan Lung Fêng, and Chou slew Prince Pi Kan. Their victims were both men who cultivated virtue themselves in order to secure the welfare of the people. But in doing this they offended their superiors; and therefore, because of that very moral culture, their superiors got rid of them, in order to guard their own reputations.

"Of old, Yao attacked the Ts'ung-chih and Hsü-ao countries, and Yü attacked the Yu-hu country. Homes were desolated and families destroyed by the slaughter of the inhabitants. Yet they fought without ceasing, and strove for victory to the last. These are instances known to all. Now if the Sages of old failed in their efforts against this love of fame, this desire for victory, — are you likely to succeed? But of course, you have a scheme. Tell it to me."

"Gravity of demeanour," replied Yen Hui, "and dispassionateness; energy and singleness of purpose, —will this do?"

"Alas!" said Confucius, "that will not do. If you make a show of being perfect and obtrude yourself, the Prince's mood will be doubtful. Ordinarily, he is not opposed, and so he has come to take actual pleasure in trampling upon the feelings of others. And if he has thus failed in the practice of routine virtues, do you expect that he will take readily to higher ones? You may insist, but without result. Outwardly you will be right, but inwardly wrong. How then will you make him mend his ways?"

"Just so," replied Yen Hui. "I am inwardly straight, and outwardly crooked, completed after the models of antiquity.

"He who is inwardly straight is a servant of God. And he who is a servant of God knows that the Son of Heaven and himself are equally the children of God. Shall then such a one trouble whether man visits him with evil or with good? Man indeed regards him as a child; and this is to be a servant of God.

"He who is outwardly crooked is a servant of man. He bows, he kneels, he folds his hands; —such is the ceremonial of a minister. What all men do, shall I dare not to do? What all men do, none will blame me for doing. This is to be a servant of man.

"He who is completed after the models of antiquity is a servant of the Sages of old. Although I utter the words of warning and take him to task, it is the Sages of old who speak, and not I. Thus, my uprightness will not bring me into trouble, the servant of the Sages of old. —Will this do?"

"Alas!" replied Confucius, "No. Your plans are too many, and are lacking in prudence. However, your firmness will secure you from harm; but that is all. You will not influence him to such an extent that he shall seem to follow the dictates of his own heart."

"Then," said Yen Hui, "I am without resource, and venture to ask for a method."

Confucius said, "*FAST*… Let me explain. You have a method, but it is difficult to practise. Those which are easy are not from God."

"Well," replied Yen Hui, "my family is poor, and for many months we have tasted neither wine nor flesh. Is not that fasting?"

"The fasting of religious observance it is," answered Confucius, "but not the fasting of the heart."

"And may I ask," said Yen Hui, "in what consists the fasting of the heart?"

"Cultivate unity," replied Confucius.

"You hear not with the ears, but with the mind; not with the mind, but with your soul.

But let hearing stop with the ears. Let the working of the mind stop with itself. Then the soul will be a negative existence, passively responsive to externals. In such a negative existence, only TAO can abide. And that negative state is the fasting of the heart."

"Then," said Yen Hui, "the reason I could not get the use of this method is my own individuality. If I could get the use of it, my individuality would have gone. Is this what you mean by the negative state?"

"Exactly so," replied the Master. "Let me tell you. If you can enter this man's domain without offending his *amour propre*, cheerful if he hears you, passive if he does not; without science, without drugs, simply living there in a state of complete indifference,—you will be near success. It is easy to stop walking: the trouble is to walk without touching the ground. As an agent of man, it is easy to deceive; but not as an agent of God. You have heard of winged creatures flying. You have never heard of flying without wings. You have heard of men being wise with wisdom. You have never heard of men wise without wisdom.

"Look at that window. Through it an empty room becomes bright with scenery; but the landscape stops outside. Were this not so, we should have an exemplification of sitting still and running away at one and the same time.

"In this sense, you may use your ears and eyes to communicate within, but shut out all wisdom from the mind.

And there where the supernatural can find shelter, shall not man find shelter too? This is the method for regenerating all creation.

It was the instrument which Yü and Shun employed. It was the secret of the success of Fu Hsi and Chi Chü. Shall it not then be adopted by mankind in general?"

Tzŭ Kao, Duke of Shê, being about to go on a mission to the Ch'i State, asked Confucius, saying, "The mission my sovereign is sending me on is a most important one. Of course, I shall be received with all due respect, but they will not take the same interest in the matter that I shall. And as an ordinary person cannot be pushed, still less a Prince, I am in a state of great alarm.

"Now you, Sir, have told me that in all undertakings great and small, TAO alone leads to a happy issue. Otherwise that, failing success, there is to be feared punishment from without, and with success, punishment from within; while exemption in case either of success or non-success falls only to the share of those who possess the virtue required.

"Well, I am not dainty with my food; neither am I always wanting to cool myself when hot. However, this morning I received my orders, and this evening I have been drinking iced water. I am so hot inside. Before I have put my hand to the business, I am suffering punishment from within; and if I do not succeed, I am sure to suffer punishment from without. Thus, I get both punishments, which is really more than I can bear. Kindly tell me what there is to be done."

"There exist two sources of safety," Confucius replied.

"One is *Destiny:* the other is *Duty.* A child's love for its parents is destiny. It is inseparable from the child's life. A subject's allegiance to his sovereign is duty. Beneath the canopy of heaven there is no place to which he can escape from it. These two sources of safety may be explained as follows. To serve one's parents without reference to *place* but only to the service, is the acme of filial piety. To serve one's prince without reference to the *act* but only to the service, is the perfection of a subject's loyalty. To serve one's own heart so as to permit neither joy nor sorrow within, but to cultivate resignation to the inevitable, —this is the climax of Virtue.

"Now a minister often finds himself in circumstances over which he has no control. But if he simply confines himself to his work, and is utterly oblivious of self, what leisure has he for loving life or hating death? And so you may safely go.

144

"But I have yet more to tell you. All intercourse, if personal, should be characterised by sincerity. If from a distance, it should be carried on in loyal terms. These terms will have to be transmitted by someone. Now the transmission of messages of good- or ill-will is the hardest thing possible. Messages of good-will are sure to be overdone with fine phrases; messages of ill-will with harsh ones. In each case the result is exaggeration, and a consequent failure to carry conviction, for which the envoy suffers. Therefore, it was said in the *Fa-yen*,

'Confine yourself to simple statements of fact, shorn of all superfluous expression of feeling, and your risk will be small.'

"In trials of skill, at first all is friendliness; but at last it is all antagonism. Skill is pushed too far. So, on festive occasions, the drinking, which is in the beginning orderly enough, degenerates into riot and disorder. Festivity is pushed too far. It is in fact the same with all things: they begin with good faith and end with contempt. From small beginnings come great endings.

"Speech is like wind to wave. Action is liable to divergence from its true goal. By wind, waves are easily excited. Divergence from the true goal is fraught with danger. Thus, angry feelings rise up without a cause. Specious words and dishonest arguments follow, as the wild random cries of an animal at the point of death. Both sides give way to passion. For where one party drives the other too much into a corner, resistance will always be provoked without apparent cause. And if the cause is not apparent, how much less will the ultimate effect be so?

"Therefore, it is said in the *Fa-yen*, 'Neither deviate from nor travel beyond your instructions.

To pass the limit is to go to excess.'

"To deviate from, or to travel beyond instructions, may imperil the negotiation. A settlement to be successful must be lasting. It is too late to change an evil settlement once made.

"Therefore, let yourself be carried along without fear, taking refuge in *no alternative* to preserve you from harm on either side. This is the utmost you can do. What need for considering your obligations? Better leave all to Destiny, difficult as this may be."

Yen Ho was about to become tutor to the eldest son of Duke Ling of the Wei State. Accordingly he observed to Chü Poh Yü,

"Here is a man whose disposition is naturally of a low order. To let him take his own unprincipled way is to endanger the State. To try to restrain him is to endanger one's personal safety. He has just wit enough to see faults in others, but not to see his own. I am consequently at a loss what to do."

"A good question indeed," replied Chü Poh Yü, "You must be careful, and begin by self-reformation. Outwardly you may adapt yourself, but inwardly you must keep up to your own standard. In this there are two points to be guarded against. You must not let the outward adaptation penetrate within, nor the inward standard manifest itself without. In the former case, you will fall, you will be obliterated, you will collapse, you will lie prostrate. In the latter case, you will be a sound, a name, a bogie, an uncanny thing. If he would play the child, do you play the child too. If he cast aside all sense of decorum, do you do so too. As far as he goes, do you go also. Thus, you will reach him without offending him.

"Don't you know the story of the praying mantis? In its rage it stretched out its arms to prevent a chariot from passing, unaware that this was beyond its strength, so admirable was its energy! Be cautious. If you are always offending others by your superiority, you will probably come to grief.

"Do you not know that those who keep tigers do not venture to give them live animals as food, for fear of exciting their fury when killing the prey? Also, that whole animals are not given, for fear of exciting the tigers' fury when rending them? The periods of hunger and repletion are carefully watched in order to prevent such outbursts. The tiger is of a different species from man; but the latter too is manageable if properly managed, unmanageable if excited to fury.

"Those who are fond of horses surround them with various conveniences. Sometimes mosquitoes or flies trouble them; and then, unexpectedly to the animal, a groom will brush them off, the result being that the horse breaks his bridle, and hurts his head and chest. The intention is good, but there is a want of real care for the horse. Against this you must be on your guard."

A certain artisan was travelling to the Ch'i State. On reaching Ch'ü-yüan, he saw a sacred *li* tree, large enough to hide an ox behind it, a hundred spans in girth, towering up ten cubits over the hill top, and carrying behind it branches, many tens of the smallest of which were of a size for boats. Crowds stood gazing at it, but our artisan took no notice, and went on his way without even casting a look behind. His apprentice however gazed his fill, and when he caught up his master, said, "Ever since I have handled an adze in your service, I have never seen such a splendid piece of timber as that. How was it that you, sir, did not care to stop and look at it?"

"It's not worth talking about," replied his master. "It's good for nothing. Make a boat of it, —it twould sink. A coffin, —it twould rot. Furniture, — it would soon break down. A door, —it would sweat. A pillar, —it would be worm-eaten. It is wood of no quality, and of no use. That is why it has attained its present age."

When the artisan reached home, he dreamt that the tree appeared to him in a dream and spoke as follows: —"What is it that you compare me with? Is it with the more elegant trees? —The cherry-apple, the pear, the orange, the pumelo, and other fruit-bearers, as soon as their fruit ripens are stripped and treated with indignity. The great boughs are snapped off, the small ones scattered abroad. Thus, do these trees by their own value injure their own lives. They cannot fulfil their allotted span of years, but perish prematurely in mid-career from their entanglement with the world around them. Thus, it is with all things. For a long period, my aim was to be useless. Many times, I was in danger, but at length I succeeded, and so became useful as I am to-day. But had I then been of use, I should not now be of the great use I am. Moreover, you and I belong both to the same category of things. Have done then with this criticism of others. Is a good-for-nothing fellow whose dangers are not yet passed a fit person to talk of a good-for-nothing tree?"

When our artisan awaked and told his dream, his apprentice said, "If the tree aimed at uselessness, how was it that it became a sacred tree?"

"What you don't understand," replied his master, "don't talk about. That was merely to escape from the attacks of its enemies. Had it not become sacred, how many would have wanted to cut it down! The means of safety adopted were different from ordinary means, and to test these by ordinary canons leaves one far wide of the mark."

Tzŭ Ch'i of Nan-poh was travelling on the Shang mountain when he saw a large tree which astonished him very much. A thousand chariot teams could have found shelter under its shade.

"What tree is this?" cried Tzŭ Ch'i. "Surely it must have unusually fine timber." Then looking up, he saw that its branches were too crooked for rafters; while as to the trunk he saw that its irregular grain made it valueless for coffins. He tasted a leaf, but it took the skin off his lips; and its odour was so strong that it would make a man as it were drunk for three days together.

"Ah!" said Tzǔ Ch'i. "This tree is good for nothing, and that is how it has attained this size. A wise man might well follow its example."

In the State of Sung there is a place called Ching-shih, where thrive the beech, the cedar, and the mulberry. Such as are of a one-handed span or so in girth are cut down for monkey-cages. Those of two or three two-handed spans are cut down for the beams of fine houses. Those of seven or eight such spans are cut down for the solid sides of rich men's coffins.

Thus, they do not fulfil their allotted span of years, but perish in mid-career beneath the axe. Such is the misfortune which overtakes worth.

For the sacrifices to the River God, neither bulls with white cheeks, nor pigs with large snouts, nor men suffering from piles, were allowed to be used. This had been revealed to the soothsayers, and these characteristics were consequently regarded as inauspicious. The wise, however, would regard them as extremely auspicious.

There was a hunchback named Su. His jaws touched his navel. His shoulders were higher than his head. His hair knot looked up to the sky. His viscera were upside down. His buttocks were where his ribs should have been. By tailoring, or washing, he was easily able to earn his living. By sifting rice he could make enough to support a family of ten.

When orders came down for a conscription, the hunchback stood unconcerned among the crowd. And similarly, in matters of public works, his deformity shielded him from being employed.

On the other hand, when it came to donations of grain, the hunchback received as much as three *chung*, and of firewood, ten faggots. And if physical deformity was thus enough to preserve his body until its allotted end, how much more would not moral and mental deformity avail!

When Confucius was in the Ch'u State, the eccentric Chieh Yü passed his door, saying, "O phœnix, O phœnix, how has thy virtue fallen!— unable to wait for the coming years or to go back into the past.

If TAO prevails on earth, prophets will fulfil their mission. If TAO does not prevail, they will but preserve themselves. At the present day they will but just escape.

"The honours of this world are light as feathers, yet none estimate them at their true value. The misfortunes of this life are weighty as the earth itself, yet none can keep out of their reach. No more, no more, seek to influence by virtue. Beware, beware, move cautiously on! O ferns, O ferns, wound not my steps! Through my tortuous journey wound not my feet! Hills suffer from the trees they produce. Fat burns by its own combustibility. Cinnamon trees furnish food: therefore, they are cut down. The lacquer tree is felled for use. All men know the use of useful things; but they do not know the use of useless things."

CHAPTER V. THE EVIDENCE OF VIRTUE COMPLETE.

Argument:

—Correspondence between inward virtue and outward influence— The virtuous man disregards externals—The possession of virtue causes oblivion of outward form—Neglect of the human—Cultivation of the divine.

IN the State of Lu there was a man, named Wang T'ai, who had had his toes cut off. His disciples were as numerous as those of Confucius.

Ch'ang Chi asked Confucius, saying, "This Wang T'ai has been mutilated, yet he divides with you, Sir, the teaching of the Lu State. He neither preaches nor discusses; yet those who go to him empty, depart full. He must teach *the doctrine which does not find expression in words;* and although his shape is imperfect, his mind is perhaps complete. What manner of man is this?"

"He is a prophet," replied Confucius, "whose instruction I have been late in seeking. I will go and learn from him. And if I, —why not those who are not equal to me? And I will take with me, not the State of Lu only, but the whole world."

"The fellow has been mutilated," said Chang Chi, "and yet people call him *Master.* He must be very different from the ordinary run. But how does he use his mind in this sense?"

149

"Life and Death are all powerful," answered Confucius, "but they cannot affect *it*.

Heaven and earth may collapse, but *that* will remain. If *this* is found to be without flaw, it will not share the fate of all things. It can cause other things to change, while preserving its own constitution intact."

"How so?" asked Chang Chi.

"From the point of view of difference," replied Confucius,

"we distinguish between the liver and the gall, between the Ch'u State and the Yüeh State. From the point of view of sameness, all things are ONE. Such is the position of Wang T'ai. He does not trouble about what reaches him through the senses of hearing and sight, but directs his whole mind towards the very climax of virtue. He beholds all things as though ONE, without observing their discrepancies. And thus the discrepancy of his toes is to him as would be the loss of so much mud."

"He devotes himself in fact to himself," said Ch'ang Chi, "and uses his wisdom to perfect his mind, until it becomes perfect. But how then is it that people make so much of him?"

"A man," replied Confucius, "does not seek to see himself in running water, but in still water. For only what is itself still can instil stillness into others.

"The grace of earth has reached only to pines and cedars; — winter and summer alike they are green. The grace of God has reached to Yao and to Shun alone; —the first and foremost of all creation. Happily, they were able to regulate their own lives and thus regulate the lives of all mankind.

"By nourishment of physical courage, the sense of fear may be so eliminated that a man will, single-handed, brave a whole army. And if such a result can be achieved in search of fame, how much more by one who extends his sway over heaven and earth and influences all things; and who, lodging within the confines of a body with its channels of sight and sound, brings his knowledge to know that all things are ONE, and that his soul endures for ever! Besides, he awaits his appointed hour, and men flock to him of their own accord. He makes no effort to attract them."

Shên T'u Chia had had his toes cut off. Subsequently, he studied under Poh Hun Wu Jen at the same time as Tzŭ Chan of the Chêng State. The latter said to him, "When I leave first, do you remain awhile. When you leave first, I will remain behind."

Next day, when they were again together in the lectureroom, Tzŭ Ch'an said, "When I leave first, do you remain awhile. When you leave first, I will remain. I am now about to go. Will you remain or not? I notice you show no respect to a Minister of State. Perhaps you think yourself my equal?"

"Dear me!" replied Shên T'u Chia, "I didn't know we had a Minister of State in the class. Perhaps you think that because you are one you should take precedence over the rest. Now I have heard that if a mirror is perfectly bright, dust and dirt will not collect on it. That if they do, it is because the mirror was not bright. He who associates for long with the wise will be without fault. Now you have been improving yourself at the feet of our Master, yet you can utter words like these. Is not the fault in you?"

"You are a fine fellow, certainly," retorted Tzŭ Ch'an, "you will be emulating the virtue of Yao next. To look at you, I should say you had enough to do to attend to your own short-comings!"

"Those who disguise their faults," said Shên T'u Chia, "so as not to lose their toes, are many in number. Those who do not disguise their faults, and so fail to keep them, are few. To recognise the inevitable and to quietly acquiesce in Destiny, is the achievement of the virtuous man alone. He who should put himself in front of the bull's-eye when Hou Yi

was shooting, would be hit. If he was not hit, it would be destiny. Those with toes who laugh at me for having no toes are many. This used to make me angry. But since I have studied under our Master, I have ceased to trouble about it. It may be that our Master has so far succeeded in purifying me. At any rate I have been with him nineteen years without being aware of the loss of my toes. Now you and I are engaged in studying the internal. Do you not then commit a fault by thus dragging me back to the external?"

At this Tzŭ Ch'an began to fidget, and changing countenance, begged Shên T'u Chia to say no more.

There was a man of the Lu State who had been mutilated, — Shu Shan *No-toes*. He came walking on his heels to see Confucius; but Confucius said, "You did not take care, and so brought this misfortune upon yourself. What is the use of coming to me now?"

"In my ignorance," replied No-toes, "I made free with my body and lost my toes. But I come with something more precious than toes which I now seek to keep. There is no man, but Heaven covers him: there is no man, but Earth supports him; —and I thought that you, sir, would be as Heaven and Earth. I little expected to hear these words from you."

"I must apologise," said Confucius. "Pray walk in and let us discuss." But No-toes walked out.

"There!" said Confucius to his disciples. "There is a criminal without toes who seeks to learn in order to make atonement for his previous misdeeds. And if he, how much more those who have no misdeeds for which to atone?" No-toes went off to Lao Tzŭ and said, "Is Confucius a sage, or is he not? How is it he has so many disciples? He aims at being a subtle dialectician, not knowing that such a reputation is regarded by real sages as the fetters of a criminal."

"Why do you not meet him with the continuity of life and death, the identity of *can* and *cannot*," answered Lao Tzŭ, "and so release him from these fetters?"

"He has been thus punished by God," replied No-toes. "It would be impossible to release him."

Duke Ai of the Lu State said to Confucius, "In the Wei State there is a leper, named Ai T'ai T'o. The men who live with him like him and make no effort to get rid of him. Of the women who have seen him, many have said to their parents, rather than be another man's wife, I would be his concubine.

"He never preaches at people, but puts himself into sympathy with them. He wields no power by which he may protect men's bodies. He has at his disposal no appointments by which to gratify their hearts. He is loathsome to a degree. He sympathises, but does not instruct. His knowledge is limited to his own State. Yet males and females alike all congregate around him.

"So, thinking that he must be different from ordinary men, I sent for him, and saw that he was indeed loathsome to a degree. Yet we had not been many months together ere my attention was fixed upon his conduct. A year had not elapsed ere I trusted him thoroughly; and as my State wanted a Prime Minister, I offered the post to him. He accepted it sullenly, as if he would much rather have declined. Perhaps he didn't think me good enough for him! At any rate, he took it; but in a very short time he left me and went away. I grieved for him as for a lost friend, and as though there were none left with whom I could rejoice. What manner of man is this?

"When I was on a mission to the Ch'u State," replied Confucius, "I saw a litter of young pigs sucking their dead mother. After a while they looked at her, and then they all left the body and went off. For their mother did not look at them anymore, nor did she any more seem to be of their kind. What they loved was their mother; not the body which contained her, but that which made the body what it was.

"When a man is killed in battle, his arms are not buried with him.

A man whose toes have been cut off does not value a present of boots. In each case the function of such things is gone.

"The concubines of the Son of Heaven do not cut their nails or pierce their ears.

He who has a marriageable daughter keeps her away from menial work. To preserve her beauty is quite enough occupation for her. How much more so for a man of perfect virtue?

"Now Ai T'ai To says nothing, and is trusted. He does nothing, and is sought after. He causes a man to offer him the government of his own State, and the only fear is lest he should decline. Truly his talents are perfect and his virtue without outward form!"

"What do you mean by his talents being perfect?" asked the Duke.

"Life and Death," replied Confucius, "existence and nonexistence, success and non-success, poverty and wealth, virtue and vice, good and evil report, hunger and thirst, warmth and cold,—these all revolve upon the changing wheel of Destiny. Day and night, they follow one upon the other, and no man can say where each one begins.

Therefore, they cannot be allowed to disturb the harmony of the organism, nor enter into the soul's domain. Swim however with the tide, so as not to offend others. Do this day by day without break, and live in peace with mankind. Thus, you will be ready for all contingencies, and may be said to have your talents perfect."

"And virtue without outward form; what is that?"

"In a water-level," said Confucius, "the water is in a most perfect state of repose. Let that be your model. The water remains quietly within, and does not overflow. It is from the cultivation of such harmony that virtue results. And if virtue takes no outward form, man will not be able to keep aloof from it."

Some days afterwards Duke Ai told Min Tzŭ, saying, "When first I took the reins of government in hand, I thought that in caring for my people's lives I had done all my duty as a ruler. But now that I have heard what a perfect man is, I fear that I have not been succeeding, but foolishly using my body and working destruction to my State. Confucius and I are not prince and minister, but merely friends with a care for each other's moral welfare."

A certain hunchback, named Wu Ch'un, whose heels did not touch the ground, had the ear of Duke Ling of Wei. The Duke took a great fancy to him; and as for well-formed men, he thought their necks were too scraggy.

Another man, with a goitre as big as a large jar, had the ear of Duke Huan of Ch'i. The Duke took a great fancy to him; and as for well-formed men, he thought their necks were too scraggy.

Thus, it is that virtue should prevail and outward form be forgotten. But mankind forgets not that which is to be forgotten, forgetting that which is not to be forgotten. This is forgetfulness indeed! And thus, with the truly wise, wisdom is a curse, sincerity like glue, virtue only a means to acquire, and skill nothing more than a commercial capacity. For the truly wise make no plans, and therefore require no wisdom. They do not separate, and therefore require no glue. They want nothing, and therefore need no virtue. They sell nothing, and therefore are not in want of a commercial capacity. These four qualifications are bestowed upon them by God and serve as heavenly food to them. And those who thus feed upon the divine have little need for the human. They wear the forms of men, without human passions. Because they wear the forms of men, they associate with men. Because they have not human passions, positives and negatives find in them no place. Infinitesimal indeed is that which makes them man: infinitely great is that which makes them divine!

Hui Tzŭ said to Chuang Tzŭ, "Are there then men who have no passions?"

Chuang Tzŭ replied, "Certainly."

"But if a man has no passions," argued Hui Tzŭ, "what is it that makes him a man?"

"TAO," replied Chuang Tzŭ, "gives him his expression, and God gives him his form. How should he not be a man?"

"If then he is a man," said Hui Tzŭ, "how can he be without passions?"

"What you mean by passions," answered Chuang Tzŭ, "is not what I mean. By a man without passions I mean one who does not permit good and evil to disturb his internal economy, but rather falls in with whatever happens, as a matter of course, and does not add to the sum of his mortality."

"But whence is man to get his body," asked Hui Tzŭ, "if there is to be no adding to the sum of mortality?"

"TAO gives him his expression," said Chuang Tzŭ, "and God gives him his form. He does not permit good and evil to disturb his internal economy. But now you are devoting your intelligence to externals, and wearing out your mental powers. You prop yourself against a tree and mutter, or lean over a table with half-closed eyes.

> God has made you a shapely sight,
> Yet your only thought is the *hard and white*."

CHAPTER VI. THE GREAT SUPREME.

Argument:

—The human and the divine—The pure men of old—Their qualifications—Their self-abstraction—All things as ONE—The known and the unknown—Life a boon—Death a transition—Life eternal open to all—The way thither—Illustrations.

HE who knows what God is, and who knows what Man is, has attained. Knowing what God is, he knows that he himself proceeded therefrom. Knowing what Man is, he rests in the knowledge of the known, waiting for the knowledge of the unknown. Working out one's allotted span, and not perishing in mid-career, —this is the fulness of knowledge.

God is a principle which exists by virtue of its own intrinsicality, and operates spontaneously, without selfmanifestation.

Herein, however, there is a flaw. Knowledge is dependent upon fulfilment. And as this fulfilment is uncertain, how can it be known that my divine is not really human, my human really divine?

> "Heaven from all creatures hides the book of Fate,
> All but the page prescribed, their present state."

We must have *pure men*, and then only can we have *pure knowledge*.

But what is a pure man? —The pure men of old acted without calculation, not seeking to secure results. They laid no plans. Therefore, failing, they had no cause for regret; succeeding, no cause for congratulation. And thus they could scale heights without fear; enter water without becoming wet; fire, without feeling hot. So far had their wisdom advanced towards TAO.

The pure men of old slept without dreams, and waked without anxiety. They ate without discrimination, breathing deep breaths. For pure men draw breath from their uttermost depths; the vulgar only from their throats.

Out of the crooked, words are retched up like vomit. If men's passions are deep, their divinity is shallow.

The pure men of old did not know what it was to love life or to hate death. They did not rejoice in birth, nor strive to put off dissolution. Quickly come, and quickly go; —no more. They did not forget whence it was they had sprung, neither did they seek to hasten their return thither. Cheerfully they played their allotted parts, waiting patiently for the end. This is what is called not to lead the heart astray from TAO, nor to let the human seek to supplement the divine.

And this is what is meant by a pure man.

Such men are in mind absolutely free; in demeanour, grave; in expression, cheerful. If it is freezing cold, it seems to them like autumn; if blazing hot, like spring. Their passions occur like the four seasons.

They are in harmony with all creation, and none know the limit thereof.

And so it is that a perfect man can destroy a kingdom and yet not lose the hearts of the people, while the benefits he hands down to ten thousand generations do not proceed from love of his fellow-man.

He who delights in man, is himself not a perfect man. His affection is not true charity.

Depending upon opportunity, he has not true worth.

He who is not conversant with both good and evil is not a superior man.

He who disregards his reputation is not what a man should be.

He who is not absolutely oblivious of his own existence can never be a ruler of men.

Thus Hu Pu Hsieh, Wu Kuang, Poh I, Shu Ch'i, Chi Tzŭ, Hsü Yü, Chi T'o, and Shên T'u Ti, were the servants of rulers, and did the behests of others, not their own.

The pure men of old did their duty to their neighbours, but did not associate with them.

They behaved as though wanting in themselves, but without flattering others. Naturally rectangular, they were not uncompromisingly hard. They manifested their independence without going to extremes. They appeared to smile as if pleased, when the expression was only a natural response.

Their outward semblance derived its fascination from the store of goodness within. They seemed to be of the world around them, while proudly treading beyond its limits. They seemed to desire silence, while in truth they had dispensed with language.

They saw in penal laws a trunk; in social ceremonies, wings; in wisdom, a useful accessory; in morality, a guide. For them penal laws meant a merciful administration; social ceremonies, a passport through the world; wisdom, an excuse for doing what they could not help; and morality, walking like others upon the path.

And thus, all men praised them for the worthy lives they led.

For what they cared for could be reduced to ONE, and what they did not care for to ONE also. That which was ONE was ONE, and that which was not ONE was likewise ONE. In that which was ONE, they were of God; in that which was not ONE, they were of Man. And so between the human and the divine no conflict ensued. This was to be a pure man.

Life and Death belong to Destiny. Their sequence, like day and night, is of God, beyond the interference of man, an inevitable law.

A man looks upon God as upon his father, and loves him in like measure. Shall he then not love that which is greater than God?

A man looks upon a ruler of men as upon some one better than himself, for whom he would sacrifice his life. Shall he not then do so for the Supreme Ruler of Creation?

When the pond dries up, and the fishes are left upon dry ground, to moisten them with the breath or to damp them with spittle is not to be compared with leaving them in the first instance in their native rivers and lakes. And better than praising Yao and blaming Chieh would be leaving them both and attending to the development of TAO.

TAO gives me this form, this toil in manhood, this repose in old age, this rest in death. And surely that which is such a kind arbiter of my life is the best arbiter of my death.

A boat may be hidden in a creek, or in a bog, safe enough.

But at midnight a strong man may come and carry away the boat on his back. The dull of vision do not perceive that however you conceal things, small ones in larger ones, there will always be a chance of losing them.

But if you conceal the whole universe in the whole universe, there will be no place left wherein it may be lost. The laws of matter make this to be so.

To have attained to the human form must be always a source of joy. And then, to undergo countless transitions, with only the infinite to look forward to, —what incomparable bliss is that! Therefore, it is that the truly wise rejoice in that which can never be lost but endures always.

For if we can accept early death, old age, a beginning, and an end, why not that which informs all creation and is of all phenomena the Ultimate Cause?

TAO has its laws, and its evidences. It is devoid both of action and of form. It may be transmitted, but cannot be received.

It may be obtained, but cannot be seen. Before heaven and earth were, TAO was. It has existed without change from all time. Spiritual beings drew their spirituality therefrom, while the universe became what we can see it now. To TAO, the zenith is not high, nor the nadir low; no point in time is long ago, nor by lapse of ages has it grown old.

Hsi Wei obtained TAO, and so set the universe in order.

Fu Hsi obtained it, and was able to establish eternal principles.

The Great Bear obtained it, and has never erred from its course. The sun and moon obtained it, and have never ceased to revolve. K'an P'i obtained it, and established the K'un-lun mountains.

P'ing I obtained it, and rules over the streams. Chien Wu obtained it, and dwells on Mount T'ai.

The Yellow Emperor obtained it, and soared upon the clouds to heaven.

Chuan Hsu obtained it, and dwells in the Dark Palace.

Yü Ch'iang obtained it, and fixed himself at the North Pole.

Hsi Wang Mu obtained it, and settled at Shao Kuang; since when, no one knows; until when, no one knows either.

P'êng Tsu obtained it, and lived from the time of Shun until the time of the Five Princes.

Fu Yüeh obtained it, and as the Minister of Wu Ting

got the empire under his control. And now, charioted upon one constellation and drawn by another, he has been enrolled among the stars of heaven.

Nan Po Tzŭ K'uei said to Nü Yü, "You are old, Sir, and yet your countenance is like that of a child. How is this?"

Nü Yü replied, "I have learnt TAO."

"Could I get TAO by studying it? " asked the other.

"I fear not," said Nü Yü. "You are not the sort of man. There was Pu Liang I. He had all the qualifications of a sage, but not TAO. Now I had TAO, though none of the qualifications. But do you imagine that much as I wished it I was able to teach TAO to him so that he should be a perfect sage? Had it been so, then to teach TAO to one who has the qualifications of a sage would be an easy matter. No, Sir. I imparted as though withholding; and in three days, for him, this sublunary state had ceased to exist.

When he had attained to this, I withheld again; and in seven days more, for him, the external world had ceased to be. And so again for another nine days, when he became unconscious of his own existence. He became first etherealised, next possessed of perfect wisdom, then without past or present, and finally able to enter there where life and death are no more,—where killing does not take away life, nor does prolongation of life add to the duration of existence.

In that state, he is ever in accord with the exigencies of his environment; and this is to be *Battered but not Bruised*. And he who can be thus battered but not bruised is on the way to perfection."

"And how did you manage to get hold of all this?" asked Nan Po Tzŭ K'uei.

"I got it from books," replied Nü Yü; "and the books got it from learning, and learning from investigation, and investigation from cö-ordination, and cö-ordination from application, and application from desire to know, and desire to know from the unknown, and the unknown from the great void, and the great void from infinity!"

Four men were conversing together, when the following resolution was suggested:—"Whosoever can make Inaction the head, Life the backbone, and Death the tail, of his existence,—that man shall be admitted to friendship with us." The four looked at each other and smiled; and tacitly accepting the conditions, became friends forthwith.

By-and-by, one of them, named Tzŭ Yü, fell ill, and another, Tzŭ Ssŭ, went to see him. "Verily God is great!" said the sick man. "See how he has doubled me up. My back is so hunched that my viscera are at the top of my body. My cheeks are level with my navel. My shoulders are higher than my neck. My hair grows up towards the sky.

The whole economy of my organism is deranged.

Nevertheless, my mental equilibrium is not disturbed." So saying, he dragged himself painfully to a well, where he could see himself, and continued, "Alas, that God should have doubled me up like this!"

"Are you afraid?" asked Tzŭ Ssŭ.

"I am not," replied Tzŭ Yü. "What have I to fear? Ere long I shall be decomposed. My left shoulder will become a cock, and I shall herald the approach of morn. My right shoulder will become a cross-bow, and I shall be able to get broiled duck. My buttocks will become wheels; and with my soul for a horse, I shall be able to ride in my own chariot. I obtained life because it was my time: I am now parting with it in accordance with the same law. Content with the natural sequence of these states, joy and sorrow touch me not. I am simply, as the ancients expressed it, hanging in the air, unable to cut myself down, bound with the trammels of material existence. But man has ever given way before God: why, then, should I be afraid?"

By-and-by, another of the four, named Tzŭ Lai, fell ill, and lay gasping for breath, while his family stood weeping around. The fourth friend, Tzŭ Li, went to see him. "Chut!" cried he to the wife and children; "begone! you balk his decomposition." Then, leaning against the door, he said, "Verily, God is great! I wonder what he will make of you now. I wonder whither you will be sent. Do you think he will make you into a rat's liver or into the shoulders of a snake?"

"A son," answered Tzŭ Lai, "must go whithersoever his parents bid him. Nature is no other than a man's parents.

If she bid me die quickly, and I demur, then I am an unfilial son. She can do me no wrong. TAO gives me this form, this toil in manhood, this repose in old age, this rest in death. And surely that which is such a kind arbiter of my life is the best arbiter of my death.

"Suppose that the boiling metal in a smelting-pot were to bubble up and say, 'Make of me an Excalibur;' I think the caster would reject that metal as uncanny. And if a sinner like myself were to say to God, 'Make of me a man, make of me a man;' I think he too would reject me as uncanny. The universe is the smelting-pot, and God is the caster. I shall go whithersoever I am sent, to wake unconscious of the past, as a man wakes from a dreamless sleep."

Tzŭ Sang Hu, Mêng Tzŭ Fan, and Tzŭ Ch'in Chang, were conversing together, when it was asked, "Who can be, and yet not be?

Who can do, and yet not do?

Who can mount to heaven, and roaming through the clouds, pass beyond the limits of space, oblivious of existence, for ever and ever without end?"

The three looked at each other and smiled; and as neither had any misgivings, they became friends accordingly.

Shortly afterwards Tzŭ Sang Hu died; whereupon Confucius sent Tzŭ Kung to take part in the mourning. But Tzŭ Kung found that one had composed a song which the other was accompanying on the lute, as follows: —

Ah! Wilt thou come back to us, Sang Hu?
Ah! Wilt thou come back to us, Sang Hu?
Thou hast already returned to thy God,

While we still remain here as men, —alas!

Tzŭ Kung hurried in and said, "How can you sing alongside of a corpse? Is this decorum?"

The two men looked at each other and laughed, saying, "What should this man know of decorum indeed?"

Tzŭ Kung went back and told Confucius, asking him, "What manner of men are these? Their object is nothingness and a separation from their corporeal frames.

They can sit near a corpse and yet sing, unmoved. There is no class for such. What are they?"

"These men," replied Confucius, "travel beyond the rule of life. I travel within it. Consequently, our paths do not meet; and I was wrong in send-you to mourn. They consider themselves as one with God, recognising no distinctions between human and divine. They look on life as a huge tumour from which death sets them free. All the same they know not where they were before birth, nor where they will be after death. Though admitting different elements, they take their stand upon the unity of all things. They ignore their passions. They take no count of their ears and eyes. Backwards and forwards through all eternity, they do not admit a beginning or end. They stroll beyond the dust and dirt of mortality, to wander in the realms of inaction. How should such men trouble themselves with the conventionalities of this world, or care what people may think of them?"

"But if such is the case," said Tzŭ Kung, "why should we stick to the rule?"

"Heaven has condemned me to this," replied Confucius. "Nevertheless, you and I may perhaps escape from it."

"By what method?" asked Tzŭ Kung.

"Fishes," replied Confucius, "are born in water. Man is born in TAO. If fishes get ponds to live in, they thrive. If man gets TAO to live in, he may live his life in peace.

Hence the saying, 'All that a fish wants is water; all that a man wants is TAO.'"

"May I ask," said Tzŭ Kung, "about divine men?"

"Divine men," replied Confucius, "are divine to man, but ordinary to God. Hence the saying that the meanest being in heaven would be the best on earth; and the best on earth, the meanest in heaven."

Yen Hui said to Confucius, "When Mêng Sun Ts'ai's mother died, he wept, but without snivelling; he grieved but his grief was not heartfelt; he wore mourning but without howling. Yet although wanting in these three points, he is considered the best mourner in the State of Lu.

Surely this is the name and not the reality. I am astonished at it."

"Mêng Sun," said Confucius, "did all that was required. He has made an advance towards wisdom.

He could not do less; while all the time actually doing less.

"Mêng Sun knows not whence we come nor whither we go. He knows not whether the end will come early or late. Passing into life as a man, he quietly awaits his passage into the unknown. What should the dead know of the living, or the living know of the dead? Even you and I may be in a dream from which we have not yet awaked.

"Then again, he adapts himself physically, while avoiding injury to his higher self.

He regards a dying man simply as one who is going home. He sees others weep, and he naturally weeps too.

"Besides, a man's personality is something of which he is subjectively conscious. It is impossible for him to say if he is really that which he is conscious of being. You dream you are a bird, and soar to heaven. You dream you are a fish, and dive into the ocean's depths. And you cannot tell whether the man now speaking is awake or in a dream.

"A pleasurable sensation precedes the smile it evokes. The smile itself is not dependent upon a reminding nudge.

Resign yourself, unconscious of all changes, and you shall enter into the pure, the divine, the ONE."

I Erh Tzŭ went to see Hsü Yu. "The latter asked him, saying, "How has Yao benefited you?"

"He bade me," replied the former, "practise charity and do my duty, and distinguish clearly between right and wrong."

"Then what do you want here?" said Hsü Yu. "If Yao has already branded you with charity and duty, and cut off your nose with right and wrong, what do you do in this free-andeasy, care-for-nobody, topsy-turvy neighbourhood?"

"Nevertheless," replied I Erh Tzŭ, "I should like to be on its confines."

"If a man has lost his eyes," retorted Hsü Yu, "it is impossible for him to join in the appreciation of beauty. A man with a film over his eyes cannot tell a blue sacrificial robe from a yellow one."

"Wu Chuang's disregard of her beauty," answered I Erh
Tzŭ, "Chü Liang's disregard of his strength, the Yellow Emperor's abandonment of wisdom, —all these were brought about by a process of filing and hammering. And how do you know but that God would rid me of my brands, and give me a new nose, and make me fit to become a disciple of yourself?"

"Ah!" replied Hsü Yu, "that cannot be known. But I will just give you an outline. The Master I serve succours all things, and does not account it *duty*. He continues his blessings through countless generations, and does not account it *charity*. Dating back to the remotest antiquity, he does not account himself old. Covering heaven, supporting earth, and fashioning the various forms of things, he does not account himself skilled. He it is whom you should seek."

"I am getting on," observed Yen Hui to Confucius.

"How so?" asked the latter.

"I have got rid of charity and duty," replied the former.

"Very good," replied Confucius, "but not perfect."

Another day Yen Hui met Confucius and said, "I am getting on."

"How so?" asked Confucius.

"I have got rid of ceremonial and music," answered Yen Hui.

"Very good," said Confucius, "but not perfect."

On a third occasion Yen Hui met Confucius and said, "I am getting on."

"How so?" asked the Sage.

"I have got rid of everything," replied Yen Hui.

"Got rid of everything!" said Confucius eagerly. "What do you mean by that?"

"I have freed myself from my body," answered Yen Hui. "I have discarded my reasoning powers. And by thus getting rid of body and mind, I have become O_{NE} with the Infinite. This is what I mean by getting rid of everything."

"If you have become O_{NE}," cried Confucius, "there can be no room for bias. If you have passed into space, you are indeed without beginning or end. And if you have really attained to this, I trust to be allowed to follow in your steps."

Tzŭ Yü and Tzŭ Sang were friends. Once when it had rained for ten days, Tzŭ Yü said, "Tzŭ Sang is dangerously ill." So he packed up some food and went to see him.

Arriving at the door, he heard something between singing and lamentation, accompanied with the sound of music, as follows: —

"O father! O mother! O Heaven! O Man!"

These words seemed to be uttered with a great effort; whereupon Tzŭ Yü went in and asked what it all meant.

"I was trying to think who could have brought me to this extreme," replied Tzŭ Sang, "but I could not guess. My father and mother would hardly wish me to be poor. Heaven covers all equally. Earth supports all equally. How can they make me in particular poor? I was seeking to know who it was, but without success. Surely then I am brought to this extreme by *Destiny*."

CHAPTER VII. How to Govern.

Argument:

—Princes should reign, not rule—Rulers find their standards of right in themselves—They thus coerce their people into obeying artificial laws, instead of leaving them to obey natural laws—By action they accomplish nothing—By inaction there is nothing which they would not accomplish—Individuals think they know what the empire wants—In reality it is the empire itself which know best—Illustrations.

Y EH CH'ÜEH asked Wang I four questions, none of which he could answer. There at the former was greatly delighted, and went off and told P'u I Tzŭ.

"Have you only just found that out?" said P'u I Tzŭ. "The Emperor Shun was not equal to T'ai Huang.

Shun was all for charity in his zeal for mankind; but although he succeeded in government, he himself never rose above the level of artificiality. Now T'ai Huang was peaceful when asleep and inactive when awake. At one time he would think himself a horse; at another, an ox. His wisdom was substantial and above suspicion. His virtue was genuine indeed. And yet he never sank to the level of artificiality."

Chien Wu meeting the eccentric Chieh Yü, the latter enquired, saying, "What did Jih Chung Shih teach you?"

"He taught me," replied Chien Wu, "about the laws and regulations which princes evolve, and which he said none would venture not to hear and obey."

"That is a false teaching indeed," replied Chieh Yü. "To attempt to govern mankind thus, —as well try to wade through the sea, to hew a passage through a river, or make a mosquito fly away with a mountain!

"The government of the truly wise man has no concern with externals. He first perfects himself, and then by virtue thereof he is enabled to accomplish what he wants.

"The bird flies high to avoid snare and dart. The mouse burrows down below the hill to avoid being smoked or cut out of its nest. Is your wit below that of these two creatures?"

T'ien Kên was travelling on the south of the Yin mountain. He had reached the river Liao when he met a certain Sage to whom he said, "I beg to ask about the government of the empire."

"Begone!" cried the Sage. "You are a low fellow, and your question is ill timed. God has just turned me out a man. That is enough for me. Borne on light pinions I can soar beyond the cardinal points, to the land of nowhere, in the domain of nothingness. And you come to worry me with government of the empire!"

But T'ien Kên enquired a second time, and the Sage replied, "Resolve your mental energy into abstraction, your physical energy into inaction. Allow yourself to fall in with the natural order of phenomena, without admitting the element of self, —and the empire will be governed."

Yang Tzŭ Chü went to see Lao Tzŭ, and said, "Suppose a man were ardent and courageous, acquainted with the order and principles of things, and untiring in the pursuit of TAO —would he be accounted a wise ruler?"

"From the point of view of a truly wise man," replied Lao Tzŭ, " such a one would be a mere handicraftsman, wearing out body and mind alike. The tiger and the pard suffer from the beauty of their skins. The cleverness of the monkey, the tractability of the ox, bring them both to the tether. It is not on such grounds that a ruler may be accounted wise."

"But in what, then," cried Yang Tzŭ Chü, "does the government of a wise man consist?"

"The goodness of a wise ruler," answered Lao Tzŭ, "covers the whole empire, yet he himself seems to know it not. It influences all creation, yet none is conscious thereof. It appears under countless forms, bringing joy to all things. It is based upon the baseless, and travels through the realms of Nowhere."

In the State of Chêng there was a wonderful magician, named Chi Han. He knew all about birth and death, gain and loss, misfortune and happiness, long life and short life, — predicting events to a day with supernatural accuracy.

The people of Chêng used to flee at his approach; but Lieh Tzŭ went to see him, and became so infatuated that on his return he said to Hu Tzŭ, "I used to look upon your TAO as perfect. Now I know something more perfect still."

"So far," replied Hu Tzŭ, "I have only taught you the ornamentals, not the essentials, of TAO; and yet you think you know all about it. Without cocks in your poultry-yard, what sort of eggs do the hens lay? If you go about trying to force TAO down people's throats, you will be simply exposing yourself. Bring your friend with you, and let me show myself to him."

So next day Lieh Tzŭ went with Chi Han to see Hu Tzŭ, and when they came out Chi Han said, "Alas! your teacher is doomed. He cannot live. I hardly give him ten days. I am astonished at him. He is but wet ashes."

Lieh Tzŭ went in and wept bitterly, and told Hu Tzŭ; but the latter said, "I showed myself to him just now as the earth shows us its outward form, motionless and still, while production is all the time going on. I merely prevented him from seeing my pent-up energy within. Bring him again."

Next day the interview took place as before; but as they were leaving Chi Han said to Lieh Tzŭ, "It is lucky for your teacher that he met me. He is better. He will recover. I saw he had recuperative power."

Lieh Tzŭ went in and told Hu Tzŭ; whereupon the latter replied, "I showed myself to him just now as heaven shows itself in all its dispassionate grandeur, letting a little energy run out of my heels. He was thus able to detect that I had some. Bring him here again."

Next day a third interview took place, and as they were leaving, Chi Han said to Lieh Tzŭ, "Your teacher is never one day like another. I can tell nothing from his physiognomy. Get him to be regular, and I will then examine him again."

This being repeated to Hu Tzŭ as before, the latter said, "I showed myself to him just now in a state of harmonious equilibrium. Where the whale disports itself, —is the abyss. Where water is at rest, —is the abyss. Where water is in motion, —is the abyss. The abyss has nine names. These are three of them."

Next day the two went once more to see Hu Tzŭ; but Chi Han was unable to stand still, and in his confusion turned and fled.

"Pursue him!" cried Hu Tzŭ; whereupon Lieh Tzŭ ran after him, but could not overtake him, so he returned and told Hu Tzŭ that the fugitive had disappeared.

"I showed myself to him just now" said Hu Tzŭ, "as TAO appeared before time was. I was to him as a great blank, existing of itself. He knew not who I was. His face fell. He became confused. And so he fled."

Upon this Lieh Tzŭ stood convinced that he had not yet acquired any real knowledge, and at once set to work in earnest, passing three years without leaving the house. He helped his wife to cook the family dinner, and fed his pigs just like human beings. He discarded the artificial and reverted to the natural. He became merely a shape. Amidst confusion.

He was unconfounded. And so he continued to the end.

By Inaction, fame comes as the spirits of the dead come to the boy who impersonates the corpse.

By Inaction, one can become the centre of thought, the focus of responsibility, the arbiter of wisdom. Full allowance must be made for others, while remaining unmoved oneself. There must be a thorough compliance with divine principles, without any manifestation thereof.

All of which may be summed up in the one-word *passivity*. For the perfect man employs his mind as a mirror. It grasps nothing: it refuses nothing. It receives, but does not keep. And thus he can triumph over matter, without injury to himself.

The ruler of the southern sea was called Shu. The ruler of the northern sea was called Hu. The ruler of the central zone was called Hun Tun.

Shu and Hu often met on Hun Tun's territory, and being always well treated by him, determined to repay his kindness.

They said, "All men have seven holes, —for seeing, hearing, eating, and breathing. Hun Tun alone has none. We will bore some for him."

So, every day they bored one hole; but on the seventh day Hun Tun died:

Outer Chapters.

◄◄●►●►◄

CHAPTER VIII. *JOINED TOES.*

Argument:

—Virtues should be natural, not artificial; passive not active.

[Chs. viii to xiii inclusive are illustrative of, or supplementary to, ch. vii.]

JOINED toes and extra fingers are an addition to nature, though, functionally speaking, superfluous. Wens and tumours are an addition to the bodily form, though, as far as nature is concerned, superfluous. And similarly, to include charity and duty to one's neighbour among the functions of man's organism, is not true TAO.

For just as joined toes are but useless lumps of flesh, and extra fingers but useless excrescences, so are any artificial additions to our internal economy but harmful adjuncts to real charity and duty to one's neighbour, and are moreover prejudicial to the right use of intelligence.

People with extra keenness of vision muddle themselves over the five colours, exaggerate the value of shades, and of distinctions of greens and yellows for sacrificial robes. Of such was Li Chu.

People with extra keenness of hearing muddle themselves over the five notes, exaggerate the tonic differences of the six pitch-pipes, and the various *timbres* of metal, stone, silk, and bamboo, of the *Huang-chung*, and of the *Ta-lü*. Of such was Shih K'uang.

People who graft on charity, force themselves to display this virtue in order to gain reputation and to enjoy the applause of the world for that which is of no account. Of such were Tsêng and Shih.

People who refine in argument do but pile up tiles or knot ropes in their maunderings over the hard and white, the like and the unlike, wearing themselves out over mere useless terms. Of such were Yang and Mih.

Therefore, every addition to or deviation from nature belongs not to the ultimate perfection of all.

He who would attain to such perfection never loses sight of the natural conditions of his existence. With him the joined is not united, nor the separated apart, nor the long in excess, nor the short wanting. For just as a duck's legs, though short, cannot be lengthened without pain to the duck, and a crane's legs, though long, cannot be shortened without misery to the crane, so that which is long in man's moral nature cannot be cut off, nor that which is short be lengthened. All sorrow is thus avoided.

Intentional charity and intentional duty to one's neighbour are surely not included in our moral nature. Yet what sorrow these have involved. Divide your joined toes and you will howl: bite off your extra finger and you will scream. In one case there is too much, in the other too little; but the sorrow is the same. And the charitable of the age go about sorrowing over the ills of the age, while the noncharitable cut through the natural conditions of things in their greed after place and wealth. Surely then intentional charity and duty to one's neighbour are not included in our moral nature. Yet from the time of the Three Dynasties downwards what a fuss has been made about them!

Those who cannot make perfect without arc, line, compasses, and square, injure the natural constitution of things. Those who require cords to bind and glue to stick, interfere with the natural functions of things. And those who seek to satisfy the mind of man by hampering with ceremonies and music and preaching charity and duty to one's neighbour, thereby destroy the intrinsicality of things.

For such intrinsicality does exist, in this sense:— Things which are curved require no arcs; things which are straight require no lines; things which are round require no compasses; things which are rectangular require no squares; things which stick require no glue; things which hold together require no cords. And just as all things are produced, and none can tell how they are produced, so do all things possess their own intrinsic qualities and none can tell how they possess them. From time immemorial this has always been so, without variation. Why then should charity and duty to one's neighbour be as it were glued or corded on, and introduced into the domain of Tag, to give rise to doubt among mankind?

Lesser doubts change the rule of life; greater doubts change man's nature.

How do we know this? By the fact that ever since the time when Shun bid for charity and duty to one's neighbour in order to secure the empire, men have devoted their lives to the pursuit thereof. Is it not then charity and duty to one's neighbour which change the nature of man?

Therefore, I have tried to show that from the time of the Three Dynasties it has always been the external which has changed the nature of man. If a mean man, he will die for gain. If a superior man, he will die for fame. If a man of rank, he will die for his ancestral honours. If a Sage, he will die for the world. The pursuits and ambitions of these men differ, but the injury to their natures involved in the sacrifice of their lives is the same.

Tsang and Ku were shepherds, both of whom lost their flocks. On inquiry, it appeared that Tsang had been engaged in reading, while Ku had gone to take part in some trials of strength. Their occupations had been different, but the result was in each case loss of the sheep.

Poh I died for fame at the foot of Mount Shou-yang.

Robber Chê died for gain on Mount T'ai.

Their deaths were not the same, but the injury to their lives and natures was in each case the same. How then can we applaud the former and blame the latter?

And so, if a man dies for charity and duty to his neighbour the world calls him a noble fellow; but if he dies for gain, the world calls him a low fellow. The dying being the same, one is nevertheless called noble and the other low. But in point of injury to life and nature, the robber Chê and Poh I are one. Where then does the distinction of noble and low come in?

Were a man to apply himself to charity and duty towards his neighbour until he was the equal of Tsêng or Shih, this would not be what I mean by perfection. Or to flavours, until he was the equal of Yü Erh.

Or to sounds, until he was the equal of Shih K'uang. Or to colours, until he was the equal of Li Chu. What I mean by perfection is not what is meant by charity and duty to one's neighbour. It is found in the cultivation of TAO. And those whom I regard as cultivators of TAO are not those who cultivate charity and duty to one's neighbour. They are those who yield to the natural conditions of things. What I call perfection of hearing is not hearing others but oneself. What I call perfection of vision is not seeing others but oneself.

For a man who sees not himself but others, takes not possession of himself but of others, thus taking what others should take and not what he himself should take.

Instead of being himself, he in fact becomes someone else. And if a man thus becomes someone else instead of himself, this is a fatal error of which both the robber Chê and Poh I can be equally guilty.

And so, conscious of my own deficiency in regard to TAO, I do not venture at my best to practise the principles of charity and duty to my neighbour, nor at my worst to fall into the fatal error above-mentioned.

CHAPTER IX. HORSES' HOOFS.

Argument:

—Superiority of the natural over the artificial—Application of this principle to government.

HORSES have hoofs to carry them over frost and snow; hair, to protect them from wind and cold. They eat grass and drink water, and fling up their heels over the champaign. Such is the real nature of horses. Palatial dwellings are of no use to them.

One day Poh Loh appeared, saying, "I understand the management of horses."

So he branded them, and clipped them, and pared their hoofs, and put halters on them, tying them up by the head and shackling them by the feet, and disposing them in stables, with the result that two or three in every ten died. Then he kept them hungry and thirsty, trotting them and galloping them, and grooming, and trimming, with the misery of the tasselled bridle before and the fear of the knotted whip behind, until more than half of them were dead.

The potter says, "I can do what I will with clay. If I want it round, I use compasses; if rectangular, a square."

The carpenter says, "I can do what I will with wood. If I want it curved, I use an arc; if straight, a line."

But on what grounds can we think that the natures of clay and wood desire this application of compasses and square, of arc and line? Nevertheless, every age extols Poh Loh for his skill in managing horses, and potters and carpenters for their skill with clay and wood. Those who *govern* the empire make the same mistake.

Now I regard government of the empire from quite a different point of view.

The people have certain natural instincts; —to weave and clothe themselves, to till and feed themselves. These are common to all humanity, and all arc agreed thereon. Such instincts are called "Heaven-sent."

And so in the days when natural instincts prevailed, men moved quietly and gazed steadily. At that time, there were no roads over mountains, nor boats, nor bridges over water. All things were produced, each for its own proper sphere. Birds and beasts multiplied; trees and shrubs grew up. The former might be led by the hand; you could climb up and peep into the raven's nest. For then man dwelt with birds and beasts, and all creation was one. There were no distinctions of good and bad men. Being all equally without knowledge, their virtue could not go astray. Being all equally without evil desires, they were in a state of natural integrity, the perfection of human existence.

But when Sages appeared, tripping people over charity and fettering with duty to one's neighbour, doubt found its way into the world. And then with their gushing over music and fussing over ceremony, the empire became divided against itself.

Was the natural integrity of things left unharmed, who could make sacrificial vessels? Was white jade left unbroken, who could make the regalia of courts? Were TAO not abandoned, who could introduce charity and duty to one's neighbour? Were man's natural instincts his guide, what need would there be for music and ceremonies? Were the five colours not confused, who would practise decoration? Were the five notes not confused, who would adopt the six pitch-pipes?

Destruction of the natural integrity of things, in order to produce articles of various kinds, —this is the fault of the artisan. Annihilation of TAO in order to practise charity and duty to one's neighbour, —this is the error of the Sage.

Horses live on dry land, eat grass and drink water. When pleased, they rub their necks together. When angry, they turn round and kick up their heels at each other. Thus far only do their natural dispositions carry them. But bridled and bitted, with a plate of metal on their foreheads, they learn to cast vicious looks, to turn the head to bite, to resist, to get the bit out of the mouth or the bridle into it. And thus their natures become depraved, —the fault of Poh Loh.

In the days of Ho Hsü the people did nothing in particular when at rest, and went nowhere in particular when they moved. Having food, they rejoiced; having full bellies, they strolled about. Such were the capacities of the people. But when the Sages came to worry them with ceremonies and music in order to rectify the form of government, and dangled charity and duty to one's neighbour before them in order to satisfy their hearts, —then the people began to develop a taste for knowledge and to struggle one with the other in their desire for gain.

This was the error of the Sages.

CHAPTER X. OPENING TRUNKS.

Argument:

>—All restrictions artificial, and therefore deceptive—Only by shaking off such fetters, and reverting to the natural, can man hope to attain.

THE precautions taken against thieves who open trunks, search bags, or ransack tills, consist of securing with cords and fastening with bolts and locks. This is what the world calls wit.

But a strong thief comes who carries off the till on his shoulders, with box and bag to boot. And his only fear is that the cords and locks should not be strong enough!

Therefore, what the world calls wit, simply amounts to assistance given to the strong thief.

And I venture to state that nothing of that which the world calls wit, is otherwise than serviceable to strong thieves; and that nothing of that which the world calls wisdom is other than a protection to strong thieves.

How can this be shown? —In the State of Ch'i a man used to be able to see from one town to the next, and hear the barking and crowing of its dogs and cocks.

The area covered by the nets of fishermen and fowlers, and pricked by the plough, was a square of two thousand and odd *li*.

And within its four boundaries not a temple or shrine was dedicated, nor a district or hamlet governed, but in accordance with the rules laid down by the Sages.

Yet one morning T'ien Ch'êng Tzŭ slew the Prince of Ch'i, and stole his kingdom. And not his kingdom only, but the wisdom-tricks which he had got from the Sages as well; so that although T'ien Ch'êng Tzŭ acquired the reputation of a thief, he lived as comfortably as ever did either Yao or Shun. The small States did not venture to blame, nor the great States to punish him; and so, for twelve generations his descendants ruled over Ch'i.

Was not this stealing the State of Ch'i and the wisdom-tricks of the Sages as well in order to secure himself from the consequences of such theft?

This amounts to what I have already said, namely that nothing of what the world esteems great wit is otherwise than serviceable to strong thieves, and that nothing of what the world calls great wisdom is other than a protection to strong thieves.

Let us take another example. Of old, Lung Fêng was beheaded, Pi Kan was disembowelled, Chang Hung was sliced to death, Tzŭ Hsü was chopped to mince-meat.

All these four were Sages, but their wisdom could not preserve them from death.

An apprentice to Robber Chê asked him saying, "Is there then TAO in thieving?"

"Pray tell me of something in which there is not TAO," Chê replied. "There is the *wisdom* by which booty is located. The *courage* to go in first, and the *heroism* of coming out last. There is the *shrewdness* of calculating success, and *justice* in the equal division of the spoil. There has never yet been a great robber who was not possessed of these five."

Thus, the doctrine of the Sages is equally indispensable to good men and to Chê. But good men are scarce and bad men plentiful, so that the good the Sages do to the world is little and the evil great.

Therefore, it has been said, "If the lips are gone, the teeth will be cold." It was the thinness of the wine of Lu which caused the siege of Han Tan.

It was the appearance of Sages which caused the appearance of great robbers.

Drive out the Sages and leave the robbers alone, —then only will the empire be governed. As when the stream ceases the gully dries up, and when the hill is levelled the chasm is filled; so, when Sages are extinct, there will be no more robbers, but the empire will rest in peace.

On the other hand, unless Sages disappear, neither will great robbers disappear; nor if you double the number of Sages wherewithal to govern the empire will you do more than double the profits of Robber Chê.

If pecks and bushels are used for measurement, they will also be stolen.

If scales and steelyards are used for weighing, they will also be stolen. If tallies and signets are used for good faith, they will also be stolen. If charity and duty to one's neighbour are used for rectification, they will also be stolen.

How is this so? —One man steals a purse and is punished. Another steals a State, and becomes a Prince. But charity and duty to one's neighbour are integral parts of princedom. Does he not then steal charity and duty to one's neighbour together with the wisdom of the Sages?

So it is that to attempt to drive out great robbers is simply to help them to steal principalities, charity, duty to one's neighbour, together with measures, scales, tallies, and signets. No reward of official regalia and uniform will dissuade, nor dread of sharp instruments of punishment will deter such men from their course. These do but double the profits of robbers like Chê, and make it impossible to get rid of them, —for which the Sages are responsible.

Therefore, it has been said, "Fishes cannot be taken away from water: the instruments of government cannot be delegated to others."

In the wisdom of Sages, the instruments of government are found. This wisdom is not fit for enlightening the world.

Away then with wisdom and knowledge, and great robbers will disappear! Discard jade and destroy pearls, and petty thieves will cease to exist. Burn tallies and break signets, and the people will revert to their natural integrity. Split measures and smash scales, and the people will not fight over quantities. Utterly abolish all the restrictions of Sages, and the people will begin to be fit for the reception of TAO.

Confuse the six pitch-pipes, break up organs and flutes, stuff up the ears of Shih K'uang, —and each man will keep his own sense of hearing to himself.

Put an end to decoration, disperse the five categories of colour, glue up the eyes of Li Chu, —and each man will keep his own sense of sight to himself.

Destroy arcs and lines, fling away square and compasses, snap off the fingers of Kung Ch'ui, —

Wherefore the saying, "Great skill is as clumsiness."

Restrain the actions of Tsêng and Shih, stop the mouths of Yang and Mih, get rid of charity and duty to one's neighbour, —and the virtue of the people will become one with God.

If each man keeps to himself his own sense of sight, the world will escape confusion. If each man keeps to himself his own sense of hearing, the world will escape entanglements. If each man keeps his knowledge to himself, the world will escape doubt. If each man keeps his own virtue to himself, the world will avoid deviation from the true path.

Tsêng, Shih, Yang, Mih, Shih K'uang, Kung Ch'ui, and Li Chu, all set up their virtue outside themselves and involve the world in such angry discussions that nothing definite is accomplished.

Have you never heard of the Golden Age, — the days of Yung Ch'êng, Ta T'ing, Poh Huang, Chung Yang, Li Lu, Li Hsü, Hsien Yüan, Hê Hsü, Tsun Lu, Chu Yung, Fu Hsi, and Shên Nung?

Then the people used knotted cords.

They were contented with what food and raiment they could get. They lived simple and peaceful lives. Neighbouring districts were within sight, and the cocks and dogs of one could be heard in the other, yet the people grew old and died without ever interchanging visits.

In those days, government was indeed perfect. But nowadays any one can excite the people by saying, "In such and such a place there is a Sage."

Immediately they put together a few provisions and hurry off, neglecting their parents at home and their master's business abroad, filing in unbroken line through territories of Princes, with a string of carts and carriages a thousand *li* in length. Such is the evil effect of an exaggerated desire for knowledge among our rulers. And if rulers aim at knowledge and neglect TAO, the empire will be overwhelmed in confusion.

How can it be shown that this is so? —Bows and cross-bows and hand-nets and harpoon-arrows, involve much

knowledge in their use; but they carry confusion among the birds of the air. Hooks and bait and nets and traps, involve much knowledge in their use; but they carry confusion among the fishes of the deep. Fences and nets and snares, involve much knowledge in their use; but they carry confusion among the beasts of the field. In the same way the sophistical fallacies of the hard and white and the like and the unlike of schoolmen involve much knowledge of argument; but they overwhelm the world in doubt.

Therefore, it is that whenever there is great confusion, love of knowledge is ever at the bottom of it. For all men strive to grasp what they do not know, while none strive to grasp what they already know; and all strive to discredit what they do not excel in, while none strive to discredit what they do excel in. The result is overwhelming confusion.

Thus, above, the splendour of the heavenly bodies is dimmed; below, the energy of land and water is disturbed; while midway the influence of the four seasons is destroyed. There is not one tiny creature which moves on earth or flies in air but becomes other than by nature it should be. So overwhelming is the confusion which desire for knowledge has brought upon the world ever since the time of the Three Dynasties downwards! The simple and the guileless have been set aside; the specious and the false have been exalted. Tranquil inaction has given place to a love of disputation; and by disputation has confusion come upon the world.

CHAPTER XI. ON LETTING ALONE.

Argument:

—The natural conditions of our existence require no artificial aids—The evils of government—Failure of coercion—TAO the refuge— Inaction the secret—The action of Inaction—Illustrations.

THERE has been such a thing as letting mankind alone; there has never been such a thing as governing mankind.

Letting alone springs from fear lest men's natural dispositions be perverted, and their virtue laid aside. But if their natural dispositions be not perverted nor their virtue laid aside, what room is there left for government?

Of old, when Yao governed the empire, he caused happiness to prevail to excess in man's nature; consequently, the people were not satisfied. When Chieh governed the empire he caused sorrow to prevail to excess in man's nature; consequently, the people were not contented. Dissatisfaction and discontent are subversive of virtue; and without virtue there is no such thing for an empire as stability.

When man rejoices greatly, he gravitates towards the positive pole. When he sorrows deeply, he gravitates towards the negative pole.

If the equilibrium of positive and negative is disturbed, the four seasons are interrupted, the balance of heat and cold is destroyed, and man himself suffers physically thereby.

Because men are made to rejoice and to sorrow and to displace their centre of gravity, they lose their steadiness, and are unsuccessful in thought and action. And thus it is that the idea of surpassing others first came into the world, followed by the appearance of such men as Robber Chê, Tsêng, and Shih, the result being that the whole world could not furnish enough rewards for the good nor distribute punishments enough for the evil among mankind. And as this great world is not equal to the demand for rewards and punishments; and as, ever since the time of the Three Dynasties downwards, men have done nothing but struggle over rewards and punishments, — what possible leisure can they have had for adapting themselves to the natural conditions of their existence?

Besides, over-refinement of vision leads to debauchery in colour; over-refinement of hearing leads to debauchery in sound; over-refinement of charity leads to confusion in virtue; over-refinement of duty towards one's neighbour leads to perversion of principle; over-refinement of ceremonial leads to divergence from the true object; over-refinement of music leads to lewdness of thought; over-refinement of wisdom leads to an extension of mechanical art; and over-refinement of shrewdness leads to an extension of vice.

If people adapt themselves to the natural conditions of existence, the above eight may be or may not be; it matters not. But if people do not adapt themselves to the natural conditions of existence, then these eight become hindrances and spoilers, and throw the world into confusion.

In spite of this, the world reverences and cherishes them, thereby greatly increasing the sum of human error. And not as a passing fashion, but with admonitions in words, with humility in prostrations, and with the stimulus of music and song. What then is left for me?

Therefore, for the perfect man who is unavoidably summoned to power over his fellows, there is naught like *Inaction*.

By means of inaction he will be able to adapt himself to the natural conditions of existence. And so it is that he who respects the State as his own body is fit to support it, and he who loves the State as his own body, is fit to govern it.

And if I can refrain from injuring my internal economy, and from taxing my powers of sight and hearing, sitting like a corpse while my dragon-power is manifested around, in profound silence while my thunder-voice resounds, the powers of heaven responding to every phase of my will, as under the yielding influence of inaction all things are brought to maturity and thrive,—what leisure then have I to set about governing the world?

Ts'ui Chü asked Lao Tzŭ, saying, "If the empire is not to be governed, how are men's hearts to be kept in order?"

"Be careful," replied Lao Tzŭ, "not to interfere with the natural goodness of the heart of man. Man's heart may be forced down or stirred up. In each case the issue is fatal.

"By gentleness, the hardest heart may be softened. But try to cut and polish it, —'twill glow like fire or freeze like ice. In the twinkling of an eye it will pass beyond the limits of the Four Seas. In repose, profoundly still; in motion, far away in the sky. No bolt can bar, no bond can bind, —such is the human heart."

"Of old, the Yellow Emperor first caused charity and duty to one's neighbour to interfere with the natural goodness of the heart of man. In consequence of which, Yao and Shun wore the hair off their legs in endeavouring to feed their people. They disturbed their internal economy in order to find room for charity and duty to one's neighbour. They exhausted their energies in framing laws and statutes. Still they did not succeed.

"Thereupon, Yao confined Huan Tou on Mount Tsung; drove the chief of San-miao and his people into San-wei, and kept them there; and banished the Minister of Works to Yu Island.

But they were not equal to their task, and through the times of the Three Princes the empire was in a state of great unrest. Among the bad men were Chieh and Chê; among the good were Tsêng and Shih. By and by, the Confucianists and the Mihists arose; and then came exultation and anger of rivals, fraud between the simple and the cunning, recrimination between the virtuous and the evil, slander between the honest and the dishonest,—until decadence set in, men fell away from their original virtue, their natures became corrupt, and there was a general rush for knowledge.

"The next thing was to coerce by all kinds of physical torture, thus bringing utter confusion into the empire, the blame for which rests upon those who would interfere with the natural goodness of the heart of man.

"In consequence, virtuous men sought refuge in mountain caves, while rulers of States sat trembling in their ancestral halls. Then, when dead men lay about pillowed on each others' corpses, when cangued prisoners and condemned criminals jostled each other in crowds,—then the Confucianists and the Mihists, in the midst of gyves and fetters, stood forth to preach!

Alas, they know not shame, nor what it is to blush!

"Until I can say that the wisdom of Sages is not a fastener of cangues, and that charity and duty to one's neighbour are not bolts for gyves, how should I know that Tsêng and Shih are not the forerunners of Chieh and Chê?

"Therefore, I said, 'Abandon wisdom and discard knowledge, and the empire will be at peace.'"

The Yellow Emperor sat on the throne for nineteen years, and his laws obtained all over the empire.

Hearing that Kuang Ch'eng Tzŭ was living on Mount K'ung-t'ung, he went thither to see him, and said, "I am told, Sir, that you are in possession of perfect TAO. May I ask in what perfect TAO consists? I desire to avail myself of the good influence of heaven and earth in order to secure harvests and feed my people. I should also like to control the Two Powers of nature in order to the protection of all living things. How can I accomplish this?"

"What you desire to avail yourself of," replied Kuang Ch'êng Tzŭ, "is the primordial integrity of matter. What you wish to control are the disintegrators thereof. Ever since the empire has been *governed* by you, the clouds have rained without waiting to thicken, the foliage of trees has fallen without waiting to grow yellow, the brightness of the sun and moon has paled, and the voice of the flatterer is heard on every side. How then speak of perfect TAO?"

The Yellow Emperor withdrew. He resigned the Throne. He built himself a solitary hut. He lay upon straw. For three months he remained in seclusion, and then went again to see Kuang Ch'êng Tzŭ.

The latter was lying down with his face to the south. The Yellow Emperor approached after the manner of an inferior, upon his knees. Prostrating himself upon the ground he said, "I am told, Sir, that you are in possession of perfect TAO. May I ask how myself may be preserved so as to last?"

Kuang Ch'êng Tzŭ jumped up with a start. "A good question indeed!" cried he. "Come, and I will speak to you of perfect TAO.

"The essence of perfect TAO is profoundly mysterious; its extent is lost in obscurity.

"See nothing; hear nothing; let your soul be wrapped in quiet; and your body will begin to take proper form. Let there be absolute repose and absolute purity; do not weary your body nor disturb your vitality, —and you will live for ever. For if the eye sees nothing, and the ear hears nothing, and the mind thinks nothing, the soul will preserve the body, and the body will live for ever.

"Cherish that which is within you, and shut off that which is without; for much knowledge is a curse. Then I will place you upon that abode of Great

Light which is the source of the positive Power, and escort you through the gate of

Profound Mystery which is the source of the negative Power. These Powers are the controllers of heaven and earth, and each contains the other.

"Cherish and preserve your own self, and all the rest will prosper of itself.

I preserve the original O~~NE~~, while resting in harmony with externals. It is because I have thus cared for myself now for twelve hundred years that my body has not decayed."

The Yellow Emperor prostrated himself and said, "Kuang Ch'êng Tzǔ is surely God…"

Whereupon the latter continued, "Come, I will tell you. That self is eternal; yet all men think it mortal. That self is infinite; yet all men think it finite. Those who possess TAO are princes in this life and rulers in the hereafter. Those who do not possess TAO, behold the light of day in this life and become clods of earth in the hereafter.

"Nowadays, all living things spring from the dust and to the dust return. But I will lead you through the portals of Eternity into the domain of Infinity. My light is the light of sun and moon. My life is the life of heaven and earth. I know not who comes nor who goes. Men may all die, but I endure for ever."

The Spirit of the Clouds when passing eastwards through the expanse of Air happened to fall in with the Vital Principle. The latter was slapping his ribs and hopping about; whereupon the Spirit of the Clouds said, "Who are you, old man, and what are you doing here?"

"Strolling! " replied the Vital Principle, without stopping.

"I want to *know* something," continued the Spirit of the Clouds.

"Ah!" uttered the Vital Principle, in a tone of disapprobation.

"The relationship of heaven and earth is out of harmony," said the Spirit of the Clouds; "the six influences do not combine, and the four seasons are no longer regular. I desire to blend the six influences so as to nourish all living beings. What am I to do?"

"I do not know!" cried the Vital Principle, shaking his head, while still slapping his ribs and hopping about; "I do not know!"

So, the Spirit of the Clouds did not press his question; but three years later, when passing eastwards through the Yusung territory, he again fell in with the Vital Principle. The former was overjoyed, and hurrying up, said, "Has your Holiness forgotten me?"

He then prostrated himself, and desired to be allowed to interrogate the Vital Principle; but the latter said, "I wander on without knowing what I want. I roam about without knowing where I am going. I stroll in this ecstatic manner, simply awaiting events. What should I know?"

"I too roam about," answered the Spirit of the Clouds; "but the people depend upon my movements. I am thus unavoidably summoned to power; and under these circumstances I would gladly receive some advice."

"That the scheme of empire is in confusion," said the Vital Principle, "that the conditions of life are violated, that the will of God does not triumph, that the beasts of the field are disorganised, that the birds of the air cry at night, that blight reaches the trees and herbs, that destruction spreads among creeping things,—this, alas! is the fault of *government*."

"True," replied the Spirit of the Clouds, "but what am I to do?"

"It is here," cried the Vital Principle, "that the poison lurks! Go back!"

"It is not often," urged the Spirit of the Clouds, "that I meet with your Holiness. I would gladly receive some advice."

"Feed then your people," said the Vital Principle, "with your heart.

Rest in inaction, and the world will be good of itself. Cast your slough. Spit forth intelligence. Ignore all differences. Become one with the infinite. Release your mind. Free your soul. Be vacuous. Be Nothing!

"Let all things revert to their original constitution. If they do this, without knowledge, the result will be a simple purity which they will never lose; but knowledge will bring with it a divergence therefrom. Seek not the names nor the relations of things, and all things will flourish of themselves."

"Your Holiness," said the Spirit of the Clouds, as he prostrated himself and took leave, "has informed me with power and filled me with mysteries. What I had long sought, I have now found."

The men of this world all rejoice in others being like themselves, and object to others not being like themselves.

Those who make friends with their likes and do not make friends with their unlikes, are influenced by a desire to differentiate themselves from others. But those who are thus influenced by a desire to differentiate themselves from others, —how will they find it possible to do so?

To subordinate oneself to the majority in order to gratify personal ambition, is not so good as to let that majority look each one after his own affairs. Those who desire to govern kingdoms, clutch at the advantages of the Three Princes without seeing the troubles involved. In fact, they trust to luck. But in thus trusting to luck not to destroy the kingdom, their chances of preserving it do not amount to one in ten thousand, while their chances of destroying it are ten thousand to nothing and even more. Such, alas! is the ignorance of rulers.

For, given territory, there is the great thing—Man. Given man, he must not be managed as if he were a mere thing; though by not managing him at all he may actually be managed as if he were a mere thing. And for those who understand that the management of man as if he were a mere thing is not the way to manage him, the issue is not confined to mere government of the empire. Such men may wander at will between the six limits of space or travel over the continent of earth, unrestrained in coming and in going. This is to be distinguished from one's fellows, and this distinction is the highest attainable by man.

The doctrine of the perfect man is to him as shadow to form, as echo to sound. Ask and it responds, fulfilling its mission as the help-mate of humanity. Noiseless in repose, objectless in motion, it guides you to the goal, free to come and free to go for ever without end. Alone in its exits and its entrances, it rivals the eternity of the sun.

As for his body, that is in accordance with the usual standard. Being in accordance with the usual standard it is not distinguished in any way. But if not distinguished in any way, what becomes of the distinction by which he is distinguished?

Those who see what is to be seen, —of such were the perfect men of old. Those who see what is not to be seen, —they are the chosen of the universe.

Spiritual sight carries them beyond the horizon where natural vision stops short.

Low in the scale, but still to be allowed for, —matter. Humble, but still to be followed, — mankind. Of others, but still to be attended to, —affairs. Harsh, but still necessary to be set forth, —the law. Far off, but still claiming our presence, —duty to one's neighbour. Near, but still claiming extension, —charity. Of sparing use, but still to be of bounteous store, —ceremony. Of middle course, but still to be of lofty scope, —virtue. One, but not to be without modification, —TAO. Spiritual, yet not to be devoid of action, — GOD.

Therefore, the true Sage looks up to God, but does not offer to aid. He perfects his virtue, but does not involve himself. He guides himself by TAO, but makes no plans. He identifies himself with charity, but does not rely on it. He extends to duty towards his neighbour, but does not store it up. He responds to ceremony, without tabooing it.

He undertakes affairs without declining them. He metes out law without confusion. He relies on his fellow-men and does not make light of them. He accommodates himself to matter and does not ignore it.

While there should be no action, there should be also no inaction.

He who is not divinely enlightened will not be sublimely pure. He who has not clear apprehension of TAO will find this beyond his reach. And he who is not enlightened by TAO, —alas indeed for him!

What then is TAO? —There is the TAO of God, and the TAO of man. Inaction and compliance make the TAO of God: action and entanglement the TAO of man. The TAO of God is fundamental: the TAO of man is accidental. The distance which separates them is great. Let us all take heed thereto!

CHAPTER XII. THE UNIVERSE.

Argument:

—The prëeminence of TAO—All things informed thereby—The true
Sage illumined thereby—His attributes—His perfection—Man's
senses his bane—Illustrations.

V AST as is the universe, its phenomena are regular. Countless though
its contents, the laws which govern these are uniform. Many though its inhabitants, that which dominates them is sovereignty. Sovereignty begins in
virtue and ends in God. Therefore, it is called divine.

Of old, the empire was under the sovereignty of inaction. There was the
virtue of God, —nothing more.

Words being in accordance with TAO, the sovereignty of the empire was
correct. Delimitations being in accordance with TAO, the duties of prince
and subject were clear. Abilities being in accordance with TAO, the officials
of the empire governed. The point of view being always in accordance with
TAO, all things responded thereto.

Thus, virtue was the connecting link between God and man, while Tao
spread throughout all creation. Men were controlled by outward circumstances, applying their in-born skill to the development of civilised life. This
skill was bound up with the circumstances of life, and these with duty, and
duty with virtue, and virtue with TAO, and TAO with God.

Therefore, it has been said, "As for those who nourished the empire of
old, having no desires for themselves, the empire was not in want. They did
nothing, and all things proceeded on their course. They preserved a dignified
repose, and the people rested in peace."

The *Record* says, "By converging to ONE, all things may be accomplished.
By the virtue, which is without intention, even the supernatural may be sub-
dued."

The Master said, "TAO covers and supports all things,"—so vast is its
extent. Each man should prepare his heart accordingly.

"To act by means of inaction is God. To speak by means of inaction is
Virtue. To love men and care for things is Charity. To recognise the unlike

as the like is breadth of view. To make no distinctions is liberal. To possess variety is wealth. And so, to hold fast to virtue is strength. To complete virtue is establishment. To follow TAO is to be prepared. And not to run counter to the natural bias of things is to be perfect.

"He who fully realises these ten points, by storing them within enlarges his heart, and with this enlargement brings all creation to himself. Such a man will bury gold on the hillside and cast pearls into the sea. He will not struggle for wealth, nor strive for fame. He will not rejoice at old age, nor grieve over early death. He will find no pleasure in success, no chagrin in failure. He will not account a throne as his own private gain, nor the empire of the world as glory personal to himself. His glory is to know that all things are O_{NE}, and that life and death are but phases of the same existence!"

The Master said, "How profound in its repose, how infinite in its purity, is TAO!

"If metal and stone were without TAO, they would not be capable of emitting sound. And just as they possess the property of sound but will not emit sound unless struck, so surely is the same principle applicable to all creation.

"The man of complete virtue remains blankly passive as regards what goes on around him. He is as originally by nature, and his knowledge extends to the supernatural. Thus, his virtue expands his heart, which goes forth to all who come to take refuge therein.

"Without TAO, form cannot be endued with life. Without virtue, life cannot be endued with intelligence. To preserve one's form, live out one's life, establish one's virtue, and realise TAO, —is not this complete virtue?

"Issuing forth spontaneously, moving without premeditation, all things following in his wake, —such is the man of complete virtue!

"He can see where all is dark. He can hear where all is still. In the darkness he alone can see light. In the stillness he alone can detect harmony. He can sink to the lowest depths of materialism. To the highest heights of spirituality, he can soar. This because he stands in due relation to all things. Though a mere abstraction, he can minister to their wants, and ever and anon receive them into rest, —the great, the small, the long, the short, for ever without end."

The Yellow Emperor travelled to the north of the Red Lake and ascended the K'un-lun Mountains. Returning south he lost his magic pearl.

He employed Intelligence to find it, but without success. He employed Sight to find it, but without success. He employed Speech to find it, but without success. Finally, he employed Nothing, and Nothing got it.

"Strange indeed," quoth the Emperor, "that Nothing should have been able to get it!"

Yao's tutor was Hsü Yu. The latter's tutor was Yeh Ch'üeh, and Yeh Ch'üeh's tutor was Wang I, whose tutor was Pei I.

Yao enquired of Hsü Yu, saying, "Would Yeh Ch'üeh do to be emperor? I am going to get Wang I to ask him."

"Alas!" cried Hsü Yu, "that would be bad indeed for the empire. Yeh Ch'üeh is a clever and capable man. He is by nature better than most men, but he seeks by means of the human to reach the divine. He strives to do no wrong; but he is ignorant of the source from which wrong springs. Emperor forsooth! He avails himself of the artificial and neglects the natural. He lacks unity in himself. He worships intelligence and is always in a state of ferment. He is a slave to circumstances and to things. Wherever he looks, his surroundings respond. He himself responds to his surroundings.

He is always undergoing modifications and is wanting in fixity. How should such a one be fit for emperor? Still every clan has its elder. He may be leader of a clan, but not a leader of leaders. A captain who has been successful in suppressing rebellion, as minister is a bane, as sovereign, a thief."

Yao went to visit Hua. The border-warden of Hua said "Ha! a Sage. My best respects to you, Sir. I wish you a long life." "Don't!" replied Yao.

"I wish you plenty of money," continued the border-warden.

"Don't!" replied Yao.

"And many sons," added he.

"Don't!" replied Yao.

"Long life, plenty of money, and many sons," cried the warden, "these are what all men desire. How is it you alone do not want them?"

"Many sons," answered Yao, "are many anxieties. Plenty of money means plenty of trouble. Long life involves much that is not pleasant to put up with. These three gifts do not advance virtue; therefore I declined them."

"At first I took you for a Sage," said the warden, "but now I find you are a mere man. God, in sending man into the world, gives to each his proper function. If you have many sons and give to each his proper function, what cause have you for anxiety?

"And similarly, if you have wealth and allow others to share it, what troubles will you have?"

"The true Sage dwells like the quail and feeds like a fledgeling.

He travels like the bird, leaving no trace behind. If there be TAO in the empire, he and all things are in harmony. If there be not TAO, he cultivates virtue in retirement. After a thousand years of this weary world, he mounts aloft, and riding upon the white clouds passes into the kingdom of God, whither the three evils do not reach, and where he rests secure in eternity. What is there to put up with in that?"

Thereupon the border-warden went off, and Yao followed him; saying, "May I ask," to which the warden only replied "Begone!"

When Yao was Emperor, Poh Ch'êng Tzŭ Kao was one of his vassals. But when Yao handed over the empire to Shun, and Shun to the Great Yü, Poh Ch'êng Tzŭ Kao resigned his fief and betook himself to agriculture.

The Great Yü going to visit him, found him working in the fields; whereupon he approached humbly, saying, "When Yao was emperor, you, Sir, were a vassal; but when Yao handed over the empire to Shun, and Shun to me, you resigned your fief and betook yourself to agriculture. May I enquire the reason of this?"

"When Yao ruled the empire," said Tzŭ Kao, "the people exerted themselves without reward and behaved themselves without punishment. But now you reward and punish them, and yet they are not good. From this point virtue will decline, the reign of force will begin, and the troubles of after ages will date their rise. Away with you! Do not interrupt my work." And he quietly went on ploughing as before.

At the beginning of the beginning, even Nothing did not exist. Then came the period of the Nameless.

When ONE came into existence, there was ONE, but it was formless. When things got that by which they came into existence, it was called their *virtue*.

That which was formless, but divided. though without interstice, was called *destiny*.

Then came the movement which gave life, and things produced in accordance with the principles of life had what is called *form*. When form encloses the spiritual part, each with its own characteristics, that is its *nature*. By cultivating this nature, we are carried back to virtue; and if this is perfected, we become as all things were in the beginning. We become unconditioned, and the unconditioned is great. As birds join their beaks in chirping, and beaks to chirp must be joined, —to be thus joined with the universe without being more conscious of it than an idiot, this is *divine virtue*, this is accordance with the eternal fitness of things.

Confucius asked Lao Tzŭ, saying, "There are persons who cultivate TAO according to fixed rules of possible and impossible, fit and unfit, just as the schoolmen speak of separating hardness from whiteness as though these could be hung up on different pegs.

Could such persons be termed sages?"

"That," replied Lao Tzŭ, "is but the skill of the handicraftsman, wearing out body and soul alike. The powers of the hunting-dog involve it in trouble; the cleverness of the monkey brings it down from the mountain.

Ch'iu, what I mean you cannot understand, neither can you put it into words.

Those who have a head and feet, but no mind nor ears, are many. Those who have a body without a body or appearance of one, and yet there they are, —are none. Movement and rest, life and death, rise and fall, are not at the beck and call of man. Cultivation of self is in his own hands. To be unconscious of objective existences and of God, this is to be unconscious of one's own personality. And he who is unconscious of his own personality, combines in himself the human and the divine."

Chiang Lü Mien went to see Chi Ch'ê, and said, "The Prince of Lu begged me to instruct him, but I declined. However, he would take no refusal, so I was obliged to do so. I don't know if I was correct in my doctrine or not. Please note what I said. I told him to be decorous and thrifty; to advance the public-spirited and loyal, and to have no partialities. Then, I said, no one would venture to oppose him."

Chi Ch'ê sniggered and said, "Your remarks on the virtues of Princes may be compared with the mantis stretching out its feelers and trying to stop a carriage, —not likely to effect the object proposed.

Besides, he would be placing himself in the position of a man who builds a lofty tower and makes a display of his valuables where all his neighbours will come and gaze at them."

"Alas! I fear I am but a fool," replied Chiang Lü Mien. "Nevertheless, I should be glad to be instructed by you in the proper course to pursue."

"The government of the perfect Sage," explained Chi Ch'ê, "consists in influencing the hearts of the people so as to cause them to complete their education, to reform their manners, to subdue the rebel mind, and to exert themselves one and all for the common good. This influence operates in accordance with the natural disposition of the people, who are thus unconscious of its operation. He who can so act has no need to humble himself before the teachings of Yao and Shun. He makes the desires of the people coincident with virtue, and their hearts rest therein."

When Tzǔ Kung went south to the Ch'u State on his way back to the Chin State, he passed through Han-yin. There he saw an old man engaged in making a ditch to connect his vegetable garden with a well. He had a pitcher in his hand, with which he was bringing up water and pouring it into the ditch, —great labour with very little result.

"If you had a machine here," cried Tzǔ Kung, "in a day you could irrigate a hundred times your present area. The labour required is trifling as compared with the work done. Would you not like to have one?"

"What is it?" asked the gardener.

"It is a contrivance made of wood," replied Tzǔ Kung, "heavy behind and light in front. It draws up water as you do with your hands, but in a constantly overflowing stream. It is called a well-sweep."

Thereupon the gardener flushed up and said, "I have heard from my teacher that those who have cunning implements are cunning in their dealings, and that those who are cunning in their dealings have cunning in their hearts, and that those who have cunning in their hearts cannot be pure and incorrupt, and that those who are not pure and incorrupt are restless in spirit, and that those who are restless in spirit are not fit vehicles for TAO. It is not that I do not know of these things. I should be ashamed to use them."

At this Tzŭ Kung was much abashed, and said nothing. Then the gardener asked him who he was, to which Tzŭ Kung replied that he was a disciple of Confucius.

"Are you not one who extends his learning with a view to being a Sage; who talks big in order to put himself above the rest of mankind; who plays in a key to which no one can sing so as to spread his reputation abroad? Rather become unconscious of self and shake off the trammels of the flesh, —and you will be near. But if you cannot govern your own self, what leisure have you for governing the empire? Begone! Do not interrupt my work."

Tzŭ Kung changed colour and slunk away, being not at all pleased with this rebuff; and it was not before he had travelled some thirty *li* that he recovered his usual appearance.

"What did the man we met do," asked a disciple, "that you should change colour and not recover for such a long time?"

"I used to think there was only one man in all the world," replied Tzŭ Kung.

"I did not know that there was also this man. I have heard the Master say that the test of a scheme is its practicability, and that success must be certain. The minimum of effort with the maximum of success, —such is the way of the Sage.

"Not so this manner of man. Aiming at TAO, he perfects his virtue. By perfecting his virtue, he perfects his body, and by perfecting his body he perfects his spiritual part. And the perfection of the spiritual part is the TAO of the Sage. Coming into life he is as one of the people, knowing not whither he is bound. How complete is his purity? Success, profit, skill, —these have no place in his heart. Such a man, if he does not will it, he does not stir; if he does not wish it, he does not act. If all the world praises him, he does not heed. If all the world blames him, he does not repine.

The praise and the blame of the world neither advantage him nor otherwise. He may be called a man of perfect virtue. As for me, I am but a mere creature of impulse."

So he went back to Lu to tell Confucius. But Confucius said, "That fellow pretends to a knowledge of the science of the ante-mundane. He knows something, but not much. His government is of the internal, not of the external. What is there wonderful in a man by clearness of intelligence becoming pure, by inaction reverting to his original integrity, and with his nature and his spiritual part wrapped up in a body, passing through this common world of ours? Besides, to you and to me the science of the ante-mundane is not worth knowing."

As Chun Mang was starting eastwards to the ocean, he fell in with Yüan Fêng on the shore of the eastern sea.

"Whither bound?" cried the latter.

"I am going to the ocean," replied Chun Mang.

"What are you going to do there?" asked Yüan Fêng.

"The ocean," said Chun Mang, "is a thing you cannot fill by pouring in, nor empty by taking out. I am simply on a trip."

"But surely you have intentions with regard to the straightbrowed people? … Come, tell me how the Sage governs."

"Oh, the government of the Sage," answered Chun Mang. "The officials confine themselves to their functions. Ability is secure of employment. The voice of the people is heard, and action is taken accordingly. Men's words and deeds are their own affairs, and so the empire is at peace. A beck or a call, and the people flock together from all sides. This is how the Sage governs."

"Tell me about the man of perfect virtue," said Yüan Fêng.

"The man of perfect virtue," replied Chun Mang, "in repose has no thoughts, in action no anxiety. He recognises no right, nor wrong, nor good, nor bad. Within the Four Seas, when all profit—that is his pleasure; when all share—that is his repose. Men cling to him as children who have lost their mothers; they rally round him as wayfarers who have missed their road. He has wealth and to spare, but he knows not whence it comes. He has food and drink more than sufficient, but knows not who provides it. Such is a man of virtue."

"And now," said Yüan Fêng, "tell me about the divine man."

"The divine man," replied Chun Mang, "rides upon the glory of the sky where his form can no longer be discerned. This is called absorption into light. He fulfils his destiny.

He acts in accordance with his nature. He is at one with God and man. For him all affairs cease to exist, and all things revert to their original state. This is called envelopment in darkness."

Mên Wu Kuei and Ch'ih Chang Man Chi were looking at Wu Wang's troops.

"He is not equal to the Great Yü," said the latter; and consequently "we are involved in all these troubles."

"May I ask," replied Mên Wu Kuei, "if the empire was under proper government when the Great Yü began to govern it, or had he first to quell disorder and then to proceed to government?"

"If the empire had all been under proper government," said the other, "what would there have been for the Great Yü to do? He was as ointment to a sore. Only bald men use wigs; only sick people want doctors. And the Sage blushes when a filial son, with anxious look, administers medicine to cure his loving father.

"In the Golden Age, good men were not appreciated; ability was not conspicuous. Rulers were mere beacons, while the people were free as the wild deer. They were upright without being conscious of duty to their neighbours. They loved one another without being conscious of charity. They were true without being conscious of loyalty. They were honest without being conscious of good faith. They acted freely in all things without recognising obligations to anyone. Thus, their deeds left no trace; their affairs were not handed down to posterity.

"A filial son does not humour his parents. A loyal minister does not flatter his prince. This is the acme of filial piety and loyalty. To assent to whatever a parent or a prince says, and to praise whatever a parent or a prince does, this is what the world calls unfilial and disloyal conduct, though apparently unaware that the principle is of universal application. For though a man assents to whatever the world says, and praises whatever the world does, he is not dubbed a toady; from which one might infer that the world is severer than a father and more to be respected than a prince! "If you tell a man he is a wheedler, he will not like it. If you tell him he is a flatterer, he will be angry. Yet he is everlastingly both. But all such sham and pretence are what the world likes, and consequently people do not punish each other for doing what they do themselves. For a man to arrange his dress, or make a display, or suit his expression so as to get into the good graces of the world, and yet not to call himself a flatterer; to identify himself in every way with the yeas and nays of his fellows, and yet not call himself one of them;—this is the height of folly.

"A man who knows that he is a fool is not a great fool. A man who knows his error is not greatly in error. Great error can never be shaken off; a great fool never becomes clearheaded. If three men are travelling and one man makes a mistake, they may still arrive at their destination, error being in the minority. But if two of them make a mistake, then they will not succeed, error being in the majority. And now, as all the world is in error, I, though I know the true path, am alas! unable to guide.

"Grand music does not appeal to vulgar ears. Give them the *Chê-yang* or the *Huang-hua*, and they will roar with laughter. And likewise, great truths do not take hold of the hearts of the masses. And great truths not finding utterance, common-places carry the day.

Two earthen instruments will drown the sound of one metal one; and the result will not be melodious.

"And now, as all the world is in error, I, though I know the true path, — how shall I guide? If I know that I cannot succeed and yet try to force success, this would be but another source of error. Better, then, to desist and strive no more. But if I strive not, who will?

"An ugly man who has a son born to him in the middle of the night will hurry up with a light, in dread lest the child should be like himself.

"An old tree is cut down to make sacrificial vessels, which are then ornamented with colour. The stump remains in a ditch. The sacrificial vessels and the stump in the ditch are very differently treated as regards honour and dishonour; equally, as far as destruction of the wood's original nature is concerned. Similarly, the acts of Robber Chê and of Tsêng and Shih are very different; but the loss of original nature is in each case the same.

"The causes of this loss are five in number; viz.—The five colours confuse the eye, and the eyes fail to see clearly. The five sounds confuse the ear, and the ear fails to hear accurately. The five scents confuse the nose, and obstruct the sense of smell. The five tastes cloy the palate, and vitiate the sense of taste. Finally, likes and dislikes cloud the understanding, and cause dispersion of the original nature.

"These five are the banes of life; yet Yang and Mih regarded them as the *summum bonum*.

They are not my *summum bonum*. For if men who are thus fettered can be said to have attained the *summum bonum*, then pigeons and owls in a cage may also be said to have attained the *summum bonum*!

"Besides, to stuff one's inside with likes and dislikes and sounds and colours; to encompass one's outside with fur caps, feather hats, the carrying of tablets, or girding of sashes—full of rubbish inside while swathed in magnificence without—and still to talk of having attained the *summum bonum*;—then the prisoner with arms tied behind him and fingers in the squeezer, the tiger or the leopard which has just been put in a cage, may justly consider that they too have attained the *summum bonum!*"

CHAPTER XIII. THE TAO OF GOD.

Argument:

—TAO is repose—Repose the secret of the universe—Cultivation of essentials—Neglect of accidentals—The sequence of TAO— Spontaneity of true virtue—TAO is unconditioned—TAO cannot be conveyed—Illustrations.

T HE TAO of GOD operates ceaselessly; and all things are produced. The TAO of the sovereign operates ceaselessly; and the empire rallies around him. The TAO of the Sage operates ceaselessly; and all within the limit of surrounding ocean acknowledge his sway. He who apprehends God, who is in relation with the Sage, and who recognises the radiating virtue of the sovereign, —his actions will be to him unconscious, the actions of repose.

The repose of the Sage is not what the world calls repose. His repose is the result of his mental attitude. All creation could not disturb his equilibrium: hence his repose.

When water is still, it is like a mirror, reflecting the beard and the eyebrows. It gives the accuracy of the water-level, and the philosopher makes it his model. And if water thus derives lucidity from stillness, how much more the faculties of the mind? The mind of the Sage being in repose becomes the mirror of the universe, the speculum of all creation.

Repose, tranquillity, stillness, inaction, —these were the levels of the universe, the ultimate perfection of TAO.

Therefore, wise rulers and Sages rest therein. Resting therein they reach the unconditioned, from which springs the conditioned; and with the conditioned comes order.

Again, from the unconditioned comes repose, and from repose comes movement, and from movement comes attainment. Further, from repose comes inaction, and from inaction comes potentiality of action.

And inaction is happiness; and where there is happiness no cares can abide, and life is long.

Repose, tranquillity, stillness, inaction, —these were the source of all things. Due perception of this was the secret of Yao's success as a ruler, and of Shun's success as his minister. Due perception of this constitutes the virtue of sovereigns on the throne, the TAO of the inspired Sage and of the uncrowned King below. Keep to this in retirement, and the lettered denizens of sea and dale will recognise your power. Keep to this when coming forward to pacify a troubled world, and your merit shall be great and your name illustrious, and the empire united into one. In your repose you will be wise; in your movements, powerful. By inaction you will gain honour; and by confining yourself to the pure and simple, you will hinder the whole world from struggling with you for show.

To fully apprehend the scheme of the universe.

This is called the great secret of being in accord with GOD, whereby the empire is so administered that the result is accord with man. To be in accord with man is human happiness; to be in accord with God is the happiness of God.

Chuang Tzŭ said, "O my exemplar! Thou who destroyest all things, and dost not account it cruelty; thou who benefitest all time, and dost not account it charity; thou who art older than antiquity and dost not account it age; thou who supportest the universe, shaping the many forms therein, and dost not account it skill;—this is the happiness of God!"

Therefore, it has been said, "Those who enjoy the happiness of God, when born into the world, are but fulfilling their divine functions; when they die, they do but undergo a physical change. In repose, they exert the influence of the Negative; in motion, they wield the power of the Positive."

Thus, those who enjoy the happiness of God have no grievance against God, no grudge against man. Nothing material injures them; nothing spiritual punishes them. Accordingly, it has been said, "Their motion is that of heaven; their repose is that of earth. Mental equilibrium gives them the empire of the world. Evil spirits do not harass them without; demons do not trouble them within. Mental equilibrium gives them sovereignty over all creation." Which signifies that in repose to extend to the whole universe and to be in relation with all creation, —this is the happiness of God. This enables the mind of the Sage to cherish the whole empire.

For the virtue of the wise ruler is modelled upon the universe, is guided by TAO, and is ever occupied in inaction. By inaction, he administers the empire, and has energy to spare; but by action he finds his energy inadequate to the administration of the empire. Therefore, the men of old set great store by inaction.

But if rulers practise inaction and the ruled also practise inaction, the ruled will equal the rulers, and will not be as their subjects. On the other hand, if the ruled practise action and rulers also practise action, rulers will assimilate themselves to the ruled, and will not be as their masters. Rulers must practise inaction in order to administer the empire. The ruled must practise action in order to subserve the interests of the empire. This is an unchangeable law.

Thus, the men of old, although their knowledge did not extend throughout the universe, were not troubled in mind. Although their intellectual powers beautified all creation, they did not rejoice. Although their abilities exhausted all things within the limits of ocean, they did not act.

Heaven has no parturitions, yet all things are evolved. Earth knows no increment, yet all things are nourished. The wise ruler practises inaction, and the empire applauds him. Therefore, it has been said, "There is nothing more mysterious than heaven, nothing richer than earth, nothing greater than the wise ruler." Wherefore also it has been said, "The virtue of the wise ruler makes him the peer of heaven and earth." Charioted upon the universe, with all creation for his team, he passes along the highway of mortality.

The essential is in the ruler; the accidental in the ruled.

The *ultima ratio* lies with the prince; representation is the duty of the minister.

Appeal to arms is the lowest form of virtue. Rewards and punishments are the lowest form of education. Ceremonies and laws are the lowest form of government. Music and fine clothes are the lowest form of happiness. Weeping and mourning are the lowest form of grief. These five should follow the movements of the mind.

The ancients indeed cultivated the study of accidentals, but they did not allow it to precede that of essentials. The prince precedes, the minister follows. The father precedes, the son follows. The elder brother precedes, the younger follows. Seniors precede, juniors follow. Men precede, women follow. Husbands precede, wives follow.

Distinctions of rank and precedence are part of the scheme of the universe, and the Sage adopts them accordingly. In point of spirituality, heaven is honourable, earth is lowly, Spring and summer precede autumn and winter: such is the order of the seasons. In the constant production of all things, there are phases of existence. There are the extremes of maturity and decay, the perpetual tide of change. And if heaven and earth, divinest of all, admit of rank and precedence, how much more man?

In the ancestral temple, parents rank before all; at court, the most honourable; in the village, the elders; in matters to be accomplished, the most trustworthy. Such is the order which appertains to TAO. He who in considering TAO disregards this order, thereby disregards TAO; and he who in considering TAO disregards TAO, — whence will he secure TAO?

Therefore, those of old who apprehended TAO, first apprehended God. TAO came next, and then charity and duty to one's neighbour, and then the functions of public life, and then forms and names, and then employment according to capacity, and then distinctions of good and bad, and then discrimination between right and wrong, and then rewards and punishments. Thus, wise men and fools met with their dues; the exalted and the humble occupied their proper places. And the virtuous and the worthless being each guided by their own natural instincts, it was necessary to distinguish capabilities, and to adopt a corresponding nomenclature, in order to serve the ruler, nourish the ruled, administer things generally, and elevate self. Where knowledge and plans are of no avail, one must fall back upon the natural.

This is perfect peace, the acme of good government. Therefore, it has been written, "Wherever there is form, there is also its name." Forms and names indeed the ancients had, but did not give precedence to them.

Thus, those of old who considered TAO, passed

M 2 through five phases before forms and names were reached, and nine before rewards and punishments could be discussed.

To rise *per saltum* to forms and names is to be ignorant of their source; to rise *per saltum* to rewards and punishments is to be ignorant of their beginning. Those who invert the process of discussing TAO, arguing in a directly contrary sense, are rather to, be governed by others than able to govern others themselves.

To rise *per saltum* to forms and names and rewards and punishments, this is to understand the instrumental part of government, but not to understand the great principle of government.

This is to be of use in the administration of the empire, but not to be able to administer the empire. This is to be a sciolist, a man of narrow views.

Ceremonies and laws were indeed cultivated by the ancients; but they were employed in the service of the rulers by the ruled. Rulers did not employ them as a means of nourishing the ruled.

Of old, Shun asked Yao, saying, "How does your Majesty employ your faculties?" "I am not arrogant towards the defenceless," replied Yao. "I do not neglect the poor. I grieve for those who die. I pity the orphan. I sympathise with the widow. Beyond this, nothing." "Good indeed!" cried Shun, "but yet not great."

"How so?" inquired Yao.

"Be passive," said Shun, "like the virtue of God. The sun and moon shine; the four seasons revolve; day and night alternate; clouds come and rain falls."

"Alas!" cried Yao, "what a muddle I have been making. You are in accord with God; I am in accord with man."

Of old, heaven and earth were considered great; and the Yellow Emperor and Yao and Shun all thought them perfection. Consequently, what did those do who ruled the empire of old? They did what heaven and earth do; no more.

When Confucius was going west to place his works in the Imperial library of the House of Chou, Tzŭ Lu counselled him, saying, "I have heard that a certain librarian of the Chêng department, by name Lao Tan, has resigned and retired into private life. Now as you, Sir, wish to deposit your works, it would be advisable to go and interview him."

"Certainly," said Confucius; and he thereupon went to see Lao Tzŭ. The latter would not hear of the proposal; so, Confucius began to expound the doctrines of his twelve canons, in order to convince Lao Tzŭ.

"This is all nonsense," cried Lao Tzŭ, interrupting him. "Tell me what are your criteria."

"Charity," replied Confucius, "and duty towards one's neighbour."

"Tell me, please," asked Lao Tzŭ, "are these part of man's original nature?"

"They are," answered Confucius. "Without charity, the superior man could not become what he is. Without duty to one's neighbour, he would be of no effect. These two belong to the original nature of a pure man. What further would you have?"

"Tell me," said Lao Tzŭ, "in what consist charity and duty to one's neighbour?"

"They consist," answered Confucius, "in a capacity for rejoicing in all things; in universal love, without the element of self. These are the characteristics of charity and duty to one's neighbour."

"What stuff!" cried Lao Tzŭ. "Does not universal love contradict itself? Is not your elimination of self a positive manifestation of self? Sir, if you would cause the empire not to lose its source of nourishment,—there is the universe, its regularity is unceasing; there are the sun and moon, their brightness is unceasing; there are the stars, their groupings never change; there are birds and beasts, they flock together without varying; there are trees and shrubs, they grow upwards without exception. Be like these; follow TAO; and you will be perfect. Why then these vain struggles after charity and duty to one's neighbour, as though beating a drum in search of a fugitive. Alas! Sir, you have brought much confusion into the mind of man."

Shih Ch'êng Ch'I visited Lao Tzŭ, and addressed him, saying, "Having heard, Sir, that you were a Sage, I put aside all thought of distance to come and visit you. Travelling many stages, the soles of my feet thickened, but I did not venture to rest. And now I see you are not a Sage. While rats feasted off your leavings, you turned your sister out of doors. This is not charity. Though you have no lack of food, raw and cooked, you are stingy beyond all bounds."

At this Lao Tzŭ was silent and made no reply; and the next day Shih Ch'êng Ch'i came again and said, "Before, I was rude to you; now, I am sorry. How is this?"

"I have no pretension," replied Lao Tzŭ, "to be possessed of cunning knowledge nor of divine wisdom. Had you yesterday called me an ox, I should have considered myself an ox. Had you called me a horse, I should have considered myself a horse.

"For if men class you in accordance with truth, and you reject the classification, you only double the reproach. My humility is natural humility. It is not humility for humility's sake."

Shih Ch'êng Ch'i moved respectfully away.

Then he advanced again, also respectfully, and said, "May I ask you about personal cultivation?"

Lao Tzŭ said, "Your countenance is a strange one. Your eyes protrude. Your jaws are heavy. Your lips are parted. Your demeanour is self-satisfied. You look like a man on a tethered horse.

You are too confident. You are too hasty. You think too much of your own powers. Such men are not trusted. Those who are found on the wrong side of a boundary line are called thieves."

Lao Tzŭ said, "TAO is not too small for the greatest, nor too great for the smallest. Thus, all things are embosomed therein; wide indeed its boundless capacity, unfathomable its depth.

"Form, and virtue, and charity, and duty to one's neighbour, these are the accidentals of the spiritual. Except he be a perfect man, who shall determine their place? The world of the perfect man, is not that vast? And yet it is not able to involve him in trouble. All struggle for power, but he does not join. Though discovering nothing false, he is not tempted astray. In spite of the utmost genuineness, he still confines himself to essentials.

"He thus places himself outside the universe, beyond all creation, where his soul is free from care. Apprehending TAO, he is in accord with virtue. He leaves charity and duty to one's neighbour alone. He treats ceremonies and music as adventitious. And so the mind of the perfect man is at peace.

"Books are what the world values as representing TAO. But books are only words, and the valuable part of words is the thought therein contained. That thought has a certain bias which cannot be conveyed in words, yet the world values words as being the essence of books. But though the world values them, they are not of value; as that sense in which the world values them is not the sense in which they are valuable.

"That which can be seen with the eye is form and colour; that which can be heard with the ear is sound and noise. But alas! the people of this generation think that form, and colour, and sound, and noise, are means by which they can come to understand the essence of TAO. This is not so. And as those who know, do not speak, while those who speak do not know, whence should the world derive its knowledge?"

Duke Huan was one day reading in his hall, when a wheelwright who was working below, flung down his hammer and chisel, and mounting the steps said, "What words may your Highness be studying?" "I am studying the words of the Sages," replied the Duke.

"Are the Sages alive?" asked the wheelwright.

"No," answered the Duke; "they are dead."

"Then the words your Highness is studying," rejoined the wheelwright, "are only the dregs of the ancients."

"What do you mean, sirrah!" cried the Duke, "by interfering with what I read? Explain yourself, or you shall die."

"Let me take an illustration," said the wheelwright, "from my own trade. In making a wheel, if you work too slowly, you can't make it firm; if you work too fast, the spokes won't fit in. You must go neither too slowly nor too fast. There must be co-ordination of mind and hand. Words cannot explain what it is, but there is some mysterious art herein. I cannot teach it to my son; nor can he learn it from me. Consequently, though seventy years of age, I am still making wheels in my old age. If the ancients, together with what they could not impart, are dead and gone, then what your Highness is studying must be the dregs."

CHAPTER XIV. THE CIRCLING SKY.

Argument:

—The Ultimate Cause—Integrity of TAO—Music and TAO—Failure of Confucianism—Confucius and Lao Tzŭ—Confucius attains to TAO—Illustrations.

[This chapter is supplementary to ch. v.]

THE sky turns round; the earth stands still; sun and moon pursue one another. Who causes this? Who directs this? Who has leisure enough to see that such movements continue?

"Some think there is a mechanical arrangement which makes these bodies move as they do. Others think that they revolve without being able to stop.

"The clouds cause rain; rain causes clouds. Whose kindly bounty is this? Who has leisure enough to see that such, result is achieved?

"Wind comes from the north. It blows now east, now west; and now it whirls aloft. Who puffs it forth? Who has leisure enough to be flapping it this way or that? I should like to know the cause of all this."

Wu Han Chao said, "Come here, and I will tell you. Above there are the Six Influences and the Five Virtues.

If a ruler keeps in harmony with these, his rule is good; if not, it is bad. By following the nine chapters of the Lo book, his rule will be a success and his virtue complete; he will watch over the interests of his people, and all the empire will owe him gratitude. This is to be an eminent ruler."

Tang, a high official of Sung, asked Chuang Tzŭ about charity. Chuang Tzŭ said, "Tigers and wolves have it."

"How so?" asked Tang.

"The natural love between parents and offspring," replied Chuang Tzŭ,— "is not that charity?"

Tang then inquired about perfect charity.

"Perfect charity," said Chuang Tzŭ, "does not admit of love for the individual."

"Without such love," replied Tang, "it appears to me there would be no such thing as affection, and without affection no filial piety. Does perfect charity not admit of filial piety?"

"Not so," said Chuang Tzŭ. "Perfect charity is the more extensive term. Consequently, it was unnecessary to mention filial piety. It was not that filial piety was omitted. It was merely not particularised.

"A man who travels southwards to Ying, cannot see Mount Ming in the north. Why? Because he is too far off.

"Therefore, it has been said that it is easy to be respectfully filial, but difficult to be affectionately filial.

But even that is easier than to become unconscious of one's natural obligations, which is in turn easier than to cause others to be unconscious of the operations thereof.

Similarly, this is easier than to become altogether unconscious of the world, which again is easier than to cause the world to be unconscious of one's influence upon it.

"True virtue does nothing, yet it leaves Yao and Shun far behind. Its good influence extends to ten thousand generations, yet no man knoweth it to exist. What boots it then to sigh after charity and duty to one's neighbour?

"Filial piety, fraternal love, charity, duty to one's neighbour, loyalty, truth, chastity, and honesty, —these are all studied efforts, designed to aid the development of virtue. They are only parts of a whole.

"Therefore, it has been said, 'Perfect honour includes all the honour a country can give. Perfect wealth includes all the wealth a country can give. Perfect ambition includes all the reputation one can desire.' And by parity of reasoning, TAO does not admit of sub-division."

Pei Mên Ch'êng; said to the Yellow Emperor, "When your Majesty played the *Han-ch'ih* in the wilds of Tung-t'ing, the first time I heard it I was afraid, the second time I was amazed, and the last time I was confused, speechless, overwhelmed."

"You are not far from the truth," replied the Yellow Emperor. "I played as a man, drawing inspiration from God.

The execution was punctilious, the expression sublime. "Perfect music first shapes itself according to a human standard; then it follows the lines of the divine; then it proceeds in harmony with the five virtues; then it passes into spontaneity. The four seasons are then blended, and all creation is brought into accord. As the seasons come forth in turn, so are all things produced. Now fulness, now decay, now soft and loud in turn, now clear, now muffled, the harmony of *Yin* and *Yang*. Like a flash was the sound which roused you as the insect world is roused, followed by a thundering peal, without end and without beginning, now dying, now living, now sinking, now rising, on and on without a moment's break. And so you were afraid.

"When I played again, it was the harmony of the *Yin* and *Yang*, lighted by the glory of sun and moon; now broken, now prolonged, now gentle, now severe, in one unbroken, unfathomable volume of sound. Filling valley and gorge, stopping the ears and dominating the senses, adapting itself to the capacities of things, —the sound whirled around on all sides, with shrill note and clear. The spirits of darkness kept to their domain. Sun, moon, and stars, pursued their appointed course. When the melody was exhausted, I stopped; if the melody did not stop, I went on.

You would have sympathised, but you could not understand. You would have looked, but you could not see. You would have pursued, but you could not overtake. You stood dazed in the middle of the wilderness, leaning against a tree and crooning, your eye conscious of exhausted vision, your strength failing for the pursuit, and so unable to overtake me. Your frame was but an empty shell. You were completely at a loss, and so you were amazed.

"Then I played in sounds which produce no amazement, the melodious law of spontaneity, springing forth like nature's countless buds, in manifold but formless joy, as though poured forth to the dregs, in deep but soundless bass. Beginning nowhere, the melody rested in void; some would say dead, others alive, others real, others ornamental, as it scattered itself on all sides in never to be anticipated chords.

"The wondering world enquires of the Sage. He is in relation with its variations and follows the same eternal law.

"When no machinery is set in motion, and yet the instrumentation is complete, this is the music of God. The mind awakes to its enjoyment without waiting to be called. Accordingly, Yu Piao praised it, saying, 'Listening you cannot hear its sound; gazing you cannot see its form.

It fills heaven and earth. It embraces the six cardinal points.' Now you desired to listen to it, but you were not able to grasp its existence. And so you were confused.

"My music first induced fear; and as a consequence, respect. I then added amazement, by which you were isolated.

And lastly, confusion; for confusion means absence of sense, and absence of sense means TAO, and TAO means absorption therein."

When Confucius travelled west to the Wei State, Yen Yüan asked Shih Chin, saying, "What think you of my Master?"

"Alas!" replied Shih Chin, "he is not a success."

"How so?" enquired Yen Yüan.

"Before the straw dog has been offered in sacrifice," replied Shih Chin, "it is kept in a box, wrapped up in an embroidered cloth, and the augur fasts before using it. But when it has once been offered up, passers-by trample over its body, and fuel-gatherers pick it up for burning. Then, if any one should take it, and again putting it in a box and wrapping it up in an embroidered cloth, watch and sleep alongside, he would not only dream, but have nightmare into the bargain.

"Now your Master has been thus treating the ancients, who are like the dog which has already been offered in sacrifice. He causes his disciples to watch and sleep alongside of them. Consequently, his tree has been cut down in Sung; they will have none of him in Wei; in fact, his chances among the Shangs and the Chous are exhausted. Is not this the dream? And then to be surrounded by the Ch'êns and the Ts'ais, seven days without food, death staring him in the face, —is not this the nightmare?

"For travelling by water there is nothing like a boat. For travelling by land there is nothing like a cart. This because a boat moves readily in water; but were you to try to push it on land you would never succeed in making it go.

Now ancient and modern times may be likened unto water and land; Chou and Lu to the boat and the cart. To try to make the customs of Chou succeed in Lu, is like pushing a boat on land: great trouble and no result, except certain injury to oneself. Your Master has not yet learnt the doctrine of non-angularity, of self-adaptation to externals.

"Have you never seen a well-sweep? You pull it, and down it comes. You release it, and up it goes. It is the man who pulls the well-sweep, and not the well-sweep which pulls the man; so that both in coming down and going up, it does not run counter to the wishes of the man. And so it was that the ceremonial and obligations and laws of the Three Emperors and Five Rulers did not aim at uniformity of application but at good government of the empire. Their ceremonial, obligations, laws, etc., were like the cherryapple, the pear, the orange, and the pumelo, —all differing in flavour but each palatable. They changed with the changing season.

"Dress up a monkey in the robes of Chou Kung, and it will not be happy until they are torn to shreds. And the difference between past and present is much the same as the difference between Chou Kung and a monkey.

"When Hsi Shih was distressed in mind, she knitted her brows. An ugly woman of the village, seeing how beautiful she looked, went home, and having worked herself into a fit frame of mind, knitted her brows. The result was that the rich people of the place barred up their doors and would not come out, while the poor people took their wives and children and departed elsewhere. That woman saw the beauty of knitted brows, but she did not see wherein the beauty of knitted brows lay. Alas! your Master is emphatically not a success."

Confucius had lived to the age of fifty-one without hearing TAO, when he went south to P'ei, to see Lao Tzŭ.

Lao Tzŭ said, "So you have come, Sir, have you? I hear you are considered a wise man up north. Have you got TAO?" "Not yet" answered Confucius.

"In what direction," asked Lao Tzŭ, "have you sought for it?"

"I sought it for five years," replied Confucius, "in the science of numbers, but did not succeed."

"And then?…" continued Lao Tzŭ.

"Then," said Confucius, "I spent twelve years seeking for it in the doctrine of the *Yin* and *Yang*, also without success."

"Just so," rejoined Lao Tzǔ. "Were TAO something which could be presented, there is no man but would present it to his sovereign, or to his parents. Could it be imparted or given, there is no man but would impart it to his brother or give it to his child. But this is impossible, for the following reason. Unless there is a suitable endowment within, TAO will not abide. Unless there is outward correctness, TAO will not operate. The external being unfitted for the impression of the internal, the true Sage does not seek to imprint. The internal being unfitted for the reception of the external, the true Sage does not seek to receive.

"Reputation is public property; you may not appropriate it in excess. Charity and duty to one's neighbour are as caravanserais established by wise rulers of old; you may stop there one night, but not for long, or you will incur reproach.

"The perfect men of old took their road through charity, stopping a night with duty to their neighbour, on their way to ramble in transcendental space. Feeding on the produce of non-cultivation, and establishing themselves in the domain of no obligations, they enjoyed their transcendental inaction. Their food was ready to hand; and being under no obligations to others, they did not put any one under obligation to themselves. The ancients called this the outward visible sign of an inward and spiritual grace.

"Those who make wealth their all in all, cannot bear loss of money. Those who make distinction their all in all, cannot bear loss of fame. Those who affect power will not place authority in the hands of others. Anxious while holding, distressed if losing, yet never taking warning from the past and seeing the folly of their pursuit, —such men are the accursed of God.

"Resentment, gratitude, taking, giving, censure of self, instruction of others, power of life and death,—these eight are the instruments of right; but only he who can adapt himself to the vicissitudes of fortune, without being carried away, is fit to use them. Such a one is an upright man among the upright. And he whose heart is not so constituted, —the door of divine intelligence is not yet opened for him."

Confucius visited Lao Tzǔ, and spoke of charity and duty to one's neighbour.

Lao Tzǔ said, "The chaff from winnowing will blind a man's eyes so that he cannot tell the points of the compass. Mosquitoes will keep a man awake all night with their biting. And just in the same way this talk of charity and duty to one's neighbour drives me nearly crazy. Sir! strive to keep the world to its own original simplicity. And as the wind bloweth where it listeth, so let Virtue establish itself. Wherefore such undue energy, as though searching for a fugitive with a big drum?

"The snow-goose is white without a daily bath. The raven is black without daily colouring itself. The original simplicity of black and of white is beyond the reach of argument. The vista of fame and reputation is not worthy of enlargement. When the pond dries up and the fishes are left upon dry ground, to moisten them with the breath or to damp them with a little spittle is not to be compared with leaving them in the first instance in their native rivers and lakes."

On returning from this visit to Lao Tzŭ, Confucius did not speak for three days. A disciple asked him, saying, "Master, when you saw Lao Tzŭ, in what direction did you admonish him?"

"I saw a Dragon," replied Confucius, "—a Dragon which by convergence showed a body, by radiation became colour, and riding upon the clouds of heaven, nourished the two Principles of Creation. My mouth was agape: I could not shut it. How then do you think I was going to admonish Lao Tzŭ?"

Upon this Tzŭ Kung remarked, "Ha! then a man can sit corpse-like manifesting his dragon-power around, his thunder-voice heard though profound silence reigns, his movements like those of the universe? I too would go and see him."

So, on the strength of his connection with Confucius, Tzŭ Kung obtained an interview. Lao Tzŭ received him distantly and with dignity, saying in a low voice, "I am old, Sir. What injunctions may you have to give me?"

"The administration of the Three Kings and of the Five Rulers," replied Tzŭ Kung, "was not uniform; but their reputation has been identical. How then, Sir, is it that you do not regard them as Sages?"

"Come nearer, my son," said Lao Tzŭ. "What mean you by *not uniform?*"

"Yao handed over the empire to Shun," replied Tzŭ Kung; "and Shun to Yü. Yü employed labour, and T'ang employed troops. Wên Wang followed Chou Hsin and did not venture to oppose him. Wu Wang opposed him and would not follow. Therefore, I said *not uniform.*"

"Come nearer, my son," said Lao Tzŭ, "and I will tell you about the Three Kings and the Five Rulers.

"The Yellow Emperor's administration caused the affections of the people to be catholic. Nobody wept for the death of his parents, and nobody found fault.

"The administration of Yao diverted the affections of the people into particular channels. If a man slew the slayer of his parents, nobody blamed him.

"The administration of Shun brought a spirit of rivalry among the people. Children were born after ten months' gestation; when five months old, they could speak; and ere they were three years of age, could already tell one person from another. And so early death came into the world.

"The administration of Yü wrought a change in the hearts of the people. Individuality prevailed, and force was called into play. Killing robbers was not accounted murder; and throughout the empire people became sub-divided into classes. There was great alarm on all sides, and the Confucianists and the Mihists arose. At first the relationships were duly observed; but what about the women of to-day?

"Let me tell you. The government of the Three Kings and Five Rulers was so only in name. In reality, it was utter confusion. The wisdom of the Three Kings was opposed to the brilliancy of the sun and moon above, destructive of the energy of land and water below, and subversive of the influence of the four seasons between.

That wisdom is more harmful than a hornet's tail, preventing the very animals from putting themselves into due relation with the conditions of their existence, —and yet they call themselves Sages! Is not their shamelessness shameful indeed?"

At this Tzŭ Kung became ill at ease.

Confucius said to Lao Tzŭ, "I arranged the Six Canons of Poetry, History, Rites, Music, Changes, and Spring and Autumn. I spent much time over them, and I am well acquainted with their purport. I used them in admonishing seventy-two rulers, by discourses on the wisdom of ancient sovereigns and illustrations from the lives of Chou and Shao. Yet not one ruler has in any way adopted my suggestions. Alas that man should be so difficult to persuade, and wisdom so difficult to illustrate."

"It is well for you, Sir," replied Lao Tzǔ, "that you did not come across any real ruler of mankind. Your Six Canons are but the worn-out foot-prints of ancient Sages. And what are foot-prints? Why, the words you now utter are as it were foot-prints. Foot-prints are made by the shoe: they are not the shoe itself.

"Fish-hawks gaze at each other with motionless eyes, —and their young are produced. The male of a certain insect chirps with the wind while the female chirps against it, — and their offspring is produced. There is another animal which, being a hermaphrodite, produces its own offspring. Nature cannot be changed. Destiny cannot be altered. Time cannot stop. TAO cannot be obstructed. Once attain to TAO, and there is nothing which you cannot accomplish. Without it, there is nothing which you can accomplish."

For three months after this Confucius did not leave his house. Then he again visited Lao Tzǔ and said, "I have attained. Birds lay eggs, fish spawn, insects undergo metamorphosis, and mammals suckle their young.

For a long time, I have not been enlightened. And he who is not enlightened himself, —how should he enlighten others?"

Lao Tzǔ said, "Ch'iu, you have attained!"

CHAPTER XV. SELF-CONCEIT.

Argument:

—Would-be sages—The vanity of effort—Method of the true Sage—
Passivity the key—The soul and mortality—Re-absorption into the
immortal.

SELF-CONCEIT and assurance, which lead men to quit society, and be different from their fellows, to indulge in tall talk and abuse of others,— these are nothing more than personal over-estimation, the affectation of recluses and those who have done with the world and have closed their hearts to mundane influences.

Preaching of charity and duty to one's neighbour, of loyalty and truth, of respect, of economy, and of humility,—this is but moral culture, affected by would-be pacificators and teachers of mankind, and by scholars at home or abroad.

Preaching of meritorious services, of fame, of ceremonial between sovereign and minister, of due relationship between upper and lower classes,—this is mere government, affected by courtiers or patriots who strive to extend the boundaries of their own State and to swallow up the territory of others.

Living in marshes or in wildernesses, and passing one's days in fishing, — this is mere inaction, affected by wanderers who have turned their backs upon the world and have nothing better to do.

Exhaling and inhaling, getting rid of the old and assimilating the new, stretching like a bear and craning like a bird, —this is but valetudinarianism, affected by professors of hygiene and those who try to preserve the body to the age of P'êng Tsu.

But in self-esteem without self-conceit, in moral culture without charity and duty to one's neighbour, in government without rank and fame, in retirement without solitude, in health without hygiene,—there we have oblivion absolute coupled with possession of all things; an infinite calm which becomes an object to be attained by all.

Such is the TAO of the universe, such is the virtue of the Sage. Wherefore it has been said, "In tranquillity, in stillness, in the unconditioned, in inaction, we find the levels of the universe, the very constitution of TAO."

Wherefore it has been said, "The Sage is a negative quantity, and is consequently in a state of passivity. Being passive he is in a state of repose. And where passivity and repose are, there sorrow and anxiety do not enter, and foul influences do not collect. And thus, his virtue is complete and his spirituality unimpaired."

Wherefore it has been said, "The birth of the Sage is the will of God; his death is but a modification of existence. In repose, he shares the passivity of the *Yin;* in action, the energy of the *Yang.* He will have nothing to do with happiness, and so has nothing to do with misfortune.

He must be influenced ere he will respond. He must be urged ere he will move. He must be compelled ere he will arise. Ignoring the future and the past, he resigns himself to the laws of God.

"And therefore, no calamity comes upon him, nothing injures him, no man is against him, no spirit punishes him. He floats through life to rest in death. He has no anxieties; he makes no plans. His honour does not make him illustrious. His good faith reflects no credit upon himself.

His sleep is dreamless, his awaking without pain. His spirituality is pure, and his soul vigorous. Thus, unconditioned and in repose, he is a partaker of the virtue of God."

Wherefore it has been said, "Sorrow and happiness are the heresies of virtue; joy and anger lead astray from TAO; love and hate cause the loss of virtue. The heart unconscious of sorrow and happiness, —that is perfect virtue. O$_{\text{NE}}$, without change, —that is perfect repose. Without any obstruction, —that is the perfection of the unconditioned. Holding no relations with the external world, —that is perfection of the negative state. Without blemish of any kind, —that is the perfection of purity."

Wherefore it has been said, "If the body toils without rest, it dies. If the mind is employed without ceasing, it becomes wearied; and being wearied, its power is gone."

Pure water is by nature clear. If untouched, it is smooth. If dammed, it will not flow, neither will it be clear. It is an emblem of the virtue of God. Wherefore it has been said, "Pure, without admixture; uniform, without change; negative, without action; moved, only at the will of God; — such would be the spirituality nourished according to TAO."

Those who possess blades from Kan or Yüeh, keep them carefully in their scabbards, and do not venture to use them. For they are precious in the extreme. The spirit spreads forth on all sides: there is no point to which it does not reach, attaining heaven above, embracing earth beneath. Influencing all creation, its form cannot be portrayed. Its name is then *Of-God*.

The TAO of the pure and simple consists in preserving spirituality. He who preserves his spirituality and loses it not, becomes one with that spirituality. And through that unity the spirit operates freely and comes into due relationship with God.

A vulgar saying has it, "The masses value money; honest men, fame; virtuous men, resolution; and Sages, the soul."

Thus, the pure is that in which there is nothing mixed; the simple is that which implies no injury to the spirituality. And he who can keep the pure and simple within himself, — he is a divine man.

CHAPTER XVI. Exercise of Faculties.

Argument:

—TAO unattainable by mundane arts—To be reached through repose
—The world's infancy—The reign of peace—Government sets in—
TAO declines—The true Sages of old—Their purity of aim.

THOSE who exercise their faculties in mere worldly studies, hoping thereby to revert to their original condition; and those who sink their aspirations in mundane thoughts, hoping thereby to reach enlightenment; —these are the dullards of the earth.

The ancients, in cultivating TAO, begat knowledge out of repose. When born, this knowledge was not applied to any purpose; and so it may be said that out of knowledge they begat repose. Knowledge and repose thus mutually producing each other, harmony and order were developed. Virtue is harmony; TAO is order.

Virtue all-embracing, —hence charity. TAO all-influencing, —hence duty to one's neighbour. From the establishment of these two springs loyalty. Then comes music, an expression of inward purity and truth; followed by ceremonial, or sincerity expressed in ornamental guise. If music and ceremonial are ill regulated, the empire is plunged into confusion. And to attempt to correct others while one's own virtue is clouded, is to set one's own virtue a task for which it is inadequate, the result being that the natural constitution of the object will suffer.

Primeval man enjoyed perfect tranquillity throughout life. In his day, the Positive and Negative principles were peacefully united; spiritual beings gave no trouble; the four seasons followed in due order; nothing suffered any injury; death was unknown; men had knowledge, but no occasion to use it. This may be called perfection of unity.

At that period, nothing was ever made so; but everything was so.

By and by, virtue declined. Sui Jen and Fu His ruled the empire. There was still natural adaptation, but the unity was gone.

A further decline in virtue. Shên Nung and Huang Ti ruled the empire. There was peace, but the natural adaptation was gone.

Again, virtue declined. Yao and Shun ruled the empire. Systems of government and moral reform were introduced. Man's original integrity was scattered. Goodness led him astray from TAO; his actions imperilled his virtue.

Then he discarded natural instinct and took up with the intellectual. Mind was pitted against mind, but it was impossible thus to settle the empire. So, art and learning were added. But art obliterated the original constitution and learning overwhelmed mind; upon which confusion set in, and man was unable to revert to his natural instincts, to the condition in which he at first existed.

Thus, it may be said that the world destroys TAO, and that TAO destroys the world. And the world and TAO thus mutually destroying each other, how can the men of TAO elevate the world, and how can the world elevate TAO? TAO cannot elevate the world; neither can the world elevate TAO. Though the Sages were not to dwell on mountain and in forest, their virtue would still be hidden; —hidden, but not by themselves.

Those of old who were called retired scholars, were not men who hid their bodies, or kept back their words, or concealed their wisdom. It was that the age was not suitable for their mission. If the age was suitable and their mission a success over the empire, they simply effaced themselves in the unity which prevailed. If the age was unsuitable and their mission a failure, they fell back upon their own resources and waited. Such is the way to preserve oneself.

Those of old who preserved themselves, did not ornament their knowledge with rhetoric. They did not exhaust the empire with their knowledge. They did not exhaust virtue. They kept quietly to their own spheres and reverted to their natural instincts. What then was left for them to *do?*

TAO does not deal with detail. Virtue does not take cognizance of trifles. Trifles injure virtue; detail injures TAO. Wherefore it has been said, "Self-reformation is enough." He whose happiness is complete has attained his desire.

Of old, attainment of desire did not mean *office.* It meant that nothing could be added to the sum of happiness. But now it does mean office, though office is external and is not a part of oneself. That which is adventitious, comes. Coming, you cannot prevent it; going, you cannot arrest it. Therefore, not to look on office as the attainment of desire, and not because of poverty to become a toady, but to be equally happy under all conditions, —this is to be without sorrow.

But now-a-days, both having and not having are causes of unhappiness. From which we may infer that even happiness is not exempt from sorrow.

Wherefore it has been said, "Those who over-estimate the external and lose their natural instincts in worldliness, —these are the people of topsy-turvydom."

CHAPTER XVII. AUTUMN FLOODS.

Argument:

—Greatness and smallness always relative—Time and space infinite—Abstract dimensions do not exist—Their expression is concrete— Terms are not absolute—Like causes produce unlike effects—In the unconditioned alone can the absolute exist—The only absolute is TAO— Illustrations.

[This chapter is supplementary to chapter ii. It is the most popular of all and has earned for its author the sobriquet of "Autumn Floods."]

IT was the time of autumn floods. Every stream poured into the river, which swelled in its turbid course. The banks receded so far from one another that it was impossible to tell a cow from a horse.

Then the Spirit of the River laughed for joy that all the beauty of the earth was gathered to himself. Down with the stream he journeyed east, until he reached the ocean. There, looking eastwards and seeing no limit to its waves, his countenance changed. And as he gazed over the expanse, he sighed and said to the Spirit of the Ocean, "A vulgar proverb says that he who has heard but part of the truth thinks no one equal to himself. And such a one am I.

"When formerly I heard people detracting from the learning of Confucius or underrating the heroism of Poh I, I did not believe. But now that I have looked upon your inexhaustibility—alas for me had I not reached your abode, I should have been for ever a laughing-stock to those of comprehensive enlightenment!"

To which the Spirit of the Ocean replied, "You cannot speak of ocean to a well-frog, —the creature of a narrower sphere. You cannot speak of ice to a summer insect, —the creature of a season. You cannot speak of TAO to a pedagogue: his scope is too restricted. But now that you have emerged from your narrow sphere and have seen the great ocean, you know your own insignificance, and I can speak to you of great principles.

"There is no body of water beneath the canopy of heaven which is greater than ocean. All streams pour into it without cease, yet it does not overflow. It is constantly being drained off, yet it is never empty. Spring and autumn bring no change; floods and droughts are equally unknown. And thus, it is immeasurably superior to mere rivers and brooks, —though I would not venture to boast on this account, for I get my shape from the universe, my vital power from the *Yin* and *Yang*. In the universe I am but as a small stone or a small tree on a vast mountain. And conscious thus of my own insignificance, what is there of which I can boast?

"The Four Seas, —are they not to the universe but like puddles in a marsh? The Middle Kingdom, —is it not to the surrounding ocean like a tare-seed in a granary? Of all the myriad created things, man is but one. And of all those who inhabit the land, live on the fruit of the earth, and move about in cart and boat, an individual man is but one. Is not he, as compared with all creation, but as the tip of a hair upon a horse's skin?

"The succession of the Five Rulers, the contentions of the Three Kings, the griefs of the philanthropist, the labours of the administrator, are but this and nothing more.

"Poh I refused the throne for fame's sake. Confucius discoursed to get a reputation for learning. This overestimation of self on their part, was it not very much your own in reference to water?"

"Very well," replied the Spirit of the River, "am I then to regard the universe as great and the tip of a hair as small?"

"Not at all," said the Spirit of the Ocean. "Dimensions are limitless; time is endless. Conditions are not invariable; terms are not final. Thus, the wise man looks into space, and does not regard the small as too little, nor the great as too much; for he knows that there is no limit to dimension. He looks back into the past, and does not grieve over what is far off, nor rejoice over what is near; for he knows that time is without end.

He investigates fulness and decay, and does not rejoice if he succeeds, nor lament if he fails; for he knows that conditions are not invariable.

He who clearly apprehends the scheme of existence, does not rejoice over life, nor repine at death; for he knows that terms are not final.

"What man knows is not to be compared with what he does not know. The span of his existence is not to be compared with the span of his non-existence. With the small to strive to exhaust the great, necessarily lands him in confusion, and he does not attain his object. How then should one be able to say that the tip of a hair is the *ne plus ultra* of smallness, or that the universe is the *ne plus ultra* of greatness?"

"Dialecticians of the day," replied the Spirit of the River, "all say that the infinitesimally small has no form, and that the infinitesimally great is beyond all measurement. Is that so?"

"If we regard greatness as compared with that which is small," said the Spirit of the Ocean, "there is no limit to it; and if we regard smallness as compared with that which is great, it eludes our sight.

The infinitesimal is a subdivision of the small; the colossal is an extension of the great. In this sense, the two fall into different categories.

"Both small and great things must equally possess form. The mind cannot picture to itself a thing without form, nor conceive a form of unlimited dimensions. The greatness of anything may be a topic of discussion, or the smallness of anything may be mentally realized. But that which can be neither a topic of discussion nor be realized mentally, can be neither great nor small.

"Therefore, the truly great man, although he does not injure others, does not credit himself with charity and mercy.

He seeks not gain but does not despise his followers who do. He struggles not for wealth but does not take credit for letting it alone. He asks help from no man, but takes no credit for his self-reliance, neither does he despise those who seek preferment through friends. He acts differently from the vulgar crowd but takes no credit for his exceptionality; nor because others act with the majority does he despise them as hypocrites. The ranks and emoluments of the world are to him no cause for joy; its punishments and shame no cause for disgrace. He knows that positive and negative cannot be distinguished, that great and small cannot be defined.

"I have heard say, the man of TAO has no reputation; perfect virtue acquires nothing; the truly great man ignores self; — this is the height of self-discipline."

"But how then," asked the Spirit of the River, "are the internal and external extremes of value and worthlessness, of greatness and smallness, to be determined?"

"From the point of view of TAO," replied the Spirit of the Ocean, "there are no such extremes of value or worthlessness. Men individually value themselves and hold others cheap. The world collectively withholds from the individual the right of appraising himself.

"If we say that a thing is great or small because it is relatively great or small, then there is nothing in all creation which is not great, nothing which is not small. To know that the universe is but as a tare-seed, and that the tip of a hair is a mountain, —this is the expression of relativity.

"If we say that something exists or does not exist, in deference to the function it fulfils or does not fulfil, then there is nothing which does not exist, nothing which does exist. To know that east and west are convertible and yet necessary terms, —this is the due adjustment of functions.

"If we say that anything is good or evil because it is either good or evil in our eyes, then there is nothing which is not good, nothing which is not evil. To know that Yao and Chieh were both good and both evil from their opposite points of view, —this is the expression of a standard.

"Of old Yao abdicated in favour of Shun, and the latter ruled. Kuei abdicated in favour of Chih, and the latter failed.

T'ang and Wu got the empire by fighting. By fighting, Poh Kung lost it.

From which it may be seen that the rationale of abdicating or fighting, of acting like Yao or like Chieh, must be determined according to the opportunity, and may not be regarded as a constant quantity.

"A battering-ram can knock down a wall, but it cannot repair the breach.

Different things are differently applied.

"Ch'ih-Chi and Hua Liu could travel 1,000 *li* in one day, but for catching rats they were not equal to a wild cat.

Different animals possess different aptitudes.

"An owl can catch fleas at night, and see the tip of a hair, but if it comes out in the daytime its eyes are so dazzled it cannot see a mountain. Different creatures are differently constituted.

"Thus, as has been said, those who would have right without its correlative, wrong; or good government without its correlative, misrule,—they do not apprehend the great principles of the universe nor the conditions to which all creation is subject. One might as well talk of the existence of heaven without that of earth, or of the negative principle without the positive, which is clearly absurd. Such people, if they do not yield to argument, must be either fools or knaves.

"Rulers have abdicated under different conditions, dynasties have been continued under different conditions. Those who did not hit off a favourable time and were in opposition to their age, —they were called usurpers. Those who did hit off the right time and were in harmony with their age, —they were called patriots. Fair and softly, my River friend; what should you know of value and worthlessness, of great and small?"

"In this case," replied the Spirit of the River, "what am I to do and what am I not to do? How am I to arrange my declinings and receivings, my takings-hold and my lettingsgo?"

"From the point of view of TAO," said the Spirit of the Ocean, "value and worthlessness are like slopes and plains.

To consider either as absolutely such would involve great injury to TAO. Few and many are like giving and receiving presents. These must not be regarded from one side, or there will be great confusion to TAO.

Be discriminating, as the ruler of a State whose administration is impartial. Be dispassionate, as the worshipped deity whose dispensation is impartial. Be expansive, like the points of the compass, to whose boundlessness no limit is set. Embrace all creation, and none shall be more sheltered than another. This is the unconditioned. And where all things are equal, how can we have the long and the short?

"TAO is without beginning, without end. Other things are born and die. They are impermanent; and now for better, now for worse, they are ceaselessly changing form. Past years cannot be recalled: time cannot be arrested.

The succession of states is endless; and every end is followed by a new beginning. Thus it may be said that man's duty to his neighbour is embodied in the eternal principles of the universe.

"The life of man passes by like a galloping horse, changing at every turn, at every hour. What should he do, or what should he not do, other than let his decomposition go on?"

"If this is the case," retorted the Spirit of the River, "pray what is the value of TAO?"

"Those who understand TAO," answered the Spirit of the

Ocean, "must necessarily apprehend the eternal principles above mentioned and be clear as to their application. Consequently, they do not suffer any injury from without.

"The man of perfect virtue cannot be burnt by fire, nor drowned in water, nor hurt by frost or sun, nor torn by wild bird or beast. Not that he makes light of these; but that he discriminates between safety and danger. Happy under prosperous and adverse circumstances alike, cautious as to what he discards and what he accepts; —nothing can harm him.

"Therefore, it has been said that the natural abides within, the artificial without. Virtue abides in the natural. Knowledge of the action of the natural and of the artificial has its root in the natural, its development in virtue. And thus, whether in motion or at rest, whether in expansion or in contraction, there is always a reversion to the essential and to the ultimate."

"What do you mean," enquired the Spirit of the River, "by the natural and the artificial?"

"Horses and oxen," answered the Spirit of the Ocean, "have four feet. That is the natural. Put a halter on a horse's head, a string through a bullock's nose, —that is the artificial.

"Therefore, it has been said, do not let the artificial obliterate the natural; do not let will obliterate destiny; do not let virtue be sacrificed to fame. Diligently observe these precepts without fail, and thus you will revert to the divine."

The walrus envies the centipede; the centipede envies the snake; the snake envies the wind; the wind envies the eye; the eye envies the mind.

The walrus said to the centipede, "I hop about on one leg, but not very successfully. How do you manage all these legs you have?"

"I don't manage them," replied the centipede. "Have you never seen saliva? When it is ejected, the big drops are the size of pearls, the small ones like mist. They fall promiscuously on the ground and cannot be counted. And so it is that my mechanism works naturally, without my being conscious of the fact."

The centipede said to the snake, "With all my legs I do not move as fast as you with none. How is that?"

"One's natural mechanism," replied the snake, "is not a thing to be changed. What need have I for legs?"

The snake said to the wind, "I can manage to wriggle along, but I have a form. Now you come blustering down from the north sea to bluster away to the south sea, and you seem to be without form. How is that?"

"'Tis true," replied the wind, "that I bluster as you say; but anyone who can point at me or kick at me, excels me.

On the other hand, I can break huge trees and destroy large buildings. That is my strong point. Out of all the small things in which I do not excel I make one great one in which I do excel. And to excel in great things is given only to the Sages."

When Confucius visited K'uang, the men of Sung surrounded him closely.

Yet he went on playing and singing to his guitar without ceasing.

"How is it, Sir," enquired Tzŭ Lu, "that you are so cheerful?"

"Come here," replied Confucius, "and I will tell you. For a long time, I have been struggling against failure, but in vain.

Fate is against me. For a long time, I have been seeking success, but in vain. The hour has not come.

"In the days of Yao and Shun, no man throughout the empire was a failure, though no one was conscious of the gain. In the days of Chieh and Chou, no man throughout the empire was a success, though no one was conscious of the loss. The times and circumstances were adapted accordingly.

"To travel by water and not avoid sea-serpents and dragons, —this is the courage of the fisherman. To travel by land and not avoid the rhinoceros and the tiger, —this is the courage of hunters. When bright blades cross, to look on death as on life, —this is the courage of the hero. To know that failure is fate and that success is opportunity, and to remain fearless in great danger, —this is the courage of the Sage. Yu! rest in this. My destiny is cut out for me."

Shortly afterwards, the captain of the troops came in and apologised, saying, "We thought you were Yang Hu; consequently, we surrounded you. We find we have made a mistake." Whereupon he again apologised and retired.

Kung Sun Lung said to Mou of Wei, "When young I studied the TAO of the ancient Sages. When I grew up I knew all about the practice of charity and duty to one's neighbour, the identification of like and unlike, the separation of hardness and whiteness, and about making the not-so so, and the impossible possible. I vanquished the wisdom of all the philosophies. I exhausted all the arguments that were brought against me. I thought that I had indeed reached the goal. But now that I have heard Chuang Tzŭ, I am lost in astonishment at his grandeur. I know not whether it is in arguing or in knowledge that I am not equal to him. I can no longer open my mouth. May I ask you to impart to me the secret?"

Kung Tzŭ Mou leant over the table and sighed. Then he looked up to heaven, and smiling replied, saying, "Have you never heard of the frog in the old well?—The frog said to the turtle of the eastern sea, 'Happy indeed am I! I hop on to the rail around the well. I rest in the hollow of some broken brick. Swimming, I gather the water under my arms and shut my mouth. I plunge into the mud, burying my feet and toes; and not one of the cockles, crabs, or tadpoles I see around me are my match. [Fancy pitting the happiness of an old well against all the water of Ocean!] Why do you not come, Sir, and pay me a visit?'

"Now the turtle of the eastern sea had not got its left leg down ere its right had already stuck fast, so it shrank back and begged to be excused. It then described the sea, saying, 'A thousand *li* would not measure its breadth, nor a thousand fathoms its depth. In the days of the Great Yü, there were nine years of flood out of ten; but this did not add to its bulk. In the days of T'ang, there were seven years out of eight of drought; but this did not narrow its span. Not to be affected by duration of time, not to be affected by volume of water, —such is the great happiness of the eastern sea.'

"At this the well-frog was considerably astonished and knew not what to say next. And for one whose knowledge does not reach to the positive-negative domain, to attempt to understand Chuang Tzŭ, is like a mosquito trying to carry a mountain, or an ant to swim a river, —they cannot succeed. And for one whose knowledge does not reach to the abstrusest of the abstruse, but is based only upon such victories as you have enumerated, —is not he like the frog in the well?

"Chuang Tzŭ moves in the realms below while soaring to heaven above. For him north and south do not exist; the four points are gone; he is engulphed in the unfathomable. For him east and west do not exist. Beginning with chaos, he has gone back to TAO; and yet you think you are going to examine his doctrines and meet them with argument! This is like looking at the sky through a tube, or pointing at the earth with an awl, —a small result.

"Have you never heard how the youth of Shouling went to study at Han-tan? They did not learn what they wanted at Han-tan, and forgot all they knew before into the bargain, so that they returned home in disgrace. And you, if you do not go away, you will forget all you know, and waste your time into the bargain."

Kung Sun Lung's jaw dropped; his tongue clave to his palate; and he slunk away.

Chuang Tzŭ was fishing in the P'u when the prince of Ch'u sent two high officials to ask him to take charge of the administration of the Ch'u State.

Chuang Tzŭ went on fishing, and without turning his head said, "I have heard that in Ch'u there is a sacred tortoise which has been dead now some three thousand years. And that the prince keeps this tortoise carefully enclosed in a chest on the altar of his ancestral temple. Now would this tortoise rather be dead and have its remains venerated, or be alive and wagging its tail in the mud?"

"It would rather be alive," replied the two officials, "and wagging its tail in the mud."

"Begone!" cried Chuang Tzŭ. "I too will wag my tail in the mud."

Hui Tzŭ was prime minister in the Liang State. Chuang Tzŭ went thither to visit him.

Someone remarked, "Chuang Tzŭ has come. He wants to be minister in your place."

Thereupon Hui Tzŭ was afraid, and searched all over the State for three days and three nights to find him.

Then Chuang Tzŭ went to see Hui Tzŭ, and said, "In the south there is a bird. It is a kind of phœnix. Do you know it? It started from the south sea to fly to the north sea. Except on the *wu-t'ung* tree, it would not alight. It would eat nothing but the fruit of the bamboo, drink nothing but the purest spring water. An owl which had got the rotten carcass of a rat, looked up as the phœnix flew by, and screeched.

Are you not screeching at me over your kingdom of Liang?"

Chuang Tzŭ and Hui Tzŭ had strolled on to the bridge over the Hao, when the former observed, "See how the minnows are darting about! That is the pleasure of fishes."

"You not being a fish yourself," said Hui Tzŭ, "how can you possibly know in what consists the pleasure of fishes?"

"And you not being I," retorted Chuang Tzŭ, "how can you know that I do not know?"

"If I, not being you, cannot know what you know," urged Hui Tzŭ, "it follows that you, not being a fish, cannot know in what consists the pleasure of fishes."

"Let us go back," said Chuang Tzŭ, "to your original question. You asked me how I knew in what consists the pleasure of fishes. Your very question shows that you knew I knew.

I knew it from my own feelings on this bridge."

CHAPTER XVIII. PERFECT HAPPINESS.

Argument:

—The uncertainty of human happiness—What the world aims at is physical well-being—This is not profitable even to the body—In inaction alone is true happiness to be found—Inaction the rule of the material universe—Acquiescence in whatever our destiny may bring forth—Illustrations.

[This chapter is supplementary to chapter vi.]

Is perfect happiness to be found on earth, or not? Are there those who can enjoy life, or not? If so, what do they do, what do they affect, what do they avoid, what do they rest in, accept, reject, like, and dislike?

What the world esteems comprises wealth, rank, old age, and goodness of heart. What it enjoys comprises comfort, rich food, fine clothes, beauty, and music. What it does not esteem comprises poverty, want of position, early death, and evil behaviour. What it does not enjoy comprises lack of comfort for the body, lack of rich food for the palate, lack of fine clothes for the back, lack of beauty for the eye, and lack of music for the ear. If men do not get these, they are greatly miserable. Yet from the point of view of our physical frame, this is folly.

Wealthy people who toil and moil, putting together more money than they can possibly use,—from the point of view of our physical frame, is not this going beyond the mark?

Officials of rank who turn night into day in their endeavours to compass the best ends;—from the point of view of our physical frame, is not this a divergence?

Man is born to sorrow, and what misery is theirs whose old age with dulled faculties only means prolonged sorrow! From the point of view of our physical frame, this is going far astray.

Patriots are in the world's opinion admittedly good. Yet their goodness does not enable them to enjoy life; and so, I know not whether theirs is veritable goodness or not. If the former, it does not enable them to enjoy life; if the latter, it at any rate enables them to cause others to enjoy theirs.

It has been said, "If your loyal counsels are not attended to, depart quietly without resistance." Thus, when Tzŭ Hsü resisted, his physical frame perished; yet had he not resisted, he would not have made his name. Is there then really such a thing as this goodness, or not?

As to what the world does and the way in which people are happy now, I know not whether such happiness be real happiness or not. The happiness of ordinary persons seems to me to consist in slavishly following the majority, as if they could not help it. Yet they all say they are happy.

But I cannot say that this is happiness or that it is not happiness. Is there then, after all, such a thing as happiness?

I make true pleasure to consist in *inaction*, which the world regards as great pain. Thus, it has been said, "Perfect happiness is the absence of happiness; perfect renown is the absence of renown."

Now in this sublunary world of ours it is impossible to assign positive and negative absolutely. Nevertheless, in inaction they can be so assigned. Perfect happiness and preservation of life are to be sought for only in inaction.

Let us consider. Heaven does nothing; yet it is clear. Earth does nothing; yet it enjoys repose. From the inaction of these two proceed all the modifications of things. How vast, how infinite is inaction, yet without source! How infinite, how vast, yet without form!

The endless varieties of things around us all spring from inaction. Therefore, it has been said, "Heaven and earth do nothing, yet there is nothing which they do not accomplish." But among men, who can attain to inaction?

When Chuang Tzŭ's wife died, Hui Tzŭ went to condole. He found the widower sitting on the ground, singing, with his legs spread out at a right angle, and beating time on a bowl.

"To live with your wife," exclaimed Hui Tzŭ, "and see your eldest son grow up to be a man, and then not to shed a tear over her corpse,—this would be bad enough. But to drum on a bowl, and sing; surely this is going too far."

"Not at all," replied Chuang Tzŭ. "When she died, I could not help being affected by her death. Soon, however, I remembered that she had already existed in a previous state before birth, without form, or even substance; that while in that unconditioned condition, substance was added to spirit; that this substance then assumed form; and that the next stage was birth. And now, by virtue of a further change, she is dead, passing from one phase to another like the sequence of spring, summer, autumn, and winter. And while she is thus lying asleep in Eternity, for me to go about weeping and wailing would be to proclaim myself ignorant of these natural laws. Therefore, I refrain."

A hunchback and a one-legged man were looking at the tombs of departed heroes, on the K'un-lun Mountains, where the Yellow Emperor rests. Suddenly, ulcers broke out upon their left elbows, of a very loathsome description.

"Do you loathe this?" asked the hunchback.

"Not I," replied the other, "why should I? Life is a loan with which the borrower does but add more dust and dirt to the sum total of existence. Life and death are as day and night; and while you and I stand gazing at the evidences of mortality around us, if the same mortality overtakes me, why should I loathe it?"

Chuang Tzŭ one day saw an empty skull, bleached, but still preserving its shape. Striking it with his riding whip, he said, "Wert thou once some ambitious citizen whose inordinate yearnings brought him to this pass?—some statesman who plunged his country in ruin and perished in the fray?—some wretch who left behind him a legacy of shame?—some beggar who died in the pangs of hunger and cold? Or didst thou reach this state by the natural course of old age?"

When he had finished speaking, he took the skull, and placing it under his head as a pillow, went to sleep. In the night, he dreamt that the skull appeared to him and said, "You speak well, Sir; but all you say has reference to the life of mortals, and to mortal troubles. In death there are none of these. Would you like to hear about death?"

Chuang Tzŭ having replied in the affirmative, the skull began:—"In death, there is no sovereign above, and no subject below. The workings of the four seasons are unknown. Our existences are bounded only by eternity. The happiness of a king among men cannot exceed that which we enjoy."

Chuang Tzŭ, however, was not convinced, and said, "Were I to prevail upon God to allow your body to be born again, and your bones and flesh to be renewed, so that you could return to your parents, to your wife, and to the friends of your youth,—would you be willing?"

At this, the skull opened its eyes wide and knitted its brows and said, "How should I cast aside happiness greater than that of a king, and mingle once again in the toils and troubles of mortality?"

When Yen Yüan went eastwards to the Ch'i State, Confucius was sad. Tzŭ Kung arose and said, "Is it, Sir, because Hui has gone east to Ch'i that you are sad?"

"A good question," replied Confucius. "There is a saying by Kuan Chung of old which I highly esteem: 'Small bags won't hold big things; short ropes won't reach down deep wells.' Thus, destiny is a pre-arrangement, just as form has its limitations. From neither, to neither, can you either take away or add.

And I fear lest Hui, on his visit to the prince of Ch'i, should preach the Tao of Yao and Shun, and dwell on the words of Sui Jen and Shên Nung. The prince will then search within himself but will not find. And not finding, he will doubt. And when a man doubts, he will kill.

"Besides, have you not heard that of old when a sea-bird alighted outside the capital of Lu, the prince went out to receive it, and gave it wine in the temple, and had the *Chiu Shao* played to amuse it, and a bullock slaughtered to feed it? But the bird was dazed and too timid to eat or drink anything; and in three days it was dead. This was treating the bird like oneself, and not as a bird would treat a bird. Had he treated it as a bird would have treated a bird, he would have put it to roost in a deep forest, to wander over a plain, to swim in a river or lake, to feed upon fish, to fly in order, and to settle leisurely. When the bird was already terrified at human voices, fancy adding music! Play the *Hsien Ch'ih* or the *Chiu Shao* in the wilds of Tung-t'ing, and birds will fly away, beasts will take themselves off, and fishes will dive down below. But men will collect to hear.

"Water, which is life to fishes, is death to man. Being differently constituted, their likes and dislikes are different. Therefore, the Sages of the past favoured not uniformity of skill or of occupation. Reputation was commensurate with reality; means were adapted to the end. This was called a due relationship with others coupled with advantage to oneself."

Lieh Tzŭ, being on a journey, was eating by the roadside, when he saw an old skull. Plucking a blade of grass, he pointed at it and said, "Only you and I know that there is no such thing as life and no such thing as death.

Are you really at peace? Or am I really happy?

"Certain germs, falling upon water, become duckweed. When they reach the junction of the land and the water, they become lichen. Spreading up the bank, they become the dog-tooth violet. Reaching rich soil, they become *wu-tsu*, the root of which becomes grubs, while the leaves comes from butter-flies, or *hsü*. These are changed into insects, born in the chimney corner, which look like skeletons. Their name is *ch'ü-to*. After a thousand days, the *ch'ü-to* becomes a bird, called *Kan-yü-ku*, the spittle of which becomes the *ssŭ-mi*. The *ssŭ-mi* becomes a wine fly, and that comes from an *i-lu*. The *huang-k'uang* produces the *chiu-yu* and the *mou-jui* produces the firefly. The *yang-ch'i* grafted to an old bamboo which has for a long time put forth no shoots, produces the *ch'ing-ning*, which produces the leopard, which produces the horse, which produces man.

"Then man goes back into the great Scheme, from which all things come and to which all things return."

CHAPTER XIX. THE SECRET OF LIFE.

Argument:

—The soul is from God—Man's body its vehicle—The soul quick-ening the body is life—Care of the internal and of the external must be simultaneous—In due nourishment of both is TAO.

[This chapter is supplementary to chapter iii.]

THOSE who understand the conditions of life devote no attention to things which life cannot accomplish. Those who understand the conditions of destiny devote no attention to things over which knowledge has no control.

For the due nourishment of our physical frames, certain things are need-ful. Yet where such things abound, the physical frame is not always nour-ished. For the preservation of life, it is necessary that there should be no abandonment of the physical frame. Yet where the physical frame is not abandoned, life does not always remain.

Life comes and cannot be declined. It goes and cannot be stopped. But alas! the world thinks that to nourish the frame is enough to keep life. And if indeed it is not enough, what then is the world to do?

Although not enough, it must still be done. It cannot be neglected. For if one is to neglect the physical frame, better far to retire at once from the world. By renouncing the world, one gets rid of the cares of the world. The result is a natural level, which is equivalent to a re-birth. And he who is re-born is near.

But what inducement is there to renounce the affairs of men, to become indifferent to life?—In the first case, the physical body suffers no wear and tear; in the second, the vitality is left unharmed. And he whose physical frame is perfect and whose vitality is in its original purity,—he is one with God.

Heaven and earth are the father and mother of all things. When they unite, the result is shape. When they disperse, the original condition is renewed.

But if body and vitality are both perfect, this state is called *fit for translation*.

Such perfection of vitality goes back to be the minister of God.

Lieh Tzŭ asked Kuan Yin, saying, "The perfect man can walk through solid bodies without obstruction. He can pass through fire without being burnt. He can scale the highest heights without fear. How does he bring himself to this?"

"It is because he is in a condition of absolute purity," replied Kuan Yin. "It is not cunning which enables him to dare such feats. Be seated, and I will tell you.

"All that has form, sound, and colour, may be classed under the head *thing*. Man differs so much from the rest, and stands at the head of all things, simply because the latter are but what they appear and nothing more. But man can attain to formlessness and vanquish death. And with that which is in possession of the eternal, how can mere things compare?

"Man may rest in the eternal fitness; he may abide in the everlasting; and roam from the beginning to the end of all creation. He may bring his nature to a condition of ONE; he may nourish his strength; he may harmonize his virtue, and so put himself into partnership with God. Then, when his divinity is thus assured, and his spirit closed in on all sides, how can anything find a passage within?

"A drunken man who falls out of a cart, though he may suffer, does not die. His bones are the same as other people's; but he meets his accident in a different way. His spirit is in a condition of security. He is not conscious of riding in the cart; neither is he conscious of falling out of it. Ideas of life, death, fear, etc., cannot penetrate his breast; and so, he does not suffer from contact with objective existences. And if such security is to be got from wine, how much more is it to be got from God. It is in God that the Sage seeks his refuge, and so he is free from harm.

"An avenger does not snap in twain the murderous weapon; neither does the most spiteful man carry his resentment to a tile which may have hit him on the head. And by the extension of this principle, the empire would be at peace; no more confusion of war, no more punishment of death.

"Do not develop your artificial intelligence but develop that intelligence which is from God. From the latter, results virtue; from the former, cunning. And those who do not shrink from the natural, nor wallow in the artificial,— they are near to perfection."

When Confucius was on his way to the Ch'u State, he came to a forest where he saw a hunch-back catching cicadas as though with his hand.

"How clever you are!" cried Confucius. "Have you any way of doing this?"

"I have a way," replied the hunchback. "In the fifth and sixth moons I practise balancing two balls one on top of the other.

If they do not fall, I do not miss many cicadas. When I can balance three balls, I only miss one in ten; and when five, then it is as though I caught the cicadas with my hand. My body is as motionless as the stump of a tree; my arms like dead branches. Heaven and earth and all creation may be around me, but I am conscious only of my cicada's wings. How should I not succeed?"

Confucius looked round at his disciples and said, "Singleness of purpose induces concentration of the faculties. Of such is the success of this hunchback."

Yen Yüan said to Confucius, "When I crossed over the Shang-shên rapid, the boatman managed his craft with marvellous skill. I asked him if handling a boat could be learnt. 'It can,' replied he. 'The way of those who know how to keep you afloat is more like sinking you. They row as if the boat wasn't there.'

"I enquired what this meant, but he would not tell me. May I ask its signification."

"It means," answered Confucius, "that such a man is oblivious of the water around him. He regards the rapid as though dry land. He looks upon an upset as an ordinary cart accident. And if a man can but be impervious to capsizings and accidents in general, whither should he not be able comfortably to go?

"A man who plays for counters will play well. If he stakes his girdle, he will be nervous; if yellow gold, he will lose his wits. His skill is the same in each case, but he is distracted by the value of his stake. And everyone who attaches importance to the external, becomes internally without resource."

T'ien K'ai Chih had an audience of Duke Wei of Chou. The Duke asked him, saying, "I have heard that Chu Hsien is studying the art of life. As you are a companion of his, pray tell me anything you know about it."

"I do but ply the broom at his outer gate," replied T'ien K'ai Chih; "what should I know about my Master's researches?"

"Don't be so modest," said the Duke. "I am very anxious to hear about it."

"Well," replied T'ien, " I have heard my master say that keeping life is like keeping a flock of sheep. You look out for the laggards and whip them up."

"What does that mean?" asked the Duke.

"In the State of Lu," said T'ien, "there was a man named Shan Pao. He lived on the mountains and drank water. All worldly interests he had put aside. And at the age of seventy, his complexion was like that of a child. Unluckily, he one day fell in with a hungry tiger who killed and ate him.

"There was also a man named Chang I, who frequented the houses of rich and poor alike. At the age of forty he was attacked by some internal disease and died.

"Shan Pao took care of his inner self, and a tiger ate his external man. Chang I took care of himself externally, but disease attacked him internally. These two individuals both omitted to whip up the laggards."

Confucius said, "Neither affecting obscurity, nor courting prominence, but unconsciously occupying the happy mean, —he who can attain to these three will enjoy a surpassing fame.

"In dangerous parts, where one wayfarer out of ten meets his death, fathers and sons and brothers will counsel each other not to travel without a sufficient escort. Is not this wisdom? And there where men are also greatly in danger, in the lists of passion, in the banquet hour, not to warn them is error indeed."

The Grand Augur, in his ceremonial robes, approached the shambles and thus addressed the pigs:——

"How can you object to die? I shall fatten you for three months. I shall discipline myself for ten days and fast for three. I shall strew fine grass and place you bodily upon a carved sacrificial dish. Does not this satisfy you?"

Then speaking from the pigs' point of view, he continued,

"It is better perhaps after all to live on bran and escape the shambles......."

"But then," added he, speaking from his own point of view, "to enjoy honour when alive one would readily die on a war-shield or in the headsman's basket."

So, he rejected the pigs' point of view and adopted his own point of view. In what sense then was he different from the pigs?

When Duke Huan was out hunting, with Kuan Chung as his charioteer, he saw a bogy. Catching hold of Kuan Chung's hand, he asked him, saying, "What do you see?"

"I see nothing," replied Kuan Chung. But when the Duke got home, he became delirious, and for many days was unable to go out.

There came a certain Huang Tzŭ Kao Ngao of the Ch'i State and said, "Your Highness is self-injured. How could a bogy injure you? When the vital strength is dissipated in anger, and is not renewed, there is a deficiency. When its tendency is in one direction upwards, the result is to incline men to wrath. When its tendency is in one direction downwards, the result is loss of memory. When it remains stagnant, in the middle of the body, the result is disease."

"Very well," said the Duke, "but are there such things as bogies?"

"There are," replied Huang. "There is the mud spirit Li; the fire spirit Kao; Lei T'ing, the spirit of the dust-bin; P'ei O and Wa Lung, sprites of the north-east; Yi Yang of the north-west; Wang Hsiang of the water; the Hsin of the hills; the K'uei of the mountain; the Pang Huang of the moor; the Wei I of the marsh."

"And what may the Wei I be like?" asked the Duke.

"The Wei I," replied Huang, " is as broad as a cart-wheel and as long as the shaft. It wears purple clothes and a red cap. It is a sentient being, and whenever it hears the rumble of thunder, it stands up in a respectful attitude. Those who see this bogy are like to be chieftains among men."

The Duke laughed exultingly and said, "The very one I saw!" Thereupon he dressed himself and sat up; and ere the day had closed, without knowing it, his sickness had left him.

Chi Hsing Tzŭ was training fighting cocks for the prince.

At the end of ten days the latter asked if they were ready. "Not yet," replied Chi; "they are in the stage of seeking fiercely for a foe."

Again, ten days elapsed, and the prince made a further enquiry. "Not yet," replied Chi; "they are still excited by the sounds and shadows of other cocks."

Ten days more, and the prince asked again. "Not yet," answered Chi; "the sight of an enemy is still enough to excite them to rage."

But after another ten days, when the prince again enquired, Chi said, "They will do. Other cocks may-crow, but they will take no notice. To look at them one might say they were of wood. Their virtue is complete. Strange cocks will not dare meet them but will run."

Confucius was looking at the cataract at Lü-liang. It fell from a height of thirty *jen*, and its foam reached forty *li* away. No scaly, finny creature could enter therein.

Yet Confucius saw an old man go in and thinking that he was suffering from some trouble and desirous of ending his life, bade a disciple run along the side to try and save him. The old man emerged about a hundred paces off, and with flowing hair went carolling along the bank. Confucius followed him and said, "I had thought, Sir, you were a spirit, but now I see you are a man. Kindly tell me, is there any way to deal thus with water?"

"No," replied the old man; "I have no way. There was my original condition to begin with; then habit growing into nature; and lastly acquiescence in destiny. Plunging in with the whirl, I come out with the swirl. I accommodate myself to the water, not the water to me. And so, I am able to deal with it after this fashion."

"What do you mean," enquired Confucius, "by your original condition to begin with, habit growing into nature, and acquiescence in destiny?"

"I was born," replied the old man, "upon dry land, and accommodated myself to dry land. That was my original condition. Growing up on the water, I accommodated myself to the water. That was what I meant by nature.

And doing as I did without being conscious of any effort so to do, that was what I meant by destiny."

Ch'ing, the chief carpenter, was carving wood into a stand for hanging musical instruments. When finished, the work appeared to those who saw it as though of supernatural execution. And the prince of Lu asked him, saying, "What mystery is there in your art?"

"No mystery, your Highness," replied Ch'ing; "and yet there is something.

"When I am about to make such a stand, I guard against any diminution of my vital power. I first reduce my mind to absolute quiescence. Three days in this condition, and I become oblivious of any reward to be gained. Five days, and I become oblivious of any fame to be acquired. Seven days, and I become unconscious of my four limbs and my physical frame. Then, with no thought of the Court present to my mind, my skill becomes concentrated, and all disturbing elements from without are gone. I enter some mountain forest. I search for a suitable tree. It contains the form required, which is afterwards elaborated. I see the stand in my mind's eye, and then set to work. Otherwise, there is nothing. I bring my own natural capacity into relation with that of the wood. What was suspected to be of supernatural execution in my work was due solely to this."

Tung Yeh Chi exhibited his charioteering skill before Duke Chuang.

Backwards and forwards he drove in lines which might have been ruled, sweeping round at each end in curves which might have been described by compasses.

The Duke, however, said that this was nothing more than weaving; and bidding him drive round and round a hundred times, returned home.

Yen Ho came upon him, and then went in and said to the Duke, "Chi's horses are on the point of breaking down."

The Duke remained silent, making no reply; and in a short time it was announced that the horses had actually broken down, and that Chi had gone away.

"How could you tell this?" said the Duke to Yen Ho.

"Because," replied the latter, "Chi was trying to make his horses perform a task to which they were unequal. Therefore, I said they would break down."

Ch'ui the artisan could draw circles with his hand better than with compasses. His fingers seemed to accommodate themselves so naturally to the thing he was working at, that it was unnecessary to fix his attention. His mental faculties thus remained ONE and suffered no hindrance.

To be unconscious of one's feet implies that the shoes are easy. To be unconscious of a waist implies that the girdle is easy. The intelligence being unconscious of positive and negative implies that the heart is at ease. No modifications within, no yielding to influences without,—this is ease under all conditions. And he who beginning with ease, is never not at ease, is unconscious of the ease of ease.

A certain Sun Hsiu went to the house of Pien Ch'ing Tzŭ and complained, saying, "In peace I am not considered wanting in propriety. In times of trouble I am not considered wanting in courage. Yet my crops fail; and officially I am not a success. From my village an outcast, I am an outlaw from my State. How have I offended against God that he should visit me with such a fate?"

"Have you not heard," replied Pien Tzŭ, "how the perfect man conducts himself? He is oblivious of his physical organisation. He is beyond the reach of sight and hearing. He moves outside the limits of this dusty world, rambling transcendentally in the domain of no-affairs. This is called acting but not from self-confidence, influencing but not from authority.

"But you, you make a show of your knowledge in order to startle fools. You cultivate yourself in contrast to the degradation of others. And you blaze along as though the sun and moon were under your arms.

Whereas, that you have a whole body in a whole skin, and have not perished in mid-career, dumb, blind, or halt, but actually hold a place among men, —this ought to be enough for you. Why rail at God? Begone!"

Sun Hsiu went away, and Pien Tzŭ went in and sat down. Shortly afterwards, he looked up to heaven and sighed; whereupon a disciple asked him what was the matter.

"When Hsiu was here just now," answered Pien Tzŭ, "I spoke to him of the virtue of the perfect man. I fear lest he be startled and so driven on to doubt."

"No, Sir," answered the disciple. "If he was right and you were wrong, wrong will never drive right into doubt. If, on the other hand, he was wrong and you were right, he brought his doubt with him, and you are not responsible." "Not so," said Pien Tzŭ. "Of old, when a bird alighted outside the capital of Lu, the prince was delighted, and killed an ox to feed it and had the *Chiu Shao* played to entertain it. The bird, however, was timid and dazed and dared not to eat or drink. This was treating the bird like oneself. But to treat a bird as a bird would treat a bird, you must put it to roost in a deep forest, let it swim in river or lake, and feed at its ease on the plain. Now Sun Hsiu is a man of small understanding; and for me to speak to him of the perfect man is like setting a mouse to ride in a coach or a band of music to play to a quail. How should he not be startled?"

CHAPTER XX. MOUNTAIN TREES.

Argument:

—The alternatives of usefulness and uselessness—TAO a *tertium quid*—The human a hindrance to the divine—Altruism—Adaptation— Destiny—Illustrations.

[This chapter is supplementary to chapter iv.]

CHUANG TZŬ was travelling over a mountain when he saw a huge tree well covered with foliage. A woodsman had stopped nearby, not caring to take it; and on Chuang Tzŭ enquiring the reason, he was told that it was of no use.

"This tree," cried Chuang Tzŭ, "by virtue of being good for nothing succeeds in completing its allotted span."

When Chuang Tzŭ left the mountain, he put up at the house of an old friend. The latter was delighted and ordered a servant to kill a goose and cook it.

"Which shall I kill?" enquired the servant; "the one that cackles or the one that doesn't?"

His master told him to kill the one which did not cackle. And accordingly, the next day, a disciple asked Chuang Tzŭ, saying, "Yesterday, that tree on the mountain, because good for nothing, was to succeed in completing its allotted span. But now, our host's goose, which is good for nothing, has to die. Upon which horn of the dilemma will you rest?"

"I rest," replied Chuang Tzŭ with a smile, "halfway between the two. In that position, appearing to be what I am not, it is impossible to avoid the troubles of mortality; though, if charioted upon TAO and floating far above mortality, this would not be so. No praise, no blame; both great and small; changing with the change of time, but ever without special effort; both above and below; making for harmony with surroundings; reaching creation's First Cause; swaying all things and swayed by none;—how then shall such troubles come? This was the method of Shên Nung and Huang Ti.

"But amidst the mundane passions and relationships of man, such would not be the case. For where there is union, there is also separation; where there is completion, there is also destruction; where there is purity, there is also oppression; where there is honour, there is also disparagement; where there is doing, there is also undoing; where there is openness, there is also underhandedness; and where there is no semblance, there is also deceit. How then can there be any fixed point? Alas indeed! Take note, my disciples, that such is to be found only in the domain of TAO."

I Liao of Shih-nan paid a visit to the prince of Lu. The latter wore a melancholy look; whereupon the philosopher of Shih-nan enquired what was the cause.

"I study the doctrines of the ancient Sages," replied the prince. "I carry on the work of my predecessors. I respect religion. I honour the good. Never for a moment do I relax in these points; yet I cannot avoid misfortune, and consequently I am sad."

"Your Highness' method of avoiding misfortune," said the philosopher of Shih-nan, "is but a shallow one. A handsome fox or a striped leopard will live in a mountain forest, hiding beneath some precipitous cliff. This is their repose. They come out at night and keep in by day. This is their caution. Though under the stress of hunger and thirst, they lie hidden, hardly venturing to slink secretly to the riverbank in search of food. This is their resoluteness. Nevertheless, they do not escape the misfortune of the net and the trap. But what crime have they committed? 'Tis their skin which is the cause of their trouble; and is not the State of Lu your Highness' skin? I would have your Highness put away body and skin alike, and cleansing your heart and purging it of passion, betake yourself to the land where mortality is not.

"In Nan-yüeh there is a district, called Established-Virtue. Its people are simple and honest, unselfish, and without passions. They can make but cannot keep. They give but look for no return. They are not conscious of fulfilling obligations. They are not conscious of subservience to etiquette.

Their actions are altogether uncontrolled, yet they tread in the way of the wise. Life is for enjoyment; death, for burial. And thither I would have your Highness proceed, power discarded, and the world left behind, only putting trust in TAO."

"The road is long and dangerous," said the prince. "Rivers and hills to be crossed, and I without boat or chariot;—what then?"

"Unhindered by body and unfettered in mind," replied the philosopher, "your Highness will be a chariot to yourself."

"But the road is long and dreary," argued the prince, "and uninhabited.

I shall have no one to turn to for help; and how, without food, shall I ever be able to get there?"

"Decrease expenditure and lessen desires," answered the philosopher, "and even though without provisions, there will be enough. And then through river and over sea your Highness will travel into shoreless illimitable space. From the borderland, those who act as escort will return; but thence onwards your Highness will travel afar.

"It is the human in ourselves which is our hindrance; and the human in others which causes our sorrow. The great Yao had not this human element himself, nor did he perceive it in others. And I would have your Highness put off this hindrance and rid yourself of this sorrow, and roam with TAO alone through the realms of Infinite Nought.

"Suppose a boat is crossing a river, and another empty boat is about to collide with it. Even an irritable man would not lose his temper. But supposing there was someone in the second boat. Then the occupant of the first would shout to him to keep clear. And if the other did not hear the first time, nor even when called to three times, bad language would inevitably follow. In the first case there was no anger, in the second there was; because in the first case the boat was empty, and in the second it was occupied. And so, it is with man. If he could only roam empty through life, who would be able to injure him?"

Pei Kung Shê, minister to Duke Ling of Wei, levied contributions for making bells. An altar was built outside the city gate; and in three months the bells, upper and lower, were all hung.

When Wang Tzŭ Ch'ing Chi saw them, he asked, saying, "How, Sir, did you manage this?"

"In the domain of ONE," replied Shê, "there may not be managing. I have heard say that which is carved and polished reverts nevertheless to its natural condition. And so, I made allowances for ignorance and for suspicion. I betrayed no feeling when welcomed or dismissed. I forbade not those who came, nor detained those who went away. I showed no resentment towards the unwilling, nor gratitude towards those who gave. Everyone subscribed what he liked; and thus in my daily collection of subscriptions, no injury was done.—How much more then those who have the great WAY?"

When Confucius was hemmed in between Ch'ên and Ts'ai, he passed seven days without food.

The minister Jen went to condole with him, and said, "You were near, Sir, to death."

"I was indeed," replied Confucius.

"Do you fear death, Sir?" enquired Jen.

"I do," said Confucius.

"Then I will try to teach you," said Jen, "the way not to die.

"In the eastern sea there are certain birds, called the *i-êrh*. They behave themselves in a modest and unassuming manner, as though unpossessed of ability. They fly simultaneously: they roost in a body. In advancing, none strives to be first; in retreating, none ventures to be last. In eating, none will be the first to begin; it is considered proper to take the leavings of others. Therefore, in their own ranks they are at peace, and the outside world is unable to harm them. And thus, they escape trouble.

"Straight trees are the first felled. Sweet wells are soonest exhausted. And you, you make a show of your knowledge in order to startle fools. You cultivate yourself in contrast to the degradation of others. And you blaze along as though the sun and moon were under your arms; consequently, you cannot avoid trouble.

"Formerly, I heard a very wise man say, Self-praise is no recommendation. In merit achieved there is deterioration. In fame achieved there is loss. Who can discard both merit and fame and become one with the rest? TAO pervades all things but is not seen. TÊ moves through all things but its place is not known. In its purity and constancy, it may be compared with the purposeless. Remaining concealed, rejecting power, it works not for merit nor for fame. Thus, not censuring others, it is not censured by others.

"And if the perfect man cares not for fame, why, Sir, should you take pleasure in it?"

"Good indeed!" replied Confucius; and forthwith he took leave of his friends and dismissed his disciples and retired to the wilds, where he dressed himself in skins and serge and fed on acorns and chestnuts. He passed among the beasts and birds and they took no heed of him. And if so, how much more among men?

Confucius asked Tzŭ Sang Hu, saying, "I have been twice expelled from Lu. My tree was cut down in Sung. I have been tabooed in Wei. I am a failure in Shang and Chou. I was surrounded between Ch'ên and Ts'ai. And in addition to all these troubles, my friends have separated from me and my disciples are gone. How is this?"

"Have you not heard," replied Sang Hu, "how when the men of Kuo fled, one of them, named Lin Hui, cast aside most valuable regalia and carried away his child upon his back? Someone suggested that he was influenced by the value of the child;—but the child's value was small. Or by the inconvenience of the regalia;—but the inconvenience of the child would be much greater. Why then did he leave behind the regalia and carry off the child?

"Lin Hui himself said, 'The regalia involved a mere question of money. The child was from God.'

"And so, it is that in trouble and calamity mere money questions are neglected, while we ever cling nearer to that which is from God. And between neglecting and clinging to, the difference is great.

"The friendship of the superior man is negative like water. The friendship of the mean man is full-flavoured like wine. That of the superior man passes from the negative to the affectionate. That of the mean man passes from the fullflavoured to nothing. The friendship of the mean man begins without due cause, and in like manner comes to an end.

"I hear and obey," replied Confucius; and forthwith he went quietly home, put an end to his studies and cast aside his books. His disciples no longer saluted him as teacher; but his love for them deepened every day.

On another occasion. Sang Hu said to him again, "When Shun was about to die, he commanded the Great Yü as follows:—Be careful. Act in accordance with your physical body. Speak in accordance with your feelings. You will thus not get into difficulty with the former nor suffer annoyance in the latter. And as under these conditions you will not stand in need of outward embellishment of any kind, it follows that you therefore will not stand in need of anything."

Chuang Tzŭ put on cotton clothes with patches in them, and arranging his girdle and tieing on his shoes, went to see the prince of Wei.

"How miserable you look, Sir!" cried the prince.

"It is poverty, not misery," replied Chuang Tzŭ. "A man who has TAO cannot be miserable. Ragged clothes and old boots make poverty, not misery. Mine is what is called being out of harmony with one's age.

"Has your Highness never seen a climbing ape? Give it some large tree, and it will twist and twirl among the branches as though monarch of all its surveys. Yi and Fêng

Mêng can never catch a glimpse of it.

"But put it in a bramble bush, and it will move autiously with sidelong glances, trembling all over with fear. Not that its muscles relax in the face of difficulty, but because it is at a disadvantage as regards position and is unable to make use of its skill. And how should anyone, living under foolish sovereigns and wicked ministers, help being miserable, even though he might wish not to be so?

"It was under such circumstances that Pi Kan was disembowelled."

When Confucius was hemmed in between Ch'ên and Ts'ai and had gone seven days without food, then, holding in his left hand a piece of dry wood and in his right hand a dry stick, he sang a ballad of Piao Shih.

He had an instrument, but the gamut was wanting. There was sound, but no tune. The sound of the wood accompanied by the voice of the man yielded a harsh result, but it was in keeping with the feelings of his audience.

Yen Hui, who was standing by in a respectful attitude, thereupon began to turn his eyes about him; and Confucius, fearing lest he should be driven by exaltation into bragging, or by a desire for safety into sorrow, spoke to him as follows:—

"Hui! it is easy to escape injury from God; it is difficult to avoid the benefits of man. There is no beginning and there is no end. Man and God are ONE. Who then was singing just now?"

"Pray, Sir, what do you mean," asked Yen Hui, "by saying that it is easy to escape injury from God?"

"Hunger, thirst, cold, and heat," replied Confucius, "are but as fetters in the path of life. They belong to the natural laws which govern the universe; and in obedience thereto I pass on my allotted course. The subject dares not disregard the mandates of his prince. And if this is man's duty to man, how much more shall it be his duty to God?"

"What is the meaning of difficult to avoid the benefits of man?" asked Yen Hui.

"If one begins," replied Confucius, "by adaptation to surroundings, rank and power follow without cease. Such advantages are external; they are not derived from oneself. And my life is more or less dependent upon the external. The superior man does not steal these; nor does the good man pilfer them. What then do I but take them as they come?

"Therefore, it has been said that no bird is so wise as the swallow. If it sees a place unfit to dwell in, it will not bestow a glance thereon; and even though it should drop food there, it will leave the food and fly away. Now swallows fear man. Yet they dwell among men. Because there they find their natural abode."

"And what is the meaning," enquired Yen Hui, "of no beginning and no end?"

"The work goes on," replied Confucius, "and no man knoweth the cause. How then shall he know the end, or the beginning? There is nothing left to us but to wait."

"And that man and God are O_{NE}," said Yen Hui. "What does that mean?"

"That man is," replied Confucius, "is from God. That God is, is also from God. That man is not God, is his nature.

The Sage quietly waits for death as the end."

When Chuang Tzŭ was wandering in the park at Tiao-ling, he saw a strange bird which came from the south. Its wings were seven feet across. Its eyes were an inch in circumference. And it flew close past Chuang Tzŭ's head to alight in a chestnut grove.

"What manner of bird is this?" cried Chuang Tzŭ. "With strong wings it does not fly away. With large eyes it does not see."

So he picked up his skirts and strode towards it with his cross-bow, anxious to get a shot. Just then he saw a cicada enjoying itself in the shade, forgetful of all else. And he saw a mantis spring and seize it, forgetting in the act its own body, which the strange bird immediately pounced upon and made its prey. And this it was which had caused the bird to forget its own nature.

"Alas!" cried Chuang Tzŭ with a sigh, "how creatures injure one another. Loss follows the pursuit of gain."

So he laid aside his bow and went home, driven away by the park-keeper who wanted to know what business he had there.

For three months after this, Chuang Tzŭ did not leave the house; and at length Lin Chü asked him, saying, "Master, how is it that you have not been out for so long?"

"While keeping my physical frame," replied Chuang Tzŭ, "I lost sight of my real self. Gazing at muddy water, I lost sight of the clear abyss. Besides, I have learnt from the Master as follows:—"When you go into the world, follow its customs."

Now when I strolled into the park at Tiao-ling, I forgot my real self. That strange bird which flew close past me to the chestnut grove, forgot its nature. The keeper of the chestnut grove took me for a thief. Consequently, I have not been out."

When Yang Tzŭ went to the Sung State, he passed a night at an inn.

The innkeeper had two concubines, one beautiful, the other ugly. The latter he loved; the former, he hated.

Yang Tzŭ asked how this was; whereupon one of the inn servants said, "The beautiful one is so conscious of her beauty that one does not think her beautiful. The ugly one is so conscious of her ugliness that one does not think her ugly."

"Note this, my disciples!" cried Yang Tzŭ. "Be virtuous, but without being consciously so; and wherever you go, you will be beloved."

CHAPTER XXI. Tien Tzŭ Fang.

Argument:

—Tao cannot be imparted in words—It is not at man's disposal—It does not consist in formal morality—It is an inalienable element of existence—Without it the soul dies—With it man is happy and his immortality secure—Illustrations.

[This chapter is supplementary to chapter vi.]

T'IEN Tzŭ Fang was in attendance upon Prince Wên of Wei.

He kept on praising Ch'i Kung, until at length Prince Wên said, "Is Ch'i Kung your tutor?"

"No," replied Tzŭ Fang; "he is merely a neighbour. He discourses admirably upon TAO. That is why I praise him."

"Have you then no tutor?" enquired the Prince.

"I have," replied Tzŭ Fang.

"And who may he be?" said Prince Wên.

"Tung Kuo Shun Tzŭ," answered Tzŭ Fang.

"Then how is it you do not praise him?" asked the Prince.

"He is perfect," replied Tzŭ Fang. "In appearance, a man; in reality, God. Unconditioned himself, he falls in with the conditioned, to his own greater glory. Pure himself, he can still tolerate others. If men are without TAO, by a mere look he calls them to a sense of error and causes their intentions to melt away. How could I praise him?"

Thereupon Tzŭ Fang took his leave, and the Prince remained for the rest of the day absorbed in silence. At length he called an officer in waiting and said, "How far beyond us is the man of perfect virtue! Hitherto I have regarded the discussion of holiness and wisdom, and the practice of charity and duty to one's neighbour, as the utmost point attainable. But now that I have heard of Tzŭ Fang's tutor, my body is relaxed and desires not movement, my mouth is closed and desires not speech. All I have learnt, verily it is mere undergrowth. And the kingdom of Wei is my bane."

When Wên Poh Hsüeh Tzŭ was on his way to Ch'i, he broke his journey in Lu. A certain man of Lu begged for an interview, but Wên Poh Hsüeh Tzŭ said, "No. I have heard that the gentlemen of the Middle Kingdom are experts in ceremonies and obligations, but wanting in knowledge of the human heart. I do not wish to see him."

So, he went on to Ch'i; but once more at Lu, on his way home, the same man again begged to have an interview.

"When I was last here," cried Wên Poh Hsüeh Tzŭ, "he asked to see me, and now again he asks to see me. Surely he must have something to communicate."

Whereupon he went and received the stranger, and on returning gave vent to sighs. Next day he received him again, and again after the interview gave vent to sighs. Then his servant asked him, saying, "How is it that whenever you receive this stranger, you always sigh afterwards?"

"I have already told you," replied Wên Poh Hsüeh Tzŭ, "that the people of the Middle Kingdom are experts in ceremonies and obligations but wanting in knowledge of the human heart. The man who visited me came in and went out as *per* compasses and square. His demeanour was now that of the dragon, now that of the tiger. He criticised me as though he had been my son. He admonished me as though he had been my father. Therefore, I gave vent to sighs.

When Confucius saw Wên Poh Hsüeh Tzŭ, the former did not utter a word. Whereupon Tzŭ Lu said, "Master, you have long wished to see Wên Poh Hsüeh Tzŭ. How is it that when you do see him you do not speak?"

"With such men as these," replied Confucius, you have only to look, and TAO abides. There is no room for speech."

Yen Yüan asked Confucius, saying, "Master, when you go at a walk, I go at a walk. When you trot, I trot. When you gallop, I gallop. But when you dash beyond the bounds of mortality, I can only stand staring behind. How is this?"

"Explain yourself," said Confucius.

"I mean," continued Yen Yüan, "that as you speak, I speak. As you argue, I argue. As you preach TAO, so I preach TAO. And by 'when you dash beyond the bounds of mortality I can only stand staring behind,' I mean that without speaking you make people believe you, without striving you make people love you, without factitious attractions you gather people around you. I cannot understand how this is so." "What is there to prevent you from finding out?" replied Confucius. "There is no sorrow to be compared with the death of the mind. The death of the body is of but secondary importance.

"The sun rises in the east and sets in the west. There is no place which he does not illuminate; and those who have eyes and feet depend upon him to use them with success. When he comes forth, that is existence; when he disappears, that is non-existence.

"And every human being has that upon which he depends for death or for life.

But if I, receiving this mind-informed body, pass without due modification to the end, day and night subject to ceaseless wear and tear like a mere thing, unknowing what the end will be, and in spite of this mind-informed body conscious only that fate cannot save me from the inevitable grave-yard,—then I am consuming life until at death it is as though you and I had but once linked arms to be finally parted for ever! Is not that indeed a cause for sorrow?

"Now you fix your attention upon something in me which, while you look, has already passed away. Yet you seek for it as though it must be still there,—like one who seeks for a horse in a market-place.

What I admire in you is transitory. Nevertheless, why should you grieve? Although my old self is constantly passing away, there remains that which does not pass away."

Confucius went to see Lao Tzŭ. The latter had just washed his head, and his hair was hanging down his back to dry. He looked like a lifeless body; so Confucius waited awhile, but at length approached and said, "Do my eyes deceive me, or is this really so? Your frame, Sir, seems like dry wood, as if it had been left without that which informs it with the life of man."

"I was wandering," replied Lao Tzŭ, "in the unborn."

"What does that mean? " asked Confucius.

"My mind is trammelled," replied Lao Tzŭ, "and I cannot know. My mouth is closed and I cannot speak. But I will try to tell you what is probably the truth.

252

"The perfect Negative principle is majestically passive. The perfect Positive principle is powerfully active. Passivity emanates from heaven above; activity proceeds from earth beneath. The interaction of the two results in that harmony by which all things are produced. There may be a First Cause, but we never see his form. His report fills space.

There is darkness and light. Days come and months go. Work is being constantly performed, yet we never witness the performance. Life must bring us from somewhere, and death must carry us back. Beginning and end follow ceaselessly one upon the other, and we cannot say when the series will be exhausted. If this is not the work of a First Cause, what is it?"

"Kindly explain," said Confucius, "what is to be got by wandering as you said."

"The result," answered Lao Tzŭ, "is perfect goodness and perfect happiness. And he who has these is a perfect man."

"And by what means," enquired Confucius, "can this be attained?"

"Animals," said Lao Tzŭ, "that eat grass do not mind a change of pasture. Creatures that live in water do not mind a change of pond. A slight change may be effected so long as the essential is untouched.

"Joy, anger, sorrow, happiness, find no place in that man's breast; for to him all creation is O~NE~. And all things being thus united in O~NE~, is body and limbs are but as dust of the earth, and life and death, beginning and end, are but as night and day, and cannot destroy his peace. How much less such trifles as gain or loss, misfortune or good fortune?

"He rejects rank as so much mud. For he knows that if a man is of honourable rank, the honour is in himself, and cannot be lost by change of condition, nor exhausted by countless modifications of existence. Who then can grieve his heart? Those who practise TAO understand the secret of this."

"Master," said Confucius, "your virtue equals that of Heaven and Earth; yet you still employ perfect precepts in the cultivation of your heart. Who among the sages of old could have uttered such words?"

"Not so," answered Lao Tzŭ. "The fluidity of water is not the result of any effort on the part of the water, but is its natural property. And the virtue of the perfect man is such that even without cultivation there is nothing which can withdraw from his sway. Heaven is naturally high, the earth is naturally solid, the sun and moon are naturally bright. Do they cultivate these attributes?"

Confucius went forth and said to Yen Hui, "In point of TAO, I am but as an animalcule in vinegar. Had not the Master opened my eyes, I should not have perceived the vastness of the universe."

When Chuang Tzŭ was at an interview with Duke Ai of Lu, the latter said, "We have many scholars, Sir, in Lu, but few of your school."

"In Lu," replied Chuang Tzŭ, "there are but few scholars."

"Look at the number who wear scholars' robes," said the Duke. "How can you say they are few?"

"Scholars who wear round hats," answered Chuang Tzŭ, "know the seasons of Heaven. Scholars who wear square shoes know the shape of Earth.

And scholars who loosely gird themselves are ready to decide whatever questions may arise. But scholars who have TAO do not necessarily wear robes; neither does the wearing of robes necessarily mean that a scholar has TAO. If your Highness does not think so, why not issue an order through the Middle Kingdom, making death the punishment for all who wear the robes without having the TAO?"

Thereupon Duke Ai circulated this mandate for five days, the result being that not a single man in Lu dared to don scholars' robes,—with the exception of one old man who, thus arrayed, took his stand at the Duke's gate.

The Duke summoned him to the presence, and asked him many questions on politics, trying to entangle him, but in vain. Then Chuang Tzŭ said, "If there is only one scholar in Lu, surely that is not many."

Rank and power had no charms for Poh Li Ch'i.

So, he took to feeding cattle. His cattle were always fat, which caused Duke Muh of Ch'in to ignore his low condition and entrust him with the administration.

Shun cared nothing for life or death. He was therefore able to influence men's hearts.

Prince Yüan of Sung desiring to draw a map, the officials of that department presented themselves, and after making obeisance stood waiting for the order, more than half of them already licking their brushes and mixing their ink.

One of them arrived late. He sauntered in without hurrying himself; and when he had made obeisance, did not wait but went off home.

The Prince sent a man to see what he did. He took off his clothes and squatted down bare-backed.

"He will do," cried the Prince. "He is a true artist."

When Wên Wang was on a tour of inspection in Tsang, he saw an old man fishing. But his fishing was not real fishing, for he did not fish to catch fish, but to amuse himself.

So, Wên Wang wished to employ him in the administration of government, but feared lest his own ministers, uncles, and brothers, might object. On the other hand, if he let the old man go, he could not bear to think of the people being deprived of such an influence.

Accordingly, that very morning he informed his ministers, saying, "I once dreamt that a Sage of a black colour and with a large beard, riding upon a parti-coloured horse with red stockings on one side, appeared and instructed me to place the administration in the hands of the old gentleman of Tsang, promising that the people would benefit greatly thereby."

The ministers at once said, "It is a command from your Highness' father."

"I think so," answered Wên Wang. "But let us try by divination."

"It is a command from your Highness' late father," said the ministers, "and may not be disobeyed. What need for divination?"

So, the old man of Tsang was received and entrusted with the administration. He altered none of the existing statutes. He issued no unjust regulations. And when, after three years, Wên Wang made another inspection, he found all dangerous organisations broken up, the officials doing their duty as a matter of course, while the use of measures of grain was unknown within the four boundaries of the State. There was thus unanimity in the public voice, singleness of official purpose, and identity of interests to all.

So Wên Wang appointed the old man Grand Tutor; and then, standing with his face to the north, asked him, saying, "Can such government be extended over the empire?"

The old man of Tsang was silent and made no reply. He then abruptly took leave, and by the evening of that same day had disappeared, never to be heard of again.

Yen Yüan said to Confucius, "If Wên Wang was unable to do this of himself, how was he able to do it by a dream?"

"Silence!" cried Confucius: "It is not for you to criticise Wên Wang who succeeded in fulfilling his mission. The dream was merely to satisfy the vulgar mind."

Lieh Yü K'ou instructed Poh Hun Wu Jên in archery. Drawing the bow to its full, he placed a cup of water on his elbow and began to let fly. Hardly was one arrow out of sight ere another was on the string, the archer standing all the time like a statue.

"But this is shooting under ordinary conditions," cried Poh Hun Wu Jên; "it is not shooting under extraordinary conditions. Now I will ascend a high mountain with you, and stand on the edge of a precipice a thousand feet in height, and see how you can shoot then."

Thereupon Wu Jên went with Lieh Tzŭ up a high mountain, and stood on the edge of a precipice a thousand feet in height, approaching it backwards until one-fifth of his feet overhung the chasm, when he beckoned to Lieh Tzŭ to come on. But the latter had fallen prostrate on the ground, with the sweat pouring down to his heels.

"The perfect man," said Wu Jên, "soars up to the blue sky, or dives down to the yellow springs, or flies to some extreme point of the compass, without change of countenance. But you are terrified, and your eyes are dazed. Your internal economy is defective."

Chien Wu said to Sun Shu Ao, "Sir, you have been three times called to office without showing any elation, and you have been three times dismissed without displaying any chagrin. At first, I doubted you; but now I notice that your breathing is perfectly regular. How do you manage thus to control your emotions?"

"I am no better than other people," replied Sun Shu Ao. "I regard office when it comes as something which may not be declined; when it goes, as something which cannot be kept. To me both the getting and losing are outside my own self; and therefore I feel no chagrin. How am I better than other people?

"Besides, I am not conscious of office being either in the hands of others or in my own. If it is in the hands of others, my own personality disappears; if in mine, theirs. And amidst the cares of deliberation and investigation, what leisure has one for troubling about rank?"

When Confucius heard this, he said, "The perfect Sages of old!—cunning men could not defeat them; beautiful women could not seduce them; robbers could not steal from them;

Fu Hsi and the Yellow Emperor could not make friends of them. Life and death are great; yet these gave them no pang.

How much less then rank and power!

"The souls of such men pierced through huge mountains as though they had been nothing; descended into the abyss without getting wet; occupied lowly stations without chagrin. They filled the whole universe; and the more they gave to others, the more they had themselves."

The Prince of Ch'u was sitting with the Prince of Fan. By and by, one of the officials of Ch'u said, "There were three indications of the destruction of the Fan State."

"The destruction of the Fan State," cried the Prince of Fan, "did not suffice to injure my existence.

And while the destruction of the Fan State did not suffice to injure my existence, the preservation of the Ch'u State will not be enough to preserve yours.

From this point of view, it will be seen that while we Fans have not begun to be destroyed, you Ch'us have not begun to exist."

CHAPTER XXII. KNOWLEDGE TRAVELS NORTH.

Argument:

—Inaction and TAO—The universe our model—Spontaneity our watchword—Omnipresence and indivisibility of TAO—External activity, internal passivity—Man's knowledge finite—Illustrations.

[This chapter is supplementary to chapter vi.]

WHEN Knowledge travelled north, across the Black Water, and over the Dark-Steep Mountain, he met Do-nothing Say-nothing and asked of him as follows:—

"Kindly tell me by what thoughts, by what cogitations, may TAO be known? By resting in what, by according in what, may TAO be approached? By following what, by pursuing what, may TAO be attained?"

To these three questions. Do-nothing Say-nothing returned no answer. Not that he would not answer, but that he could not. So when Knowledge got no reply, he turned round and went off to the south of the White Water and up the Kuchüeh Mountain, where he saw All-in-extremes, and to him he put the same questions.

"Ha!" cried All-in-extremes, "I know. I will tell you . . . . . ." But just as he was about to speak, he forgot what he wanted to say. So, when Knowledge got no reply, he went back to the palace and asked the Yellow Emperor. The latter said, "By no thoughts, by no cogitations, TAO may be known. By resting in nothing, by according in nothing, TAO may be approached. By following nothing, by pursuing nothing, TAO may be attained."

Then Knowledge said to the Yellow Emperor, "Now you and I know this, but those two know it not. Who is right?"

"Of those two," replied the Yellow Emperor, "Do-nothing Say-nothing is genuinely right, and All-in-extremes is near. You and I are wholly wrong. Those who understand it do not speak about it, those who speak about it do not understand it.

Therefore, the Sage teaches a doctrine which does not find expression in words.

258

TAO cannot be made to come. Virtue cannot be reached.

Charity can be evoked. Duty to one's neighbour can be wrongly directed. Ceremonies are mere shams.

"Therefore, it has been said, 'If TAO perishes, then TÊ will perish. If Tê perishes, then charity will perish. If charity perishes, then duty to one's neighbour will perish. If duty to one's neighbour perishes, then ceremonies will perish. Ceremonies are but a showy ornament of TAO, while ofttimes the source of trouble.'

"Therefore, it has been said, 'Those who practise TAO suffer daily loss. If that loss proceeds until inaction ensues, then by that very inaction there is nothing which cannot be done.'

"Now, we are already beings. And if we desire to revert to our original condition, how difficult that is! 'Tis a change to which only the greatest among us are equal.

"Life follows upon death. Death is the beginning of life. Who knows when the end is reached? "The life of man results from convergence of the vital fluid. Its convergence is life; its dispersion, death. If then life and death are but consecutive states, what need have I to complain?

"Therefore, all things are O_{NE}. What we love is animation.

What we hate is corruption. But corruption in its turn becomes animation, and animation once more becomes corruption.

"Therefore, it has been said, The world is permeated by a single vital fluid, and Sages accordingly venerate ONE."

Then Knowledge said to the Yellow Emperor, "I asked Donothing Say-nothing, but he did not answer me. Not that he would not; he could not. So I asked All-in-extremes. He was just going to tell me, but he did not tell me. Not that he would not; but just as he was going to do so, he forgot what he wanted to say. Now I ask you, and you tell me. How then are you wholly wrong?"

"Of those two," replied the Yellow Emperor, "the former was genuinely right, inasmuch as he did not *know*. The latter was near, inasmuch as he *forgot*. You and I are wholly wrong, inasmuch as we *know*.

When All-in-extremes heard of this, he considered that the Yellow Emperor had spoken well.

The universe is very beautiful, yet it says nothing. The four seasons abide by a fixed law, yet they are not heard. All creation is based upon absolute principles, yet nothing speaks.

And the true Sage, taking his stand upon the beauty of the universe, pierces the principles of created things. Hence the saying that the perfect man does nothing, the true Sage performs nothing, beyond gazing at the universe.

For man's intellect, however keen, face to face with the countless evolutions of things, their death and birth, their squareness and roundness,—can never reach the root. There creation is, and there it has ever been.

The six cardinal points, reaching into infinity, are ever included in TAO. An autumn spikelet, in all its minuteness, must carry TAO within itself. There is nothing on earth which does not rise and fall, but it never perishes altogether.

The *Yin* and the *Yang*, and the four seasons, keep to their proper order. Apparently destroyed, yet really existing; the material gone, the immaterial left;—such is the law of creation, which passeth all understanding. This is called the root, whence a glimpse may be obtained of God.

Yeh Ch'üeh enquired of P'i I about TAO.

The latter said, "Keep your body under proper control, your gaze concentrated upon O$_{NE}$,—and the peace of God will descend upon you. Keep back your knowledge, and concentrate your thoughts upon O$_{NE}$,—and the holy spirit shall abide within you. Virtue shall beautify you, Tao shall establish you, aimless as a new-born calf which recks not how it came into the world."

While P'i I was still speaking, Yeh Ch'üeh had gone off to sleep; at which the former rejoiced greatly, and departed singing,

> "Body like dry bone, Mind like dead ashes;
> This is true knowledge.
> Not to strive after knowing the whence.
> In darkness, in obscurity.
> The mindless cannot plan;—
> What manner of *man* is that?"

Shun asked Ch'êng, saying, "Can one get TAO so as to have it for one's own?"

"Your very body," replied Ch'eng, "is not your own. How should TAO be?"

"If my body," said Shun, "is not my own, pray whose is it?"

"It is the delegated image of God," replied Ch'êng. "Your life is not your own. It is the delegated harmony of God.

Your individuality is not your own. It is the delegated adaptability of God.

Your posterity is not your own. It is the delegated exuviæ of God.

You move, but know not how. You are at rest, but know not why. You taste, but know not the cause. These are the operation of God's laws. How then should you get Tag so as to have it for your own?"

Confucius said to Lao Tzŭ, "To-day you are at leisure. Pray tell me about perfect TAO."

"Purge your heart by fasting and discipline," answered Lao Tzŭ. "Wash your soul as white as snow. Discard your knowledge. TAO is abstruse and difficult of discussion. I will try, however, to speak to you of its outline.

"Light is born of darkness. Classification is born of formlessness. The soul is born of TAO. The body is born of the vital essence.

"Thus, all things produce after their kind. Creatures with nine channels of communication are born from the womb.

Creatures with eight are born from the egg.

Of their coming there is no trace. In their departure there is no goal. No entrance gate, no dwelling house, they pass this way and that, as though at the meeting of cross-roads.

"Those who enter herein become strong of limb, subtle of thought, and clear of sight and hearing. They suffer no mental fatigue, nor meet with physical resistance.

"Heaven cannot but be high. Earth cannot but be broad. The sun and moon cannot but revolve. All creation cannot but flourish. To do so is their TAO.

"But it is not from extensive study that this may be known, nor by dialectic skill that this may be made clear. The true Sage will have none of these. It is in addition without gain, in diminution without loss, that the true Sage finds salvation.

"Unfathomable as the sea, wondrously ending only to begin again, informing all creation without being exhausted, the TAO of the perfect man is spontaneous in its operation. That all creation can be informed by it without exhaustion, is its TAO.

"In the Middle Kingdom there are men who recognise neither positive nor negative. They abide between heaven and earth. They act their part as mortals, and then return to the Cause.

"From that standpoint, life is but a concentration of the vital fluid, whose longest and shortest terms of existence vary by an inappreciable space,— hardly enough for the classification of Yao and Chieh.

"Tree-fruits and plant-fruits exhibit order in their varieties; and the relationships of man, though more difficult to be dealt with, may still be reduced to order.

The true Sage who meets with these, does not violate them. Neither does he continue to hold fast by them.

Adaptation by arrangement is Tê. Spontaneous adaptation is TAO, by which sovereigns flourish and princes succeed.

"Man passes through this sublunary life as a white horse passes a crack. Here one moment, gone the next. Neither are there any not equally subject to the ingress and egress of mortality. One modification brings life; then another, and it is death. Living creatures cry out; human beings sorrow. The bow-sheath is slipped off; the clothes-bag is dropped; and in the confusion the soul wings its flight, and the body follows, on the great journey home!

"The reality of the formless, the unreality of that which has form,—this is known to all. Those who are on the road to attainment care not for these things, but the people at large discuss them. Attainment implies non-discussion: discussion implies non-attainment. Manifested, TAO has no objective value; hence silence is better than argument. It cannot be translated into speech; better then say nothing at all. This is called the great attainment."

Tung Kuo Tzŭ asked Chuang Tzŭ, saying, "What you call TAO,—where is it?"

"There is nowhere," replied Chuang Tzŭ, "where it is not."

"Tell me one place at any rate where it is," said Tung Kuo Tzŭ.

"It is in the ant," replied Chuang Tzŭ.

"Why go so low down?" asked Tung Kuo Tzŭ.

"It is in a tare," said Chuang Tzŭ.

"Still lower," objected Tung Kuo Tzŭ.

"It is in a potsherd," said Chuang Tzŭ.

"Worse still!" cried Tung Kuo Tzŭ.

"It is in ordure," said Chuang Tzŭ. And Tung Kuo Tzŭ made no reply.

"Sir," continued Chuang Tzŭ, "your question does not touch the essential. When Huo, inspector of markets, asked the managing director about the fatness of pigs, the test was always made in parts least likely to be fat. Do not therefore insist in any particular direction; for there is nothing which escapes. Such is perfect TAO; and such also is ideal speech. *Whole, entire, all,* are three words which sound differently but mean the same. Their purport is ONE.

"Try to reach with me the palace of Nowhere, and there, amidst the identity of all things, carry your discussions into the infinite. Try to practise with me inaction, wherein you may rest motionless, without care, and be happy. For thus my mind becomes an abstraction. It wanders not, and yet is not conscious of being at rest. It goes and comes and is not conscious of stoppages. Backwards and forwards without being conscious of any goal. Up and down the realms of Infinity, wherein even the greatest intellect would fail to find an end.

"That which makes things the things they are, is not limited to such things. The limits of things are their own limits in so far as they are things. The limits of the limitless, the limitlessness of the limited,—these are called fulness and emptiness, renovation and decay. TAO causes fulness and emptiness, but it is not either. It causes renovation and decay, but it is not either. It causes beginning and end, but it is not either. It causes accumulation and dispersion, but it is not either."

O Ho Kan was studying with Shên Nung under Lao Lung Chi.

Shên Nung used to remain shut up, with his head on the table, absorbed in daydreams. On one occasion, O Ho Kan knocked at the door, and entering said, "Lao Lung is dead!"

Thereupon Shên Nung, leaning on his staff, arose; and flinging down his staff with a bang, smiled and said, "O my Master, thou knewest me to be worthless and self-sufficient, and thou didst leave me and die. Now I, having no scope for my vain talk, I too will die."

When Yen Kang Tiao heard this, he said, "Those who exemplify TAO are sought after by all the best men in the empire. Now if one who has not attained to more TAO than the ten-thousandth part of the tip of an autumn spikelet, is still wise enough to withhold vain talk and die,—how much more those who exemplify TAO? To the eye it is formless, and to the ear it is noiseless. Those who discuss it, speak of it as 'the obscure.' But the mere fact of discussing Tao makes it not TAO."

At this the Empyrean asked Without-end, saying, "Do you know TAO?"

"I do not," replied Without-end; whereupon the Empyrean proceeded to ask Inaction.

"I do know TAO," said Inaction.

"Is there any method," asked the Empyrean, "by which you know TAO?"

"There is," replied Inaction.

"What is it?" asked the Empyrean.

"I know," answered Inaction, "that TAO may honour and dishonour, bind and loose. That is the method by which I know TAO."

The Empyrean repeated these words to No-beginning, and asked him which was right, the ignorance of Without-end or the knowledge of Inaction.

"Not to know," replied No-beginning, "is profound. To know is shallow. Not to know is internal. To know is external."

Here the Empyrean broke in with a sigh, "Then ignorance is knowledge, and knowledge ignorance! But pray whose knowledge is the knowledge of not knowing?"

"TAO," said No-beginning, "cannot be heard. Heard, it is not TAO. It cannot be seen. Seen, it is TAO. It cannot be spoken. Spoken, it is not TAO. That which imparts form to forms is itself formless; therefore, TAO cannot have a name."

No-beginning continued, "He who replies to one asking about TAO, does not know TAO. Although one may hear about TAO, he does not really hear about TAO. There is no such thing as asking about TAO. There is no such thing as answering such questions. To ask a question which cannot be asked is vain. To answer a question which cannot be answered is unreal. And one who thus meets the vain with the unreal is one who has no physical perception of the universe, and no mental perception of the origin of existence,—unfit alike to roam over the K'un-lun peak or to soar into the Supreme Void."

Light asked Nothing, saying, "Do you, Sir, exist, or do you not exist?"

But getting no answer to his question, Light set to work to watch for the appearance of Nothing.

Hidden, vacuous,—all day long he looked but could not see it, listened but could not hear it, grasped at but could not seize it.

"Bravo!" cried Light. "Who can equal this? I can get to be nothing, but I cannot get as far as the absence of nothing. Assuming that Nothing has an objective existence, how can it reach this next stage?"

The man who forged swords for the Minister of War was eighty years of age. Yet he never made the slightest slip in his work.

The Minister of War said to him, "Is it your skill, Sir, or have you any method?"

"It is concentration," replied the man. "When twenty years old, I took to forging swords. I cared for nothing else. If a thing was not a sword, I did not notice it. I availed myself of whatever energy I did not use in other directions in order to secure greater efficiency in the direction required. Still more of that which is never without use;—

So that there was nothing which did not lend its aid.

Jen Ch'iu asked Confucius, saying, "Can we know about the time before the universe existed?"

"We can," replied Confucius. "Time was of old precisely what it is now."

At this rebuff, Jen Ch'iu withdrew. Next day he again visited Confucius and said, "Yesterday when I asked you that question and you answered me, I was quite clear about it. To-day I am confused. How is this?"

"Your clearness of yesterday," answered Confucius, "was because my answer appealed direct to your natural intelligence. Your confusion of to-day results from the intrusion of something other than the natural intelligence. There is no past, no present, no beginning, no end. To have posterity before one has posterity,—is that possible?"

Jen Ch'iu made no answer, and Confucius continued, "That will do. Do not reply. If life did not give birth to death, and if death did not put an end to life, surely life and death would be no longer correlates, but would each exist independently. What there was before the universe, was TAO. TAO makes things what they are, but is not itself a thing. Nothing can produce TAO; yet everything has TAO within it, and continues to produce it without end.

And the endless love of the Sage for his fellow-man is based upon the same principle."

Yen Yüan asked Confucius, saying, "Master, I have heard you declare that there may be no eagerness to conform, no effort to adapt. If so, pray how are we to get along?"

"The men of old," replied Confucius, "practised physical, but not moral, modification.

The men of to-day practise moral, not physical modification.

Let your modification extend to the external only. Internally, be constant without modification.

"How shall you modify, and how shall you not modify? How reconcile the divergence?—By not admitting division.

"There was the garden of Hsi Wei, the park of the Yellow Emperor, the palace of Shun, the halls of T'ang and Wu.

These were perfect men; but had they been taught by Confucianists and Mihists, they would have hammered one another to pieces over scholastic quibbles. How much more then the men of to-day?

"The perfect Sage, in his relations with the external world, injures nothing. Neither does anything injure him. And only he who is thus exempt can be trusted to conform and to adapt.

"Mountain forests and loamy fields swell my heart with joy. But ere the joy be passed, sorrow is upon me again.

Joy and sorrow come and go, and over them I have no control.

"Alas! the life of man is but as a stoppage at an inn. He knows that which comes within the range of his experience. Otherwise, he knows not. He knows that he can do what he can do, and that he cannot do what he cannot do. But there is always that which he does not know and that which he cannot do; and to struggle that it shall not be so,—is not this a cause for grief?

"The best language is that which is not spoken, the best form of action is that which is without deeds.

Spread out your knowledge and it will be found to be shallow."

Mixed Chapters.

CHAPTER XXIII. *KÊNG SANG CH'U.*

Argument:

—The operation of TAO is not seen—Spheres of action vary—TAO remains the same—Spontaneity essential—TAO can be divided but remains entire—It is infinite as Time and Space—It is unconditioned—The external and the internal—Illustrations.

AMONG the disciples of Lao Tzŭ was one named Kêng Sang Ch'u. He alone had attained to the TAO of his Master. He lived up north, on the Wei-lei Mountains. Of his attendants, he dismissed those who were systematically clever or conventionally charitable. The useless remained with him; the incompetent served him. And in three years the district of Wei-lei was greatly benefited.

One of the inhabitants said in conversation, "When Mr. Kêng Sang first came among us, we did not know what to make of him. Now, we could not say enough about him in a day, and even a year would leave something unsaid. Surely, he must be a true Sage. Why not pray to him as to the spirits, and honour him as a tutelary god of the land?"

On hearing of this, Kêng Sang Ch'u turned his face to the south in shame, at which his disciples were astonished. But Kêng Sang said, "What cause have you for astonishment? The influence of spring quickens the life of plants, and autumn brings them to maturity. In the absence of any agent, how is this so? It is the operation of TAO.

"I have heard that the perfect man may be pent up like a corpse in a tomb, yet the people will become unartificial and without care.

But now these poor people of Wei-lei wish to exalt me among their wise and good. Surely then I am but a shallow vessel; and therefore I was shamed for the doctrine of Lao Tzŭ."

The disciples said, "Not so. In a sixteen-foot ditch a big fish has not room to turn round; but 'tis the very place for an eel. On a six or seven-foot hillock a large beast finds no shelter, while the uncanny fox gladly makes its lair therein. Besides, ever since the days of Yao and Shun it has always been customary to honour the virtuous, advance the able, give precedence to the good and useful. Why not then among the people of Wei-lei? Let them do it, Sir."

"Come here, my children," said Kêng Sang Ch'u. "A beast big enough to swallow a cart, if it wanders alone from the hills, will not escape the sorrow of the snare. A fish big enough to gulp down a boat, if stranded on the dry shore will become a prey to ants. Therefore, it is that birds and beasts love height, and fishes and turtles love depth. And the man who cares for himself hides his body. He loves the occult.

"As to Yao and Shun, what claim have they to praise? Their fine distinctions simply amounted to knocking a hole in a wall in order to stop it up with brambles; to combing each individual hair; to counting the grains for a rice pudding! How in the name of goodness did they profit their generation?

"If the virtuous are honoured, emulation will ensue. If knowledge be fostered, the result will be theft.

These things are of no use to make people good. The struggle for wealth is so severe. Sons murder their fathers; ministers their princes; men rob in broad daylight, and bore through walls at high noon. I tell you that the root of this great evil is from Yao and Shun, and that its branches will extend into a thousand ages to come. A thousand ages hence, man will be feeding upon man!"

Nan Yung Ch'u sadly straightened his seat and said, "But what is one of my age to do that he may attain to this?"

"Preserve your form complete," said Kêng Sang, "your vitality secure. Let no anxious thoughts intrude. And then in three years' space you may attain to this."

"I do not know," said Nan Yung, "that there is any difference in the form of eyes; yet blind men cannot see. I do not know that there is any difference in the form of ears; yet deaf men cannot hear. I do not know that there is any difference in the form of hearts; yet fools cannot use theirs to any purpose. The forms are alike; yet there is something which differentiates them. One will succeed, and another will not. Yet you tell me to preserve my form complete, my vitality secure, and let no anxious thoughts intrude. But so far I only hear TAO with my ears."

"Well said!" cried Kêng Sang; and then he added, "Small wasps cannot transform huge caterpillars.

Bantams cannot hatch the eggs of geese. The fowls of Lu can. Not that there is any difference in the hatching power of chickens. One can and another cannot, because one is naturally fitted for working on a large, the other on a small scale. My talents are of the latter order. I cannot transform you. Why not go south and see Lao Tzŭ?"

So, Nan Yung took some provisions, and after a seven days' journey arrived at the abode of Lao Tzŭ.

"Have you come from Kêng Sang Ch'u?" said the latter.

"I have," replied Nan Yung.

"But why," said Lao Tzŭ, "bring all these people with you?"

Nan Yung looked back in alarm, and Lao Tzŭ continued, "Do you not understand what I say?"

Nan Yung bent his head abashed, and then looking up, said with a sigh, "I have now forgotten how to answer, in consequence of missing what I came to ask."

"What do you mean?" said Lao Tzŭ.

"If I do not know," replied Nan Yung, "men call me a fool. If I do know, I injure myself. If I am not charitable, I injure others. If I am, I injure myself. If I do not do my duty to my neighbour, I injure others. If I do it, I injure myself. My trouble lies in not seeing how to escape from these three dilemmas. On the strength of my connection with Kêng Sang, I would venture to ask advice."

"When I saw you," said Lao Tzŭ, "I knew in the twinkling of an eye what was the matter with you. And now what you say confirms my view. You are confused, as a child that has lost its parents. You would fathom the sea with a pole. You are astray. You are struggling to get back to your natural self, but cannot find the way. Alas! alas!"

Nan Yung begged to be allowed to remain, and set to work to cultivate the good and eliminate the evil within him. At the expiration of ten days, with sorrow in his heart, he again sought Lao Tzŭ.

"Have you thoroughly cleansed yourself? " said Lao Tzŭ. "But this grieved look...... There is some evil obstruction yet.

"If the disturbances are external,

do not be always combating them, but close the channels to the mind. If the disturbances are internal, do not strive to oppose them, but close all entrance from without.

If the disturbances are both internal and external, then you will not even be able to hold fast to TAO, still less practise
it."

"If a rustic is sick," said Nan Yung, "and another rustic goes to see him; and if the sick man can say what is the matter with him,—then he is not seriously ill. Yet my search after TAO is like swallowing drugs which only increase the malady.

I beg therefore merely to ask the art of preserving life."

"The art of preserving life," replied Lao Tzŭ, "consists in being able to keep all in ONE, to lose nothing, to estimate good and evil without divination, to know when to stop, and how much is enough, to leave others alone and attend to oneself, to be without cares and without knowledge,—to be in fact as a child. A child will cry all day and not become hoarse, because of the perfection of its constitutional harmony.

It will keep its fist tightly closed all day and not open it, because of the concentration of its virtue. It will gaze all day without taking off its eyes, because its sight is not attracted by externals. In motion, it knows not whither it is bound; at rest, it is not conscious of doing anything; but unconsciously adapts itself to the exigencies of its environment. This is the art of preserving life."

"Is this then the virtue of the perfect man?" cried Nan Yung.

"Not so," said Lao Tzŭ. "I am, as it were, but breaking the ice.

"The perfect man shares the food of this earth, but the happiness of God. He does not incur trouble either from men or things. He does not join in censuring, in plotting, in toadying. Free from care he comes, and unconscious he goes;—this is the art of preserving life."

"This then is perfection?" inquired Nan Yung.

"Not yet," said Lao Tzŭ. "I specially asked if you could be as a child. A child acts without knowing what it does; moves without knowing whither. Its body is like a dry branch; its heart like dead ashes. Thus, good and evil fortune find no lodgment therein; and there where good and evil fortune are not, how can the troubles of mortality be?

"Those whose hearts are in a state of repose give forth a divine radiance, by the light of which they see themselves as they are. And only by cultivating such repose can man attain to the constant.

"Those who are constant are sought after by men and assisted by God. Those who are sought after by men are the people of God; those who are assisted by God are his chosen children.

"To study this is to study what cannot be learnt. To practise this is to practise what cannot be accomplished. To discuss this is to discuss what can never be proved. Let knowledge stop at the unknowable. That is perfection. And for those who do not follow this, God will destroy them!

"With such defences for the body, ever prepared for the unexpected, deferential to the rights of others,—if then calamities overtake you, these are from God, not from man. Let them not disturb what you have already achieved. Let them not penetrate into the soul's abode. For there resides the Will. And if the will knows not what to will, it will not be able to will.

"Whatsoever is not said in all sincerity, is wrongly said. And not to be able to rid oneself of this vice is only to sink deeper towards perdition.

"Those who do evil in the open light of day,—men will punish them. Those who do evil in secret,—God will punish them. Who fears both man and God, he is fit to walk alone.

Those who are devoted to the internal, in practice acquire no reputation. Those who are devoted to the external, strive for pre-eminence among their fellows. Practice without reputation throws a halo around the meanest. But he who strives for pre-eminence among his fellows, he is as a huckster whose weariness all perceive though he himself puts on an air of gaiety.

"He who is naturally in sympathy with man, to him all men come. But he who forcedly adapts, has no room even for himself, still less for others. And he who has no room for others, has no ties. It is all over with him.

"There is no weapon so deadly as man's will. Excalibur is second to it. There is no bandit so powerful as Nature.

In the whole universe there is no escape from it. Yet it is not Nature which does the injury. It is man's own heart.

"TAO informs its own subdivisions, their successes and their failures. What is feared in subdivision is separation.

What is feared in separation, is further separation.

Thus, to issue forth without return, this is development of the supernatural. To issue forth and attain the goal, this is called death. To be annihilated and yet to exist, this is convergence of the supernatural into ONE. To make things which have form appear to all intents and purposes formless,—this is the sum of all things.

"Birth is not a beginning; death is not an end. There is existence without limitation; there is continuity without a starting-point. Existence without limitation is *Space*. Continuity without a starting-point is *Time*. There is birth, there is death, there is issuing forth, there is entering in. That through which one passes in and out without seeing its form, that is the Portal of God.

"The Portal of God is Non-Existence. All things sprang from Non-Existence. Existence could not make existence existence. It must have proceeded from Non-Existence, And Non-Existence and Nothing are ONE.

Herein is the abiding-place of the Sage.

"The knowledge of the ancients reached the highest point, —the time before anything existed. This is the highest point. It is exhaustive. There is no adding to it.

"The second best was that of those who started from existence. Life was to them a misfortune. Death was a return home. There was already separation.

"The next in the scale said that at the beginning there was nothing. Then life came, to be quickly followed by death. They made Nothing the head, Life the trunk, and Death the tail of existence, claiming as friends whoever knew that existence and non-existence, and life and death were all ONE.

"These three classes, though different, were of the same clan; as were Chao Ching who inherited fame, and Chia who inherited territory.

"Man's life is as the soot on a kettle.

Yet men speak of the subjective point of view. But this subjective point of view will not bear the test. It is a point of knowledge we cannot reach.

"At the winter sacrifice, the tripe may be separated from the great toe; yet these cannot be separated.

He who looks at a house, visits the ancestral hall, and even the latrines. Thus every point is the subjective point of view.

"Let us try to formulate this subjective point of view. It originates with life, and, with knowledge as its tutor, drifts into the admission of right and wrong.

But one's own standard of right is *the* standard, and others have to adapt themselves to it. Men will die for this. Such people look upon the useful as appertaining to wisdom, the useless as appertaining to folly; upon success in life as honourable, upon failure as dishonourable.

The subjective point of view is that of the present generation, who like the cicada and the young dove see things only from their own standpoint.

"If a man treads upon a stranger's toe in the market-place, he apologises on the score of hurry. If an elder brother does this, he is quit with an exclamation of sympathy. And if a parent does so, nothing whatever is done.

"Therefore, it has been said, 'Perfect politeness is not
artificial; perfect duty to one's neighbour is not a matter of calculation; perfect wisdom takes no thought; perfect charity recognises no ties; perfect trust requires no pledges.' "Discard the stimuli of purpose. Free the mind from disturbances. Get rid of entanglements to virtue. Pierce the obstructions to TAO.

"Honours, wealth, distinction, power, fame, gain,—these six stimulate purpose.

"Mien, carriage, beauty, arguments, influence, opinions,— these six disturb the mind.

"Hate, ambition, joy, anger, sorrow, pleasure,—these six are entanglements to virtue.

"Rejecting, adopting, receiving, giving, knowledge, ability, —these six are obstructions to TAO.

"If these twenty-four be not allowed to run riot, then the mind will be duly ordered. And being duly ordered, it will be in repose. And being in repose, it will be clear of perception. And being clear of perception, it will be unconditioned. And being unconditioned, it will be in that state of inaction by which there is nothing which cannot be accomplished.

"TAO is the sovereign lord of TÊ.

Life is the glorifier of TÊ.

Nature is the substance of life.

The operation of that nature is action. The perversion of that action is error.

"People who know put forth physical power. People who know employ mental effort. But what people who know do not know is to be as the eye.

"Emotion which is spontaneous is called virtue passive. Emotion which is not evoked by the external is called virtue active. The names of these are antagonistic; but essentially they are in accord.

"Yi was skilled in hitting the bull's-eye; but stupid at preventing people from praising him for so doing.

The Sage devotes himself to the natural and neglects the artificial. For only the Perfect Man can devote himself profitably to the natural and artificial alike. Insects influence insects; because insects are natural. When the Perfect Man hates the natural, it is the artificially natural which he hates. How much more man's alternate naturalness and artificiality?

"If a bird falls in with Yi, Yi will get it. Such is his skill. And if the world were made into a cage, birds would have no place of escape. So it was that by cookery T'ang got hold of I Yin, and by five rams' skins Duke Muh of Ch'in got Poh Li Ch'i. But had these princes not been themselves successful at getting, they never would have got these men.

"A one-legged man discards ornament, his exterior not being open to commendation. Condemned criminals will go up to great heights without fear, for they no longer regard life and death from their former point of view. And those who pay no attention to their moral clothing and condition become oblivious of their own personality; and by thus becoming oblivious of their personality, they proceed to be the people of God.

"Wherefore, if men revere them, they rejoice not. If men insult them, they are not angered. But only those who have passed into the eternal harmony of God are capable of this.

"If your anger is external, not internal, it will be anger proceeding from not-anger. If your actions are external, not internal, they will be actions proceeding from inaction,

"If you would attain peace, level down your emotional nature. If you desire spirituality, cultivate adaptation of the intelligence. If you would have your actions in accordance with what is right, allow yourself to fall in with the dictates of necessity. For necessity is the TAO of the Sage."

CHAPTER XXIV. Hsü Wu Kuei.

Argument:

—TAO is passionless—Immorality of the moral—Obstructions to natural virtue—The evils of action—Too much zeal—The outward and visible—The inward and spiritual—Illustrations.

Hsü WU KUEI, introduced by Nü Shang, went to see Wu Hou of Wei.

The Prince greeted him sympathisingly, and said, "You are suffering. Sir. You must have endured great hardships in your mountain life that you should be willing to leave it and visit me."

"It is I who should sympathise with your Highness, not your Highness with me," answered Hsü Wu Kuei. "If your Highness gives free play to passion and yields to loves and hates, then the natural conditions of your existence will suffer.

And if your Highness puts aside passion and abjures loves and hates, then your senses of sight and hearing will suffer.

It is I who should sympathise with your Highness, not your Highness with me."

The Prince was too astonished to reply; and after a while Hsü Wu Kuei continued, "I will try to explain to your Highness how I judge of dogs. The lowest in the scale will eat their fill and then stop, like a cat. Those of the middle class are as though staring at the sun. The highest class are as though they had parted with their own individuality.

"But I do not judge of dogs as well as I judge of horses. I judge of horses as follows. Their straightness must be that of a line. Their curve must be that of an arc. Their squareness, that of the square. Their roundness, that of the compasses.

These are the horses of the State. They are not equal to the horses of the Empire. The horses of the Empire are splendid. They move as though anxious to get along, as though they had lost the way, as though they had parted with their own individuality. Thus, they outstrip all competitors, over the unstirred dust, out of sight!"

The Prince was greatly pleased and smiled. But when Hsü Wu Kuei went out, Nü Shang asked him, saying, "What can you have been saying to his Highness? Whenever I address him, it is either in a pacific sense, based upon the Canons of *Poetry*, *History*, *Rites*, and *Music*; or in a belligerent sense, based upon the *Golden Roster* or the *Six Plans of Battle*.

I have transacted with great success innumerable matters entrusted to me, yet his Highness has never vouchsafed a smile. What can you have been saying to make him so pleased as all this?"

"I merely told him," replied Hsü Wu Kuei, "how I judged of dogs and horses."

"Was that all? " enquired Nü Shang, incredulously.

"Have you not heard," said Hsü Wu Kuei, "of the outlaw of Yüeh? After several days' absence from his State, he was glad to meet any one he had known there. After a month, he was glad to meet any one he had even seen there. And after a year, he was glad to meet any one who was in any way like to his fellow-countrymen. Is not this a case of absence from one's kind increasing the desire to be with them?

"Thus a man who had fled into the wilderness, where bishop-wort chokes the path of the weasel and stoat, now advancing, now stopping,—how he would rejoice if the footfall of a fellow-creature broke upon his ear. And how much more were he to hear the sound of a brother's, of a relative's voice at his side. Long it is, I ween, since his Highness has heard the voice of a pure man at his side!"

Hsü Wu Kuei went to visit the Prince. The latter said, "Living, Sir, up in the hills, and feeding upon berries or satisfying yourself with leeks, you have long neglected me. Are you now growing old? Or do you hanker after flesh-pots and wine? Or is it that mine is such a well-governed State?"

"I am of lowly birth," replied Hsü Wu Kuei. "I could not venture to eat and drink your Highness' meat and wine. I came to sympathise with your Highness."

"What do you mean?" cried the Prince? "What is there to sympathise about?"

"About your Highness' soul and body," replied Hsü Wu Kuei.

"Pray explain," said the Prince.

"Nourishment is nourishment," said Hsü Wu Kuei.

"Being high up does not make one high, nor does being low make one low. Your Highness is the ruler of a large State, and you oppress the whole population thereof in order to satisfy your sensualities. But your soul is not a party to this. The soul loves harmony and hates disorder. For disorder is a disease. Therefore, I came to sympathise. How is it that your Highness alone is suffering?"

"I have long desired to see you," answered the Prince. "I wish to love my people, and by cultivation of duty towards one's neighbour to put an end to war. Can this be done?"

"It cannot," replied Hsü Wu Kuei. "Love for the people is the root of all evil to the people. Cultivation of duty towards one's neighbour in order to put an end to war is the origin of all fighting. If your Highness starts from this basis, the result can only be disastrous.

"Everything that is made good, turns out bad. And although your Highness should make charity and duty to one's neighbour, I fear they would be spurious articles. For the inward intention would appear in the outward manifestation. The adoption of a fixed standard would lead to complications. And revolutions within lead to fighting without. Surely your Highness would not make a bower into a battlefield, nor a shrine of prayer into a scene of warfare!

"Have nothing within which is obstructive of virtue. Seek not to vanquish others in cunning, in plotting, in war. If I slay a whole nation and annex the territory in order to find nourishment for my passions and for my soul,—irrespective of military skill, wherein does the victory lie?

"If your Highness will only abstain, that will be enough. Cultivate the sincerity that is within your breast, so as to be responsive to the conditions of your environment, and be not aggressive. The people will thus escape death; and what need then to put an end to war?"

When the Yellow Emperor went to see TAO upon the Chütz'ŭ Mountain, Fang Ming was his charioteer, Chang Yü sat on his right, Chang Jo and Hsi P'êng were his outriders, and K'un Hun and Hua Chi brought up the rear.

On reaching the wilds of Hsiang-cheng, these seven Sages lost their way and there was no one of whom to ask the road. By and by, they fell in with a boy who was grazing horses, and asked him, saying, "Do you know the Chü-tz'ŭ Mountain?"

"I do," replied the boy.

"And can you tell us," continued the Sages, "where TAO abides?"

"I can," replied the boy.

"This is a strange lad," cried the Yellow Emperor. "Not only does he know where the Chü-tz'ŭ Mountain is, but also where TAO abides! Come tell me, pray, how would you govern the empire?"

"I should govern the empire," said the boy, "just the same as I look after my horses. What else should I do?

"When I was a little boy and used to live within the points of the compass, my eyes got dim of sight. An old man advised me to mount the chariot of the sun and visit the wilds of Hsiang-ch'êng. My sight is now much better, and I continue to dwell without the points of the compass. I should govern the empire in just the same way. What else should I do?"

"Of course," said the Yellow Emperor, "government is not your trade. Still I should be glad to hear what you would do."

The boy declined to answer, but on being again urged, cried out, "What difference is there between governing the empire and looking after horses? See that no harm comes to the horses, that is all!"

Thereupon the Emperor prostrated himself before the boy; and addressing him as Divine Teacher, took his leave.

If schemers have nothing to give them anxiety, they are not happy. If dialecticians have not their premises and conclusion, they are not happy. If critics have none on whom to vent their spleen, they are not happy. Such men are the slaves of objective existences.

Those who attract the sympathies of the world, start new dynasties. Those who win the people's hearts, take high official rank. Those who are strong undertake difficulties. Those who are brave encounter dangers. Men of arms delight in war. Men of peace think of nothing but reputation. Men of law strive to improve the administration. Professors of ceremony and music cultivate deportment. Moralists devote themselves to the obligations between man and man.

Take away agriculture from the husbandman, and his classification is gone. Take away trade from the merchant, and his classification is gone. Daily work is the stimulus of the labourer. The skill of the artisan is his pride. If money cannot be made, the avaricious man is sad. If his power meets with a check, the boaster will repine. Ambitious men love change.

Thus, men are always doing something; inaction is to them impossible. They observe in this the same regularity as the seasons, ever without change. They hurry to destruction, dissipating in all directions their vital forces, alas! never to return.

Chuang Tzŭ said, "If archers who aimed at nothing and hit something were accounted good shots, everybody in the world would be another Yi. Could this be so?"

"It could," replied Hui Tzŭ.

"If there was no general standard of right in the world," continued Chuang Tzŭ, "but each man had his own, then everybody would be a Yao. Could this be so?"

"It could," replied Hui Tzŭ.

"Very well," said Chuang Tzŭ. "Now there are the Confucianists, the Mihists, the schools of Yang and Ping, making with your own five in all. Pray which of these is right?

"Possibly it is a similar case to that of Lu Chü?—A disciple said to him, 'Master, I have attained to your TAO. I can do without fire in winter: I can make ice in summer.'

"'You merely avail yourself of latent heat and latent cold,' replied Lu Chü. 'That is not what I call TAO. I will demonstrate to you what my TAO is.'

"Thereupon he tuned two lutes, and placed one in the hall and the other in the adjoining room. And when he struck the *Kung* note on one, the *Kung* note on the other sounded; when he struck the *chio* note on one, the *chio* note on the other sounded. This because they were both tuned to the same pitch.

"But if he changed the interval of one string, so that it no longer kept its place in the octave, and then struck it, the result was that all the twenty-five strings jangled together. There was sound as before, but the influence of the keynote was gone. Is this your case?"

"The Confucianists, the Mihists, and the followers of Yang and Ping," replied Hui Tzŭ, "are just now engaged in discussing this matter with me. They try to overwhelm me with argument or howl me down with noise. Yet they have not proved me wrong. Why then should you?"

"A man of the Ch'i State," replied Chuang Tzŭ, "sent away his son into the Sung State, to be a door-keeper, with maimed body.

But a vase, which he valued highly, he kept carefully wrapped up.

"He who would seek for a stray child, but will not leave his home, is like to lose him.

"If a man of Ch'u, who was sent away to be a door-keeper, began, in the middle of the night, when no one was about, to fight with the boatman, I should say that before his boat left the shore he would already have got himself into considerable trouble."

Chuang Tzŭ was once attending a funeral, when he passed by the grave of Hui Tzŭ. Turning to his attendants, he said, "A man of Ying who had his nose covered with a hard scab, no thicker than a fly's wing, sent for a stone-mason to chip it off. The stonemason plied his adze with great dexterity while the patient sat still and let him chip. When the scab was all off, the nose was found to be uninjured, the man of Ying never having moved a muscle.

"When Yüan, prince of Sung, heard of this, he summoned the stone-mason and said, 'Try to do the same for me.'

"'I used to be able to do it Sire,' replied the stone-mason, 'but my material has long since perished.'

"And I too, ever since he perished, have been without my material, having no one with whom I can speak."

"There was no one," says Lin Hsi Chung," in all Chuang Tzŭ's generation who could understand him; neither is there any one now, at this late date, any more than there was then."

Kuan Chung being at the point of death, Duke Huan went to see him.

"You are ill, venerable Sir," said the Duke, "really ill. You had better say to whom, in the event of your getting worse, I am to entrust the administration of the State"

"Whom does your Highness wish to choose?" enquired Kuan Chung.

"Will Pao Yü do?" asked the Duke.

"He will not," said Kuan Chung. "He is pure, incorruptible, and good. With those who are not like himself, he will not associate. And if he has once heard of a man's wrong-doing, he never forgets it. If you employ him in the administration of the empire, he will get to loggerheads with his prince and to sixes and sevens with the people. It would not be long before he and your Highness fell out."

"Whom then can we have?" asked the Duke.

"There is no alternative," replied Kuan Chung; "it must be Hsi P'êng. He is a man who forgets the authority of those above him, and makes those below him forget his. Ashamed that he is not the peer of the Yellow Emperor, he grieves over those who are not the peers of himself.

"To share one's virtue with others is called true wisdom. To share one's wealth with others is reckoned meritorious. To exhibit superior merit is not the way to win men's hearts. To exhibit inferior merit is the way. There are things in the State he does not hear; there are things in the family he does not see. There is no alternative; it must be Hsi P'êng."

The prince of Wu took a boat and went to the Monkey Mountain, which he ascended. When the monkeys saw him, they fled in terror and hid themselves in the thicket. One of them, however, disported himself carelessly, as though showing off its skill before the prince. The prince took a shot at it; but the monkey, with great rapidity, seized the flying arrow with its hand. Then the prince bade his guards try, the result being that the monkey was killed.

Thereupon the prince turned to his friend Yen Pu I, and said, "That monkey flaunted its skill and its dexterity in my face. Therefore it has come to this pass. Beware! Do not flaunt your superiority in the faces of others."

Yen Pu I went home, and put himself under the tuition of Tung Wu, with a view to get rid of such superiority. He put aside all that gave him pleasure and avoided gaining reputation. And in three years his praise was in everybody's mouth.

Tzŭ Ch'i of Nan-poh was sitting leaning on a table. He looked up to heaven and sighed, at which juncture Yen Ch'êng Tzŭ entered and said, "How, Sir, can such an important person as yourself be in body like dry wood, in mind like dead ashes?"

"I used to live in a cave on the hills," replied Tzŭ Ch'i. "At that time, T'ien Ho, because he once saw me, was thrice congratulated by the people of Ch'i. Now I must have given some indication by which he recognised me. I must have sold for him to buy. For had I not manifested myself, how would he have recognised me? Had I not sold, how could he have bought?

"Alas! I grieve over man's self-destruction. And then I grieve over one who grieves for another. And then I grieve over him who grieves over one who grieves for another! And so I get daily farther and farther away."

When Confucius went to Ch'u, the prince entertained him at a banquet. Sun Shu Ao stood up with a goblet of wine in his hand, and I Liao of Shihnan poured a libation, saying, "On such occasions as this, the men of old were wont to make some utterance."

"Mine," replied Confucius, "is the doctrine of wordless utterances. Shall I who make no utterances, make utterance now?

"I Liao of Shih-nan played with his ball, and the trouble of two houses was arranged.

Sun Shu Ao remained quietly in repose, and the men of Ying threw down their arms.

I should want a three-foot tongue indeed!

"Theirs was the TAO of inaction. His was the argument of silence. Wherefore, for Tɛ̇ to rest in undivided TAO, and for speech to stop at the unknowable,—this is perfection.

"With undivided TAO, TÊ cannot be coincident.

No argument can demonstrate the unknowable. Subdivision into Confucianists and Mihists only makes confusion worse confounded.

"The sea does not reject the streams which flow eastward into it. Therefore it is immeasurably great. The true Sage folds the universe in his bosom. His good influence benefits all throughout the empire, without respect to persons. Born without rank, he dies without titles. He does not take credit for realities.

He does not establish a name. This is to be a great man.

"A dog is not considered a good dog because he is a good barker. A man is not considered a good man because he is a good talker. How much less in the case of greatness? And if doing great things is not enough to secure greatness, how much less shall it secure virtue?

"In point of greatness, there is nothing to be compared with the universe. Yet what does the universe seek in order to be great?

"He who understands greatness in this sense, seeks nothing, loses nothing, rejects nothing, never suffers injury from without. He takes refuge in his own inexhaustibility. He finds safety in according with his nature. This is the essence of true greatness."

Tzŭ Ch'i had eight sons. He ranged them before him, and summoning Chiu Fang Yin, said to him, "Examine my sons physiognomically, and tell me which will be the fortunate one."

"K'un," replied Chiu Fang Yin, "will be the fortunate one."

"In what sense?" asked the father, beaming with delight.

"K'un," said Chiu Fang Yin, "will eat at the table of a prince, and so end his days."

Thereupon Tzŭ Ch'i burst into tears and said, "What has my son done that this should be his fate?"

"Eating at the table of a prince," replied Chiu Fang Yin, "will benefit the family for three generations. How much more his father and mother! But for you, Sir, to go and weep is enough to turn back the luck from you. The son's fortune is good, but the father's bad."

"Yin," said Tzǔ Ch'i, "I should like to know what you mean by calling K'un fortunate. Wine and meat gratify the palate, but you do not say how these are to come.

"Supposing that to me, not being a shepherd, a lamb were born in the south-west corner of my hall; or that to me, not being a sportsman, quails were hatched in the north-east corner. If you did not call that uncanny, what would you call it?

"My sons and I do but roam through the universe. With them I seek the joys of heaven; with them I seek the fruits of earth. With them I engage in no business; with them I concoct no plots; with them I attempt nothing out-of-theway. With them I mount upon the truth of the universe, and do not offer opposition to the exigencies of our environment. With them I accommodate myself naturally; but with them I do not become a slave to circumstances. Yet now the world is rewarding me!

"Every uncanny effect must be preceded by some uncanny cause. Alas! my sons and I have done nothing. It must be the will of God. Therefore I weep."

Shortly afterwards, when K'un was on his way to the Yen State, he was captured by brigands. To sell him as he was, would be no easy matter. To sell him without his feet would be easy enough. So they cut off his feet and sold him into the Ch'i State, where he became door-keeper to Duke Chü and had meat to his dinner for the rest of his life.

Yeh Ch'üeh meeting Hsü Yu, said to him, "Where are you going?"

"Away from Yao!" replied the latter.

"What do you mean?" asked Yeh Ch'üeh.

"Yao," said Hsü Yu, "thinks of nothing but charity. I fear he will become a laughing-stock to the world, and that in future ages men will eat one another.

"There is no difficulty in winning the people. Love them and they will draw near. Profit them and they will come up. Praise them and they will vie with one another. But introduce something they dislike, and they will be gone.

"Love and profit are born of charity and duty to one's neighbour. Those who ignore charity and duty to one's neighbour are few; those who make capital out of them are many.

"For the operation of these virtues is not disinterested. It is like lending gear to a sportsman.

Wherefore, for one man to dogmatise for the good of the whole empire, is like splitting a thing at a single blow.

"Yao knows that good men benefit the empire. But he does not know that they injure it. Only those on a higher level than good men know this.

"There are nincompoops; there are parasites; there are enthusiasts.

"A man who learns from a single teacher, and then goes off exultant, satisfied with his acquirements though ignorant that there was a time when nothing existed,—such a one is a nincompoop.

"Parasites are like the lice on a pig's back. They choose bald patches, which are to them palaces and parks. The parts between the toes, the joints, the dugs, and the buttocks, are to them so many comfortable and convenient resting-places. They know not that one day the butcher will tuck up his sleeves and spread straw and apply fire, and that they will perish in the singeing of the pig. As they sow, so do they reap. This is to be a parasite.

"Of enthusiasts, Shun is an example. Mutton does not care for ants; it is the ants which care for the mutton. Mutton has a frowsy smell; and there is a frowsiness about Shun which attracts the people. Therefore it was that after three changes of residence, when he came to the Teng district, he had some hundred thousand families with him.

"Then Yao, hearing of his goodness, appointed him to a barren region, trusting, as he said, that Shun's arrival would enrich it. When Shun took up this appointment, he was already old, and his intellect was failing; yet he would not cease work and retire from office. He was, in fact, an enthusiast.

"So it is that the spiritual man dislikes a crowd. For where there is a crowd there is diversity, and where there is diversity advantage does not accrue. He is therefore neither very intimate, nor very distant. He clings to virtue and nourishes a spirit of harmony, in order to be in accord with his fellow-men. This is to be a divine man.

"Leave wisdom to ants. Strive for what fishes desire.

Leave attractiveness to mutton. Use your eyes to contemplate, your ears to listen to, your mind to consider, their own internal workings. For him who can do these things, his level will be that of a line, his modifications in due and proper season.

"Therefore, the divine man trusts to the natural development of events. He does not strive to introduce the artificial into the domain of the natural. Accordingly, life is a gain and death a loss, or death is a gain and life a loss.

"For instance, drugs. They are characteristically poisonous. Such are *Chieh-Kêng*, *Chi-Yung*, and *Shih-Ling*. Circumstances, however, make of each a sovereign remedy. The list is inexhaustible.

"When Kou Chien encamped with three thousand armed warriors at Kuei-ch'i, only Chung saw that defeat would be followed by a rally. Yet he could not foresee the evil that was to come upon himself. Wherefore it has been said, 'An owl's eyes are adapted to their use. A crane's leg is of the length required. 'Twould be disastrous to shorten it.'

"Thus it has been said, 'The wind blows and the river suffers. The sun shines and the river suffers.' But though wind and sun be both brought into relation with the river, it does not really suffer therefrom. Fed from its source, it still continues to flow on.

"The relation between water and earth is determinate. The relation between a man and his shadow is determinate. The relation between thing and thing is determinate.

"The relation between eye and vision is baneful. The relation between ear and hearing is baneful. The relation between mind and object is baneful. The relation between all kinds of capacity and man's inner self is baneful. If such banefulness be not corrected, disasters will spring up on all sides. Retrogression is hard to achieve, and success long in coming. Yet alas! men regard such capacities as valuable possessions.

"The destruction of States and the ceaseless slaughter of human beings result from an inability to examine into this.

"The foot treads the ground in walking; nevertheless it is the ground not trodden on which makes up the good walk.

A man's knowledge is limited; but it is upon what he does not know that he depends to extend his knowledge to the apprehension of God.

"Knowledge of the great O$_{NE}$, of the great Negative, of the great Nomenclature, of the great Uniformity, of the great Space, of the great Truth, of the great Law,—this is perfection.

"The great ONE is omnipresent. The great Negative is omnipotent. The great Nomenclature is all-inclusive. The great Uniformity is all-assimilative. The great Space is allreceptive. The great Truth is all-exacting. The great Law is all-binding.

"The ultimate end is God. He is manifested in the laws of nature. He is the hidden spring. At the beginning, he was.

This, however, is inexplicable. It is unknowable. But from the unknowable we reach the known.

"Investigation must not be limited, nor must it be unlimited.

In this vague undefinedness there is an actuality. Time does not change it. It cannot suffer diminution. May we not then call it our great Guide?

"Why not bring our doubting hearts to investigation thereof? And then, using certainty to dispel doubt, revert to a state without doubt, in which doubt is doubly dead?"

CHAPTER XXV. TSÊ YANG.

Argument:

—Influence of virtue concealed—The true Sage a negative quantity —The great, the small, the infinite—Crime and Capital—Rulers and their vices—What is Society? Predestination or Chance?—Illustrations.

WHEN Tsê Yang visited the Ch'u State, I Chieh spoke of him to the prince; but the latter refused an audience.

Upon I Chieh's return, Tsê Yang went to see Wang Kuo, and asked him to obtain an interview with the prince.

"I am not so fitted for that," replied Wang Kuo, "as Kung Yüeh Hsiu."

"What sort of a man is he?" enquired. Tsê Yang.

"In winter," said Wang Kuo, "he catches turtles on the river. In summer, he reposes in some mountain copse. If any passers-by ask of him, he tells them, "This is my home." Where I Chieh could not succeed, still less should I. I am not equal even to him.

"He is a man without virtue, but possessed of knowledge. Were it not for an air of arrogance, he would be very popular with his superiors. But help without virtue is a hindrance. Shivering people borrowing clothes in the coming spring! Hot people thinking of last winter's icy blast!

"The prince of Ch'u is dignified and severe. In punishing, he is merciless as a tiger. Only a very practised or a very perfect man could influence him.

"The true Sage, when in obscurity, causes those around him to forget their poverty. When in power, he causes princes to forget ranks and emoluments, and to become as though of low estate. He rejoices exceedingly in all creation. He exults to see TAO diffused among his fellow-men, while suffering no loss himself.

"Thus, although silent, he can instil peace; and by his mere presence cause men to be to each other as father and son. From his very return to passivity comes this active influence for good. So widely does he differ in heart from ordinary men. Wherefore I said, 'Wait for Kung Yüeh Hsiu.'

"The true Sage is free from all embarrassments. All things are to him as O$_{\text{NE}}$. Yet he knows not that this is so. It is simply nature, In the midst of action he remains the same. He makes God his guide, and men make him theirs. He grieves that wisdom carries one but a short distance, and at times comes altogether to a deadlock.

"To a beauty, mankind is the mirror in which she sees herself. If no one tells her she is beautiful, she does not know that she is so. But whether she knows it or whether she does not know it, whether she hears it or whether she does not hear it, her joy will never cease, neither will mankind ever cease to take pleasure therein. It is nature.

"The love of a Sage for his fellows likewise finds expression among mankind. Were he not told so, he would not know that he loved his fellows. But whether he knows it or whether he does not know it, whether he hears it or whether he does not hear it, his love for his fellows is without end, and mankind cease not to repose therein.

"The old country, the old home, gladden a wanderer's eyes. Nay, though nine-tenths of it be a howling wilderness, still his eye will be glad. How much more to see sight and hear hearing, from a lofty dais suspended in their very midst!"

Jen Hsiang Shih reached the centre and attained. He recognised no beginning, no end, no quantity, no time. Daily modified together with his environment, as part of ONE he knew no modification. Why not rest in this?

To strive to follow God and not to succeed is to display an activity fatal to itself. How can success ever be thus achieved?

The true Sage ignores God. He ignores man. He ignores a beginning. He ignores matter. He moves in harmony with his generation and suffers not. He takes things as they come and is not overwhelmed. How are we to become like him?

T'ang appointed his Equerry, Mên Yin Têng Hêng, to be his tutor, listening to his counsels but not being restricted by them. He got TAO for himself and a reputation for his tutor. But the reputation was a violation of principle, and landed him in the domain of alternatives.

As a tutor, Confucius pushed care and anxiety to an extreme limit.

Yung Ch'êng Shih said, "Take away days, and there would be no years. No inside, no outside."

Prince Hui of Wei had made a treaty with prince Wei of Ch'i, which the latter broke.

Thereupon prince Hui was wroth, and was about to send a man to assassinate him. But the Captain-General heard of this, and cried out in shame, "Sire, you are ruler over a mighty State, yet you would seek the vengeance of a common man. Give me two hundred thousand warriors, and

I will do the work for you. I will take his people prisoners, and carry off their oxen and horses. I will make the heat of the prince's mind break out on his back. Then I will seize his country, and he will flee. Then you can wring his neck as you please."

When Chi Tzǔ heard this, he cried out in shame and said, "If you are building a ten-perch wall, and when the wall is near completion, destroy it, you inflict great hardship on the workmen.

Now for seven years the troops have not been called out. That is, as it were, your Highness' foundation work. Listen not to the Captain-General. He is a mischievous fellow."

When Hua Tzŭ heard this, he was very indignant and said, "He who argued in favour of punishing the Ch'i State was a mischievous fellow. And he who argued against punishing the Ch'i State was a mischievous fellow. And he who says that either of the above is a mischievous fellow, is a mischievous fellow himself."

"Where then shall I find what to do?" enquired the prince.

"In TAO alone," said Hua Tzŭ.

When Hui Tzŭ heard this, he introduced Tai Chin Jen to the prince.

"There is a creature called a snail," said Tai Chin Jen. "Does your Highness know what I mean? "

"I do," replied the prince.

"There is a kingdom on its left horn," continued Tai Chin Jen, "ruled over by *Aggression*, and another on its right horn, ruled over by *Violence*. These two rulers are constantly fighting for territory. In such cases, corpses lie about by thousands, and one party will pursue the other for fifteen days before returning."

"Whew!" cried the prince. "Surely you are joking."

"Sire," replied Tai Chin Jen, "I beg you to regard it as fact. Does your Highness recognise any limit to space? "

"None," said the prince, "It is boundless."

"When, therefore," continued Tai Chin Jen, "the mind descends from the contemplation of boundless space to the contemplation of a kingdom with fixed boundaries, that kingdom must seem to be of dimensions infinitesimally small?"

"Of course," replied the prince.

"Well then," said Tai Chin Jen, "in a kingdom with fixed boundaries there is the Wei State. In the Wei State there is the city of Liang. In the city of Liang there is a prince. In what does that prince differ from Violence?"

"There is no difference," said the prince.

Thereupon Tai Chin Jen took his leave, and the prince remained in a state of mental perturbation, as though he had lost something.

When Tai Chin Jen had gone, Hui Tzŭ presented himself, and the prince said, "Our friend is truly a great man. Sages are not his equal."

"If you blow through a tube," replied Hui Tzŭ, "the result will be a note. If you blow through the hole in a sword-hilt, the result will be simply *whssh*. Yao and Shun have been belauded by mankind; yet compared with Tai Chin Jen they are but *whssh*."

When Confucius went to Ch'u, he stopped at a restaurant on Mount I. The servant to a man and his wife who lived next door, got up on top of the house.

"Whatever is he doing up there?" asked Tzŭ Lu.

"He is a Sage," replied Confucius," under the garb of a menial. He buries himself among the people.

He effaces himself at the wayside. Fame, he has none; but his perseverance is inexhaustible. Though his mouth speaks, his heart speaks not. He has turned his back upon mankind, not caring to abide amongst them. He has drowned himself on dry land. I think 'tis I Liao of Shih-nan."

Tzŭ Lu asked to be allowed to go and call him; but Confucius stopped him, saying, "No. He knows that I know what he is. He knows that I have come to Ch'u to recommend him to the prince. And he looks on me as a toady. Under the circumstances, as he would scorn to hear the words of a toady, how much more would he scorn to see him in the flesh! How could you keep him?"

Tzŭ Lu went to see, but the house was empty.

The border-warden of Ch'ang-wu said to Tzŭ Lao, "A prince in his administrative details must not lack thoroughness; in his executive details he must not be inefficient. Formerly, in my ploughing I lacked thoroughness, and the results also lacked thoroughness. In my weeding I was inefficient, and the results were also inefficient. By and by, I changed my system. I ploughed deep, and weeded carefully, the result being an excellent harvest, more than I could get through in a year."

Chuang Tzŭ, upon hearing this, observed, "The men of today in their self-regulation and their self-organisation are mostly as the Border-warden has described. They put their Godhead out of sight. They abandon their natural dispositions. They get rid of all feeling. They part with their souls, carried away by the fashion of the hour.

"Those who lack thoroughness in regard to their natural dispositions suffer an evil tribe to take the place thereof.

These grow up rank as reeds and rushes, at first of apparent value to the body, but afterwards to destroy the natural disposition. Then they break out, at random, like sores and ulcers carrying off pent-up humours."

Poh Chü was studying under Lao Tzŭ. "Let us go," said he, "and wander over the world."

"No," replied Lao Tzŭ, "the world is just as you see it here." But as he again urged it, Lao Tzŭ said, "Where would you go to begin with?"

"I would begin," answered Poh Chü, "by going to the Ch'i State. There I would view the dead bodies of their malefactors. I would push them to make them rise. I would take off my robes and cover them. I would cry to God and bemoan their lot, as follows:—'O sirs, O sirs, there was trouble upon earth, and you were the first to fall into it!'

"I would say, 'Perhaps you were robbers, or perhaps murderers?' .... Honour and disgrace were set up, and evil followed. Wealth was accumulated, and contentions began. Now the evil which has been set up and the contentions which have accumulated, endlessly weary man's body and give him no rest. What escape is there from this?

"The rulers of old set off all success to the credit of their people, attributing all failure to themselves. All that was right went to the credit of their people, all that was wrong they attributed to themselves. Therefore, if any matter fell short of achievement, they turned and blamed themselves.

"Not so the rulers of to-day. They conceal a thing and blame those who cannot see it. They impose dangerous tasks and punish those who dare not undertake them. They inflict heavy burdens and chastise those who cannot bear them. They ordain long marches and slay those who cannot make them.

"And the people, feeling that their powers are inadequate, have recourse to fraud. For when there is so much fraud about, how can the people be otherwise than fraudulent? If their strength is insufficient, they will have recourse to fraud. If their knowledge is insufficient, they will have recourse to deceit. If their means are insufficient, they will steal. And for such robbery and theft, who is really responsible?"

When Chu Poh Yü reached his sixtieth year, he changed his opinions. What he had previously regarded as right, he now came to regard as wrong. But who shall say whether the right of to-day may not be as wrong as the wrong of the previous fifty-nine years?

Things are produced around us, but no one knows the whence. They issue forth, but no one sees the portal. Men one and all value that part of knowledge which is known. They do not know how to avail themselves of the unknown in order to reach knowledge. Is not this misguided?

Alas! alas! the impossibility of escaping from this state results in what is known as elective affinity.

Confucius asked the historiographers Ta T'ao, Poh Chang Ch'ien, and Hsi Wei, saying, "Duke Ling of Wei was fond of wine and given up to pleasure, and neglected the administration of his State. He spent his time in hunting, and did not cultivate the goodwill of the other feudal princes. How was it he came to be called *Ling*?"

"For those very reasons," replied Ta T'ao.

"The Duke," said Poh Chang Ch'ien, "had three wives. He was having a bath together with them when Shih Ch'iu, summoned by his Highness, entered the apartment. Thereupon the Duke covered himself and the ladies. So outrageously did he behave on the one hand, and yet so respectful was he towards a virtuous man. Hence he was called *Ling*."

"When the Duke died," said Hsi Wei, "divination showed that it would be inauspicious to bury him in the old family burying-ground, but auspicious to bury him at Sha-ch'iu. And upon digging a grave there, several fathoms deep, a stone coffin was found, which, being cleaned, yielded the following inscription:—*Posterity cannot be trusted. Duke Ling of Wei will seize this for his tomb.*

"As a matter of fact, Duke Ling of Wei had been named Ling long before. What should these two persons know about it?"

Shao Chih asked T'ai Kung Tiao, saying, "What is meant by society?"

"Society," replied T'ai Kung Tiao, "is an agreement of a certain number of families and individuals to abide by certain customs. Discordant elements unite to form a harmonious whole. Take away this unity and each has a separate individuality.

"Point at any one of the many parts of a horse, and that is not a horse, although there is the horse before you. It is the combination of all which makes the horse.

"Similarly, a mountain is high because of its individual particles. A river is large because of its individual drops. And he is a just man who regards all parts from the point of view of the whole.

"Thus, in regard to the views of others, he holds his own opinion, but not obstinately. In regard to his own views, while conscious of their truth, he does not despise the opinions of others.

"The four seasons have different characteristics. but God shows no preference for either, and therefore we have the year complete.

The functions of the various classes of officials differ; but the sovereign shows no partiality, and therefore the empire is governed. There are the civil and the military; but the truly great man shows no preference for either, and therefore their efficacy is complete. All things are under the operation of varying laws; but TAO shows no partiality and therefore it cannot be identified.

Not being able to be identified, it consequently does nothing. And by doing nothing all things can be done.

"Seasons have their beginnings and their ends. Generations change and change. Good and evil fortune alternate, bringing sorrow here, happiness there.

He who obstinately views things from his own standpoint only, may be right in one case and wrong in another. Just as in a great jungle all kinds of shrubs are found together; or as on a mountain you see trees and stones indiscriminately mixed,—so is what we call society."

"Would it not do then," asked Shao Chih, "if we were to call this TAO?"

"It would not," replied T'ai Kung Tiao. "All creation is made up of more than ten thousand things. We speak of creation as the *Ten Thousand Things* merely because it is a convenient term by which to express a large number. In point of outward shape the universe is vast. In point of influence the Positive and Negative principles are mighty. Yet TAO folds them all in its embrace. For convenience' sake the bond of society is called great. But how can that which is thus conditioned be compared with TAO? There is as wide a difference between them as there is between a horse and a dog."

"Whence then," enquired Shao Chih, "comes the vitality of all things between the four points of the compass, between heaven above and earth beneath?"

"The Positive and Negative principles," answered T'ai Kung Tiao, "influence, act upon, and regulate each other. The four seasons alternate with, give birth to, and destroy one another. Hence, loves and hates, and courses rejected and courses adopted. Hence too, the intercourse of the sexes.

"States of peril and safety alternate. Good and evil fortune give birth to one another. Slowness and speed are mutually exclusive. Collection and dispersion are correlates. The actuality of these may be noted.

The essence of each can be verified. There is regular movement forward, modified by deflection into a curve. Exhaustion leads to renewal. The end introduces a new beginning. This is the law of material existences. The force of language, the reach of knowledge, cannot pass beyond the bounds of such material existences. The disciple of TAO refrains from prying into the states after or before. Human speculation stops short of this,"

"Chi Chên," said Shao Chih, "taught *Chance;* Chieh Tzŭ taught *Predestination.*

In the speculations of these two schools, on which side did right lie?"

"The cock crows," replied T'ai Kung Tiao, "and the dog barks. So much we know. But the wisest of us could not say why one crows and the other barks, nor guess why they crow or bark at all.

"Let me explain. The infinitely small is inappreciable; the infinitely great is immeasurable. Chance and Predestination must refer to the conditioned. Consequently, both are wrong.

"Predestination involves a real existence. Chance implies an absolute absence of any principle. To have a name and the embodiment thereof,—this is to have a material existence. To have no name and no embodiment,— of this one can speak and think; but the more one speaks the farther off one gets.

"The unborn creature cannot be kept from life. The dead cannot be tracked. From birth to death is but a span; yet the secret cannot be known. Chance and Predestination are but *à priori* solutions.

"When I seek for a beginning, I find only time infinite. When I look forward to an end, I see only time infinite. Infinity of time past and to come implies no beginning and is in accordance with the laws of material existences. Predestination and Chance give us a beginning, but one which is compatible only with the existence of matter.

"TAO cannot be existent. If it were existent, it could not be non-existent. The very name of TAO is only adopted for convenience' sake. Predestination and Chance are limited to material existences. How can they bear upon the infinite?

"Were language adequate, it would take but a day to fully set forth TAO. Not being adequate, it takes that time to explain material existences. TAO is something beyond material existences. It cannot be conveyed either by words or by silence. In that state which is neither speech nor silence, its transcendental nature may be apprehended."

CHAPTER XXVI. CONTINGENCIES.

Argument:

—The external uncertain—The internal alone without harm—Life and death are external—The soul only is under man's control—Folly of worldliness—Illustrations.

CONTINGENCIES are uncertain. Hence the decapitation of Lung Fêng, the disembowelment of Pi Kan, the enthusiasm of Chi Tzŭ, the death of Wu Lai, the flights of Chieh and Chou.

No sovereign but would have loyal ministers; yet loyalty does not necessarily inspire confidence. Hence Wu Yüan found a grave in the river; and Ch'ang Hung perished in Shu, his blood, after being preserved three years, turning into green jade.

No parent but would have filial sons; yet filial piety does not necessarily inspire love. Hence Hsiao Chi sorrrowed, and Tsêng Shên grieved.

Wood rubbed with wood produces fire. Metal exposed to fire will liquefy. If the Positive and Negative principles operate inharmoniously, heaven and earth are greatly disturbed. Thunder crashes, and with rain comes lightning, scorching up the tall locust-trees. One fears lest sky and land should collapse and leave no escape. Unable to lie *perdu*, the heart feels as though suspended between heaven and earth.

So in the struggle between peace and unrest, the friction between good and evil, much fire is evolved which consumes the inner harmony of man. But the mind is unable to resist fire. It is destroyed, and with it TAO comes to an end.

Chuang Tzǔ's family being poor, he went to borrow some corn from the prince of Chien-ho.

"Yes," said the prince. "I am just about collecting the revenue of my fief, and will then lend you three hundred ounces of silver. Will that do?"

At this Chuang Tzǔ flushed with anger and said, "Yesterday, as I was coming along, I heard a voice calling me. I looked round, and in the cart-rut I saw a stickleback.

" 'And what do you want, stickleback?' said I.

" 'I am a denizen of the eastern ocean,' replied the stickleback. 'Pray, Sir, a pint of water to save my life.'

" 'Yes,' said I. 'I am just going south to visit the princes of Wu and Yüeh. I will bring you some from the west river. Will that do?'

"At this the stickleback flushed with anger and said, 'I am out of my element. I have nowhere to go. A pint of water would save me. But to talk to me like this,—you might as well put me in a dried-fish shop at once.' "

Jên Kung Tzǔ got a huge hook on a big line, which he baited with fifty oxen. He squatted down at Kuei-chi, and cast into the eastern ocean. Every day he fished, but for a whole year he caught nothing. Then came a great fish which swallowed the bait, and dragging the huge hook dived down below. This way and that way it plunged about, erecting the dorsal fin. The white waves rolled mountain high. The great deep was shaken up. The noise was like that of so many devils, terrifying people for many miles around.

But when Jên Kung Tzǔ had secured his fish, he cut it up and salted it. And from Chih-ho eastwards, and from Ts'ang-wu northwards, there was none but ate his fill of that fish. Even among succeeding generations, *goube-mouches* of the day recounted the marvellous tale.

To take a rod and line, and go to a pool, and catch small fry is a very different thing from catching big fish. And by means of a little show of ability to secure some small billet is a very different thing from really pushing one's way to the front. So that those who do not imitate the example of Jên Kung Tzŭ will be very far from becoming leaders in their generation.

When some Confucianists were opening a grave in accordance with their Canons of *Poetry* and *Rites*, the master shouted out, "Day is breaking. How are you getting on with the work?"

"Not got off the burial-clothes yet," answered an apprentice. "There is a pearl in the mouth."

Now the Canon of *Poetry* says—

> The greenest corn
> Grows over graves.
> In life, no charity;
> In death, no pearl.

So seizing the corpse's brow with one hand, and forcing down its chin with the other, these Confucianists proceed to tap its cheeks with a metal hammer, in order to make the jaws open gently and not injure the pearl!

A disciple of Lao Lai Tzŭ while out gathering fuel, chanced to meet Confucius. On his return, he said, "There is a man over there with a long body and short legs, round shoulders and drooping ears. He looks as though he were sorrowing over mankind. I know not who he can be."

"It is Confucius!" cried Lao Lai Tzŭ. "Bid him come hither."

When Confucius arrived, Lao Lai Tzŭ addressed him as follows:—

"Ch'iu! Get rid of your dogmatism and your specious knowledge, and you will be really a superior man."

Confucius bowed and was about to retire, when suddenly his countenance changed and he enquired, "Shall I then be able to enter upon TAO?"

"The wounds of one generation being too much," answered Lao Lai Tzŭ, "you would take to yourself the sorrows of all time. Are you not weary? Is your strength equal to the task?

"To employ goodness as a passport to influence through the gratification of others, is an everlasting shame. Yet this is the common way of all, to lure people by fame, to bind them by ties of gratification.

"Better than extolling Yao and cursing Chieh is oblivion of both, keeping one's praises to oneself. These things react injuriously on self; the agitation of movement results in deflection.

"The true Sage is a passive agent. If he succeeds, he simply feels that he was provided by no effort of his own with the energy necessary to success."

Prince Yüan of Sung dreamed one night that a man with dishevelled hair peeped through a side door and said, "I have come from the waters of Tsai-lu. I am a marine messenger attached to the staff of the River God. A fisherman, named Yü Ch'ieh, has caught me."

When the prince awaked, he referred his dream to the soothsayers, who said, "This is a divine tortoise."

"Is there any fisherman," asked the prince, "whose name is Yü Ch'ieh?"

Being told there was, the prince gave orders for his appearance at court; and the next day Yü Ch'ieh had an audience.

"Fisherman," said the prince, "what have you caught?"

"I have netted a white tortoise," replied the fisherman, "five feet in semi-circumference."

"Bring your tortoise," said the prince. But when it came, the prince could not make up his mind whether to kill it or keep it alive. Thus in doubt, he had recourse to divination, and received the following response:—

Slay the tortoise for purposes of divination and good fortune will result.

So the tortoise was despatched. After which, out of seventytwo omens taken, not a single one proved false.

"A divine tortoise," said Confucius, "can appear to prince Yüan in a dream, yet it cannot escape the net of Yü Ch'ieh. Its wisdom can yield seventy-two faultless omens, yet it cannot escape the misery of being cut to pieces. Truly wisdom has its limits; spirituality, that which it cannot reach.

"In spite of the highest wisdom, there are countless snares to be avoided. If a fish has not to fear nets, there are always pelicans. Get rid of small wisdom, and great wisdom will shine upon you. Put away goodness and you will be naturally good. A child does not learn to speak because taught by professors of the art, but because it lives among people who can themselves speak."

Hui Tzŭ said to Chuang Tzŭ, "Your theme, Sir, is the useless."

"You must understand the useless," replied Chuang Tzŭ, "before you can discuss the useful.

"For instance, the earth is of huge proportions, yet man uses of it only as much as is covered by the sole of his foot. By and by, he turns up his toes and goes beneath it to the Yellow Spring. Has he any further use for it?"

"He has none," replied Hui Tzŭ.

"And in like manner," replied Chuang Tzŭ, "may be demonstrated the use of the useless.

"Could a man transcend the limits of the human," said Chuang Tzŭ, "would he not do so? Unable to do so, how should he succeed?

"The determination to retire, to renounce the world,—such alas! is not the fruit of perfect wisdom or immaculate virtue. From cataclysms ahead, these do not turn back; nor do they heed the approach of devouring flame. Although there are class distinctions of high and low, these are but for a time, and under the changed conditions of a new sphere are unknown.

"Wherefore it has been said, 'The perfect man leaves no trace behind.'

"For instance, to glorify the past and to condemn the present has always been the way of the scholar.

Yet if Hsi Wei Shih and individuals of that class were caused to re-appear in the present day, which of them but would accommodate himself to the age?

"Only the perfect man can transcend the limits of the human and yet not withdraw from the world, live in accord with mankind and yet suffer no injury himself. Of the world's teachings he learns nothing. He has that within which makes him independent of others.

"If the eye is unobstructed, the result is sight. If the ear is unobstructed the result is hearing. If the nose is unobstructed, the result is sense of smell.

If the mouth is unobstructed, the result is sense of taste. If the mind is unobstructed, the result is wisdom. If wisdom is unobstructed, the result is T<small>Ê</small>.

"TAO may not be obstructed. To obstruct is to strangle. This affects the base, and all evils spring into life.

"All sentient beings depend upon breath. If this does not reach them in sufficient quantity, it is not the fault of God. God supplies it day and night without cease, but man stops the passage.

"Man has for himself a spacious domain. His mind may roam to heaven. If there is no room in the house, the wife and her mother-in-law run against one another. If the mind cannot roam to heaven, the faculties will be in a state of antagonism. Those who would benefit mankind from deep forests or lofty mountains are simply unequal to the strain upon their higher natures.

"Ill-regulated virtue ends in reputation. Ill-regulated reputation ends in notoriety. Scheming leads to confusion. Knowledge begets contentions. Obstinacy produces stupidity. Organised government is for the general good of all.

"Spring rains come in due season, and plants and shrubs burst up from the earth. Weeding and tending do not begin until such plants and shrubs have reached more than half their growth, and without being conscious of the fact.

"Repose gives health to the sick. Rubbing the eyelids removes the wrinkles of old age. Quiet will dispel anxieties. These remedies however are the resource only of those who need them. Others who are free from such ills pay no attention thereto.

"That which the true Sage marvels at in the empire, claims not the attention of the Divine man. That which the truly virtuous man marvels at in his own sphere, claims not the attention of the true Sage. That which the superior man marvels at in his State, claims not the attention of the truly virtuous man. How the mean man adapts himself to his age, claims not the attention of the superior man.

"The keeper of the Yen gate, having maltreated himself severely in consequence of the death of his parents, received a high official post.

His relatives thereupon maltreated themselves, and some half of them died.

"Yao offered the empire to Hsü Yu, but Hsü Yu fled. T'ang offered it to Wu Kuang, but Wu Kuang declined with anger.

"When Chi T'o heard of Hsü Yu's flight, he took all his disciples with him and jumped into the river K'uan; upon which the various feudal princes mourned for three years, and Shên T'u Ti had the river filled up.

"The *raison d'être* of a fish-trap is the fish. When the fish is caught, the trap may be ignored. The *raison d'être* of a rabbit-snare is the rabbit. When the rabbit is caught the snare may be ignored. The *raison d'être* of language is an idea to be expressed. When the idea is expressed, the language may be ignored. But where shall I find a man to ignore language, with whom I may be able to converse?"

CHAPTER XXVII. LANGUAGE.

Argument:

—Speech, natural and artificial—Natural speech in harmony with the divine—Destiny—The ultimate cause—Purification of the soul—Illustrations.

OF language put into other people's mouths, nine tenths will succeed. Of language based upon weighty authority, seven tenths. But language which flows constantly over, as from a full goblet, is in accord with God.

When language is put into other people's mouths, outside support is sought. Just as a father does not negotiate his son's marriage; for any praise he could bestow would not have the same value as praise by an outsider. Thus, the fault is not mine, but that of others.

To that which agrees with our own opinions we assent; from that which does not we dissent. We regard that which agrees with our own opinion as right. We regard that which differs from our opinion as wrong. Language based on weighty authority is used to bar further argument. The authorities are our superiors, our elders in years. But if they lack the requisite knowledge and experience, being our superiors only in the sense of age, then they are not our superiors. And if men are not the superiors of their fellows, no one troubles about them. And those about whom no one troubles are merely stale.

Language which flows constantly over, as from a full goblet, is in accord with God.

Because it spreads out on all sides, it endures for all time. Without language, contraries are identical. The identity is not identical with its expression: the expression is not identical with its identity. Therefore it has been said, Language not expressed in language is not language. Constantly spoken, it is as though not spoken. Constantly unspoken, it is not as though not spoken.

From the subjective point of view, there are possibilities and impossibilities, there are suitabilities and unsuitabilities. This results from the natural affinity of things for what they are and their natural antagonism to what they are not. For all things have their own particular constitutions and potentialities. Nothing can exist without these. But for language that constantly flows over, as from a full goblet, and is in accord with God, how should the permanent be attained?

All things spring from germs. Under many diverse forms these things are ever being reproduced. Round and round, like a wheel, no part of which is more the starting-point than any other. This is called the equilibrium of God. And he who holds the scales is God.

Chuang Tzŭ said to Hui Tzŭ, "When Confucius reached his sixtieth year he changed his opinions. What he had previously regarded as right, he ultimately came to regard as wrong. But who shall say whether the right of to-day may not be as wrong as the wrong of the previous fifty-nine years?"

"He was a persevering worker," replied Hui Tzŭ, "and his wisdom increased day by day."

"Confucius," replied Chuang Tzŭ, "discarded both perseverance and wisdom, but did not attempt to formulate the doctrine in words. He said, 'Man has received his talents from God, together with a soul to give them life. He should speak in accordance with established laws. His words should be in harmony with fixed order. Personal advantage and duty to one's neighbour lie open before us. Likes and dislikes, rights and wrongs, are but as men choose to call them. But to bring submission into men's hearts, so that they shall not be stiff-necked, and thus fix firmly the foundations of the empire,—to that, alas! I have not attained.' "

Tseng Tzŭ held office twice. His emotions varied in each case.

"As long as my parents were alive," said he, "I was happy on a small salary. When I had a large salary, but my parents were no more, I was sad."

A disciple said to Confucius, "Can we call Tsêng Tzŭ a man without cares to trouble him?"

"He had cares to trouble him," replied Confucius. "Can a man who has no cares to trouble him feel grief? His small salary and his large salary were to him like a heron or a mosquito flying past."

Yen Ch'êng Tzŭ Yu said to Tung Kuo Tzŭ Ch'i, "One year after receiving your instructions I became naturally simple. After two years, I could adapt myself as required. After three years, I understood. After four years, my intelligence developed. After five years, it was complete. After six years, the spirit entered into me. After seven, I knew God. After eight, life and death existed for me no more. After nine, perfection.

"Life has its distinctions; but in death we are all made equal. That death should have an origin, but that life should have no origin,—can this be so? What determines its presence in one place, its absence in another?

"Heaven has its fixed order. Earth has yielded up its secrets to man. But where to seek whence am I?

"Not knowing the hereafter, how can we deny the operation of Destiny? Not knowing what preceded birth, how can we assert the operation of Destiny? When things turn out as they ought, who shall say that the agency is not supernatural? When things turn out otherwise, who shall say that it is?"

The various Penumbræ said to the Umbra, "Before you were looking down, now you are looking up. Before you had your hair tied up, now it is all loosed. Before you were sitting, now you have got up. Before you were moving, now you are stopping still. How is this?"

"Gentlemen," replied the Umbra, "the question is hardly worth asking.

I do these things, but I do not know why. I am like the scaly back of the cicada, the shell of the locust,—apparently independent, but not really so. By firelight or in daylight I am seen: in darkness or by night I am gone. And if I am dependent on these, how much more are they dependent on something else? When they come, I come with them. When they go, I go with them. When they live, I live with them. But who it is that gives the life, how shall we seek to know?"

Yang Tzŭ Chü went southwards to P'ei, and when Lao Tzŭ was travelling westwards to Ch'in, hastened to receive him outside the city. Arriving at the bridge, he met Lao Tzŭ; and the latter standing in the middle of the road, looked up to heaven and said with a sigh, "At first, I thought you could be taught. I think so no more."

Yang Tzŭ Chü made no reply, but when they reached the inn, handed Lao Tzŭ water for washing and rinsing, and a towel and comb. He then removed his own boots outside the door, and crawling on his knees into the Master's presence, said, "I have been wishing to ask for instruction, Sir, but as you were travelling and not at leisure, I did not venture. You are now, Sir, at leisure. May I enquire the reason of what you said?"

"You have an overbearing look," said Lao Tzŭ. "Who would live with such a man? He who is truly pure behaves as though he were sullied. He who has virtue in abundance behaves as though it were not enough."

Yang Tzŭ Chü changed countenance at this, and replied, "I hear and obey."

Now when Yang Tzŭ Chü first went to the inn, the visitors there had come out to receive him. Mine host had arranged his mat, while the landlady held towel and comb. The visitors had given him up the best seats, and those who were cooking had left the stove free for him. But when he went back, the other visitors struggled to get the best seats for themselves.

CHAPTER XXVIII. ON DECLINING POWER.

[Spurious.]

Y AO offered to resign the empire to Hsü Yu, but the latter declined.

He then offered it to Tzŭ Chou Chih Fu, who said, "There is no objection to making me emperor. But just now I am suffering from a troublesome disease, and am engaged in trying to cure it. I have no leisure to look after the empire."

Now the empire is of paramount importance. Yet here was a man who would not allow it to injure his chance of life. How much less then would he let other things do so? Yet it is only he who would do nothing in the way of government who is fit to be trusted with the empire.

Shun offered to resign the empire to Tzŭ Chou Chih Poh. The latter said, "Just now I am suffering from a troublesome disease, and am engaged in trying to cure it. I have no leisure to look after the empire."

Now the empire is a great trust; but not to sacrifice one's life for it is precisely where the man of TAO differs from the man of the world.

Shun offered to resign the empire to Shan Chuan. Shan Chuan said, "I am a unit in the sum of the universe. In winter I wear fur clothes. In summer I wear grass-cloth. In spring I plough and sow, toiling with my body. In autumn I gather in the harvest, and devote myself to rest and enjoyment. At dawn I go to work; at sunset I leave off. Contented with my lot I pass through life with a light heart. Why then should I trouble myself with the empire? Ah, Sir, you do not know me."

So he declined, and subsequently hid himself among the mountains, nobody knew where.

Shun offered the empire to a friend, a labourer of Shih-hu.

"Sire," said the latter, "you exert yourself too much. The chief thing is to husband one's strength;"—meaning that in point of real virtue Shun had not attained.

Then, husband and wife, bearing away their household gods and taking their children with them, went off to the sea and never came back.

When T'ai Wang Shan Fu was occupying Pin, he was attacked by savages. He offered them skins and silk, but they declined these. He offered them dogs and horses, but they declined these also. He then offered them pearls and jade, but these too they declined. What they wanted was the territory.

"To live with a man's elder brother," said T'ai Wang Shan Fu, "and slay his younger brother; to live with a man's father and slay his son,—this I could not bear to do. Make shift to remain here. To be my subjects or the subjects of these savages, where is the difference? Besides I have heard say that we ought not to let that which is intended to nourish life become injurious to life."

Thereupon he took his staff and went off. His people all followed him, and they founded a new State at the foot of Mount Ch'i.

Now T'ai Wang Shan Fu undoubtedly had a proper respect for life. And those who have a proper respect for life, if rich and powerful, do not let that which should nourish injure the body. If poor and lowly, they do not allow gain to involve them in physical wear and tear.

But the men of the present generation who occupy positions of power and influence, are all afraid of losing what they have got. Directly they see a chance of gain, away goes all care for their bodies. Is not that a cause for confusion?

In three successive cases the people of Yüeh had put their prince to death. Accordingly, Shou, the son of the last prince, was much alarmed, and fled to Tan-hsüeh, leaving the State of Yüeh without a ruler.

Shou was at first nowhere to be found, but at length he was traced to Tan-hsüeh. He was, however, unwilling to come forth, so they smoked him out with moxa. They had a royal carriage ready for him; and as Shou seized the cord to mount the chariot, he looked up to heaven and cried, "Oh! ruling, ruling, could I not have been spared this?"

It was not that Shou objected to be a prince. He objected to the dangers associated with such positions. Such a one was incapable of sacrificing life to the State, and for that very reason the people of Yüeh wanted to get him.

The States of Han and Wei were struggling to annex each other's territory when Tzŭ Hua Tzŭ went to see prince Chao Hsi. Finding the latter very downcast, Tzŭ Hua Tzŭ said, "Now suppose the representatives of the various States were to sign an agreement before your Highness, to the effect that although cutting off the left hand would involve loss of the right, while cutting off the right would involve loss of the left, nevertheless that whosoever would cut off either should be emperor over all,—would your Highness cut?"

"I would not," replied the prince.

"Very good," said Tzŭ Hua Tzŭ. "It is clear therefore that one's two arms are worth more than the empire. And one's body is worth more than one's arms, while the State of Han is infinitely less important than the empire. Further, what you are struggling over is of infinitely less importance than the State of Han. Yet your Highness is wearing out body and soul alike in fear and anxiety lest you should not get it."

"Good indeed!" cried the prince. "Many have counselled me, but I have never heard the like of this."

From which we may infer that Tzŭ Hua Tzŭ knew the difference between what was of importance and what was not.

The prince of Lu, hearing that Yen Ho had attained to TAO, despatched messengers with presents to open communications.

Yen Ho lived in a hovel. He wore clothes of coarse grass, and occupied himself in tending oxen.

When the messengers arrived. Yen Ho went out to meet them; whereupon they enquired, "Is this where Yen Ho lives?"

"This is Yen Ho's house," replied the latter.

The messengers then produced the presents; but Yen Ho said, "I fear you have made a mistake. And as you might get into trouble, it would be as well to go back and make sure."

This the messengers accordingly did. When however they returned, there was no trace to be found of Yen Ho. Thus it is that men like Yen Ho hate wealth and power.

Wherefore it has been said that the best part of TAO is for self-culture, the surplus for governing a State, and the dregs for governing the empire. From which we may infer that the great deeds of kings and princes are but the leavings of the Sage. For preserving the body and nourishing vitality, they are of no avail. Yet the superior men of today endanger their bodies and throw away their lives in their greed for the things of this world. Is not this pitiable?

The true Sage in all his actions considers the why and the wherefore. But there are those now-a-days who use the pearl of the prince of Sui to shoot a bird a thousand yards off.

And the world of course laughs at them. Why? Because they sacrifice the greater to get the less. But surely life is of more importance even than the prince's pearl!

Lieh Tzŭ was poor. His face wore a hungry look.

A visitor one day mentioned this to Tzŭ Yang of Chêng, saying, "Lieh Tzŭ is a scholar who has attained to TAO. He lives in your Excellency's State, and yet he is poor. Can it be said that your Excellency does not love scholars?"

Thereupon Tzŭ Yang gave orders that Lieh Tzŭ should be supplied with food. But when Lieh Tzŭ saw the messengers, he bowed twice and declined.

When the messengers had gone, and Lieh Tzŭ went within, his wife gazed at him, and beating her breast said, "I have heard that the wife and children of a man of TAO are happy and joyful. But see how hungry I am. His Excellency sent you food, and you would not take it. Is not this flying in the face of Providence?"

"His Excellency did not know me personally," answered Lieh Tzŭ with a smile. "It was because of what others said about me that he sent me the food. If then men were to speak ill of me, he would also act upon it. For that reason I refused the food."

Subsequently, there was trouble among the people of Cheng, and Tzŭ Yang was slain.

When Prince Chao of the Ch'u State lost his kingdom, he was followed into exile by his butcher, named Yüeh.

On his restoration, as he was distributing rewards to those who had remained faithful to him, he came to the name of Yüeh.

Yüeh, however, said, "When the prince lost his kingdom, I lost my butchery. Now that the prince has got back his kingdom, I have got back my butchery. I have recovered my office and salary. What need for further reward?"

On hearing this, the prince gave orders that he should be made to take his reward.

"It was not through my fault," argued Yüeh, "that the prince lost his kingdom, and I should not have taken the punishment. Neither was it through me that he got it back, and I cannot therefore accept the reward."

When the prince heard this answer, he commanded Yüeh to be brought before him. But Yüeh said, "The laws of the Ch'u State require that a subject shall have deserved exceptionally well of his prince before being admitted to an audience. Now my wisdom was insufficient to preserve this kingdom, and my courage insufficient to destroy the invaders. When the Wu soldiers entered Ying, I feared for my life and fled. That was why I followed the prince. And if now the prince wishes to set law and custom aside and summon me to an audience, this is not my idea of proper behaviour on the part of the prince."

"Yüeh," said the prince to Tzŭ Ch'i, his master of the horse, "occupies a lowly position; yet his principles are of the most lofty. Go, make him a San Ching."

"I am aware," replied Yüeh to the master of the horse, "that the post of San Ching is more honourable than that of butcher. And I am aware that the emolument is larger than what I now receive. Still, because I want preferment and salary, I cannot let my prince earn the reputation of being injudicious in his patronage. I must beg to decline. Let me go back to my butchery."

And he adhered to his refusal.

Yüan Hsien dwelt in Lu,—in a mud hut, with a grass-grown roof, an apology for a door, and two mulberry-trees for door-posts. The windows which lighted his two rooms were no bigger than the mouth of a jar, and were closed by a wad of old clothes. The hut leaked from above and was damp under foot; yet Yüan Hsien sat gravely there playing on the guitar.

Tzŭ Kung came driving up in a fine chariot, in a white robe lined with purple; but the hood of the chariot was too big for the street.

When he went to see Yüan Hsien, the latter came to the door in a flowery cap, with his shoes down at heel, and leaning on a stalk.

"Good gracious!" cried Tzŭ Kung, "whatever is the matter with you?"

"I have heard," replied Yüan Hsien, "that he who is without wealth is called poor, and that he who learns without being able to practise is said to have something the matter with him. Now I am merely poor; I have nothing the matter with me."

Tzŭ Kung was much abashed at this reply; upon which Yüan Hsien smiling continued, "To try to thrust myself forward among men; to seek friendship in mutual flattery; to learn for the sake of others; to teach for my own sake; to use benevolence and duty to one's neighbour for evil ends; to make a great show with horses and carriages,—these things I cannot do."

Tsêng Tzŭ lived in the Wei State. His wadded coat had no outside cloth. His face was bloated and rough. His hands and feet were horny hard. For three days he had had no fire; no new clothes for ten years. If he set his cap straight the tassel would come off. If he drew up his sleeve his elbow would poke through. If he pulled up his shoe, the heel would come off. Yet slipshod he sang the *Sacrificial Odes of Shang*, his voice filling the whole sky, as though it had been some instrument of metal or stone.

The Son of Heaven could not secure him as a minister. The feudal princes could not secure him as a friend. For he who nourishes his purpose becomes oblivious of his body. He who nourishes his body becomes oblivious of gain. And he who has attained TAO becomes oblivious of his mind.

"Come hither," said Confucius to Yen Hui. "Your family is poor, and your position lowly. Why not go into official life?"

"I do not wish to," replied Yen Hui. "I have fifty acres of land beyond the city walls, which are enough to supply me with food. Ten more within the walls provide me with clothes. My lute gives me all the amusement I want; and the study of your doctrines keeps me happy enough. I do not desire to go into official life."

"Bravo! well said!" cried Confucius with beaming countenance. "I have heard say that those who are contented do not entangle themselves in the pursuit of gain. That those who have really obtained do not fear the contingency of loss. That those who devote themselves to cultivation of the inner man, though occupying no position, feel no shame. Thus indeed I have long preached. Only now, that I have seen Yen Hui, am I conscious of the realisation of these words."

Prince Mou of Chung-shan said to Chan Tzŭ, "My body is in the country, but my heart is in town. What am I to do?"

"Make life of paramount importance," answered Chan Tzŭ, "and worldly advantage will cease to have weight."

"That I know," replied the Prince; "but I am not equal to the task."

"If you are not equal to this," said Chan Tzŭ, "then it were well for you to pursue your natural bent. Not to be equal to a task, and yet to force oneself to stick to it,—this is called adding one injury to another. And those who suffer such two-fold injury do not belong to the class of the long-lived."

Prince Mou of Wei was heir to the throne of a large State. For him to become a hermit among the hills was more difficult than for an ordinary cotton-clothed scholar. And although he had not attained to TAO, he may be said to have been on the way thither.

When Confucius was caught between the Ch'êns and the Ts'ais, he went seven days without proper food. He ate soup of herbs, having no rice. He looked very much exhausted, yet he sat within playing his guitar and singing to it.

Yen Hui was picking over the herbs, while Tzŭ Lu and Tzŭ Kung were talking together. One of them said, "Our Master has twice been driven out of Lu. They will have none of him in Wei. His tree was cut down in Sung. He got into trouble in Shang and Chou. And now he is surrounded by the Ch'êns and the Ts'ais. Whoever kills him is to be held guiltless. Whoever takes him prisoner is not to be interfered with. Yet all the time he goes on playing and singing without cease. Is this the right thing, for a superior man to do?"

Yen Hui said nothing, but went inside and told Confucius, who laid aside his guitar and said with a loud sigh, "Yu and Tz'ŭ are ignorant fellows.

Bid them come, and I will speak to them."

When they entered Tzŭ Lu said, "We seem to have made a thorough failure."

"What do you mean?" cried Confucius. "The superior man who succeeds in TAO, has success. If he fails in TAO, he makes a failure. Now I, holding fast to the TAO of charity and duty towards one's neighbour, have fallen among the troubles of a disordered age. What failure is there in that?

"Therefore it is that by cultivation of the inner man there is no failure in TAO, and when danger comes there is no loss of virtue. It is the chill winter weather, it is frost, it is snow, which bring out the luxuriance of the pine and the fir.

I regard it as a positive blessing to be thus situated as I am."

Thereupon he turned abruptly round and went on playing and singing.

At this Tzŭ Lu hastily seized a shield and began dancing to the music, while Tzŭ Kung said, "I had no idea of the height of heaven and of the depth of earth."

The ancients who attained TAO were equally happy under success and failure. Their happiness had nothing to do with their failure or their success. TAO once attained, failure and success became mere links in a chain, like cold, heat, wind, and rain. Thus Hsü Yu enjoyed himself at Ying-yang, and Kung Poh found happiness on the hill-top.

Shun offered to resign the empire to his friend Pei Jen Wu Tsê.

"What a strange manner of man you are!" cried the latter. "Living in the furrowed fields, you exchanged such a life for the throne of Yao. And as if that was not enough, you now try to heap indignity upon me. I am ashamed of you." Thereupon he drowned himself in the waters of Ch'ing-ling.

When T'ang was about to attack Chieh, he went to consult with Pien Sui.

"It is not a matter in which I can help you," said the latter.

"Who can?" asked T'ang.

"I do not know," replied Pien Sui.

T'ang then went to consult with Wu Kuang.

"It is not a matter in which I can help you," said the latter.

"Who can?" asked T'ang,

"I do not know," replied Wu Kuang.

"What do you think of I Yin?" asked T'ang.

"He forces himself," said Wu Kuang, "to put up with obloquy. Beyond this I know nothing of him."

So T'ang took I Yin into his counsels. They attacked Chieh, and vanquished him.

Then T'ang offered to resign the empire in favour of Pien Sui. But Pien Sui declined, saying, "When your Majesty consulted with me about attacking Chieh, you evidently looked on me as a robber.

Now that you have vanquished him, and you offer to resign in my favour, you evidently regard me as covetous. I was born indeed in a disordered age. But for a man without TAO to thus insult me twice, is more than I can endure."

So he drowned himself in the river Chou.

Then T'ang offered to resign in favour of Wu Kuang, saying, "The wise plan, the brave execute, the good rest therein,—such was the TAO of the ancients. Why, Sir, should not you occupy the throne?"

But Wu Kuang declined, saying, "To depose a ruler is not to do one's duty to one's neighbour. To slay the people is not charity. For others to suffer these wrongs, while I enjoy the profits, is not honest. I have heard say that one should not accept a wage unless earned in accordance with right; and that if the world is without Tao, one should not put foot upon its soil, still less rule over it! I can bear this no longer."

Thereupon he took a stone on his back and jumped into the river Lu.

At the rise of the Chou dynasty there were two scholars, named Po I and Shu Ch'i, who lived in Ku-tu.

One of these said to the other, "I have heard that in the west there are men who are apparently in possession of TAO. Let us go and see them."

When they arrived at Ch'i-yang, Wu Wang heard of their arrival and sent Shu Tan to enter into a treaty with them. They were to receive emoluments of the second degree and rank of the first degree. The treaty was to be sealed with blood and buried.

At this the two looked at each other and smiled. "Ah!" said one of them, "this is strange indeed. It is not what we call TAO.

"When Shên Nung ruled the empire, he worshipped God without asking for any reward. Sometimes it was the law he put in force; sometimes it was his personal influence he brought to bear. He was loyal and faithful to his people without seeking any return. He did not build his success upon another's ruin, nor mount high by means of another's fall, nor seize opportunities to secure his own advantage.

"But now that the Chous, beholding the iniquities of the Yins, have taken upon themselves to govern, we have intrigues above and bribes below. Troops are mobilised to protect prestige. Victims are slaughtered to give good faith to a treaty. A show of virtue is made to amuse the masses. Fighting and slaughter are made the means of gain. Confusion has simply been exchanged for disorder.

"I have heard tell that the men of old, living in quiet times, never shirked their duties; but lighting upon troublous times, nothing could make them stay. The empire is now in darkness. The virtue of the Chous has faded. For the empire to be united under the Chous would be a disgrace to us. Better flee away and keep our actions pure."

Accordingly, these two philosophers went north to Mount Shou-yang, where they subsequently starved themselves to death.

Men like Poh I and Shu Ch'i, if wealth and honour came to them so that they could properly accept, would assuredly not have recourse to such heroic measures, nor would they be content to follow their own bent, without giving their services to their generation. Such was the purity of these two scholars.

CHAPTER XXIX. ROBBER CHÊ.

[Spurious.]

CONFUCIUS was on terms of friendship with Liu Hsia Chi, whose younger brother was known as "Robber Chê."

Robber Chê had a band of followers nine thousand strong. He ravaged the whole empire, plundering the various nobles and breaking into people's houses. He drove off oxen and horses. He stole men's wives and daughters. Family ties put no limit to his greed. He had no respect for parents nor for brothers. He neglected the worship of his ancestors. Wherever he passed, the greater States flew to arms, the smaller ones to places of safety. All the people were sore distressed.

"A father," said Confucius to Liu Hsia Chi, "should surely be able to admonish his son; an elder brother to teach his younger brother. If this be not so, there is an end of the value attached to these relationships.

"Now you, Sir, are one of the scholars of the age, while your younger brother is the Robber Chê, the scourge of the empire. You are unable to teach him, and I blush for you. Let me go and have a talk with him on your behalf."

"As to what you say, Sir, about fathers and elder brothers," answered Liu Hsia Chi, "if the son will not listen to his father, nor the younger brother to his elder brother, what becomes of your arguments then?

"Besides, Chê's passions are like a bubbling spring. His thoughts are like a whirlwind. He is strong enough to defy all foes. He can argue until wrong becomes right. If you follow his inclinations, he is pleased. If you oppose them he is angry. He is free with the language of abuse. Do not go near him."

Confucius paid no attention to this advice; but with Yen Hui as charioteer and Tzŭ Kung on his right, went off to see Robber Chê.

The latter had just encamped to the south of T'ai-shan, and was engaged in devouring a dish of minced human liver. Confucius alighted from his chariot, and advancing addressed the doorkeeper as follows:—

"I am Confucius of the Lu State. I have heard of the high character of your captain."

He then twice respectfully saluted the doorkeeper, who went in to announce his arrival.

When Robber Chê heard who it was, he was furious. His eyes glared like stars. His hair raised his cap from his head as he cried out, "What! that crafty scoundrel Confucius of Lu? Go, tell him from me that he is a mere word-monger. That he talks nonsense about Wen Wang and Wu Wang. That he wears an extravagant cap, with a thong from the side of a dead ox. That what he says is mostly rhodomontade. That he consumes where he does not sow, and wears clothes he does not weave. That his lips patter and his tongue wags. That his rights and wrongs are of his own coining, whereby he throws dust in the eyes of rulers and prevents the scholars of the empire from reverting to the original source of all things.

That he makes a great stir about filial piety and brotherly love, glad enough himself to secure some fat fief or post of power. Tell him that he deserves the worst, and that if he does not take himself off his liver shall be in my morning stew."

But Confucius sent in again, saying, "I am a friend of Liu Hsia Chi. I am anxious to set eyes upon your captain's shoestrings."

When the doorkeeper gave this second message, Robber Chê said, "Bring him before me!" Thereupon Confucius hurried in, and avoiding the place of honour stepped back and made two obeisances.

Robber Chê, flaming with anger, straddled out his two legs, and laying his hand upon his sword glared at Confucius and roaring like a tigress with young, said, "Ch'iu! come here. If what you say suits my ideas, you will live. Otherwise you will die."

"I have heard," replied Confucius, "that the world contains three classes of virtue. To grow up tall, of a beauty without compare, and thus to be the idol of young and old, of noble and lowly alike,—this is the highest class. To be possessed of wisdom which embraces the universe and can explain all things,—this is the middle class. To be possessed of courage which will stand test and gather followers around, —this is the lowest class.

"Now any man whose virtue belongs to either of these classes is fit to occupy the place and title of ruler. But you. Captain, unite all three in your-self. You are eight feet two in height. Your expression is very bright. Your lips are like vermilion. Your teeth like a row of shells. Your voice is like a beautiful bell;—yet you are known as Robber Chê. Captain, I blush for you.

"Captain, if you will hearken to me I will go south for you to Wu and Yüeh, north to Ch'i and Lu, east to Sung and Wei, and west to Chin and Ch'u. I will have a great wall built for you of many *li* in extent, enclosing hamlets of many hundreds of thousands of inhabitants, over which State you shall be ruler. Your relations with the empire will enter upon a new phase. You will disband your men. You will gather your brothers around you. You will join in worship of your ancestors. Such is the behaviour of the true Sage and the man of parts, and such is what the world desires."

"Ch'iu! come here," cried Robber Chê in a great rage. "Those who are squared by offers and corrected by words are the stupid vulgar masses. The height and the beauty which you praise in me are legacies from my parents. Even though you did not praise them, do you think I should be ignorant of their existence? Besides, those who flatter to the face speak evil behind the back. Now all you have been saying about the great State and its numerous population simply means squaring me by offers as though one of the common herd. And of course it would not last.

"There is no State bigger than the empire. Yao and Shun both got this, yet their descendants have not territory enough to insert an awl's point. Tang and Wu Wang both sat upon the Imperial throne, yet their posterity has been obliterated from the face of the earth.

Was not this because of the very magnitude of the prize?

"I have also heard that in olden times the birds and animals outnumbered man, and that the latter was obliged to seek his safety by building his domicile in trees. By day he picked up acorns and chestnuts. At night he slept upon a branch. Hence the name *Nest-builders*.

"Of old, the people did not know how to make clothes. In summer they collected quantities of fuel, and in winter warmed themselves by fire. Hence the name *Provident*.

"In the days of Shên Nung, they lay down without caring where they were and got up without caring whither they might go. A man knew his mother but not his father. He lived among the wild deer. He tilled the ground for food. He wove cloth to cover his body. He harboured no thought of injury to others. These were the glorious results of an age of perfect virtue.

"The Yellow Emperor, however, could not attain to this virtue. He fought with Ch'ih Yu at Chŏ-lu, and blood flowed for a hundred *li*. Then came Yao and Shun with their crowd of ministers. Then T'ang who deposed his sovereign, and Wu Wang who slew Chou. After which time the strong took to oppressing the weak, the many to coercing the few, In fact, ever since T'ang and Wu Wang we have had none other than disturbers of the peace.

"And now you come forward preaching the old dogmas of Wên Wang and palming off sophistries without end, in order to teach future generations. You wear patched clothes and a narrow girdle, you talk big and act falsely, in order to deceive the rulers of the land, while all the time you yourself are aiming at wealth and power! You are the biggest thief I know of; and if the world calls me Robber Chê, it most certainly ought to call you Robber Ch'iu.

"By fair words you enticed Tzŭ Lu to follow you. You made him doff his martial cap, and ungird his long sword, and sit a disciple at your feet. And all the world cried out that Confucius could stop violence and prevent wrong-doing. By and by, when Tzŭ Lu wished to slay the prince of Wei, but failed, and was himself hacked to pieces and exposed over the eastern gate of Wei,—that was because you had not properly instructed him.

"You call yourself a man of talent and a Sage forsooth! Twice you have been driven out of Lu. You were tabooed in Wei. You were a failure in Ch'i. You were surrounded by the Ch'êns and the Ts'ais. In fact, the empire won't have you anywhere. It was your teaching which brought Tzŭ Lu to his tragical end. You cannot take care, in the first place, of yourself, nor, in the second place, of others. Of what value can your doctrine be?

"There is none to whom mankind has accorded a higher place than to the Yellow Emperor. Yet his virtue was not complete. He fought at <u>Chŏ-lu</u>, and blood ran for a hundred *li*. Yao was not paternal.

Shun was not filial.

The great Yü was deficient in one respect.

T'ang deposed his sovereign. Wu Wang vanquished Chou. Wên Wang was imprisoned at Yin-li.

"Now these six worthies enjoy a high reputation among men. Yet a fuller investigation shows that in each case a desire for advantage disturbed their original purity and forced it into a contrary direction. Hence the shamelessness of their deeds.

"Among those whom the world calls virtuous were Poh I and Shu Ch'i. They declined the sovereignty of Ku-chu and died of starvation on Mount Shou-yang, their corpses deprived of burial.

"Pao Chiao made a great show of virtue and abused the world in general. He grasped a tree and died.

"Shên T'u Ti, when no heed was paid to his counsels, jumped into the river with a stone on his back and became food for fishes.

"Chieh Tzŭ T'ui was truly loyal. He cut a slice from his thigh to feed Wen Wang. Afterwards, when Wen Wang turned his back upon him, he retired in anger, and grasping a tree, was burnt to death.

"Wei Shêng made an assignation with a girl beneath a bridge. The girl did not come, and the water rose. But Wei Shêng would not leave. He grasped a buttress and died.

"These four differed in no way from dogs and pigs going about begging to be slaughtered. They all exaggerated reputation and disregarded death. They did not reflect upon their original nature and seek to preserve life into the old age allotted.

"Among ministers whom the world calls loyal, none can compare with Wang Tzŭ, Pi Kan, and Wu Tzŭ Hsü. The last-mentioned drowned himself. Pi Kan was disembowelled. These two worthies are what men call loyal ministers; yet, as a matter of fact, all the world laughs at them!

"Thus, from the most ancient times down to Tzŭ Hsü and Pi Kan, there have been none deserving of honour. And as to the sermon you, Ch'iu, propose to preach to me,—if it is on ghostly subjects, I shan't understand them, and if it is on human affairs, why there is nothing more to be said. I know it all already.

"I will now tell you a few things. The lust of the eye is for beauty. The lust of the ear is for music. The lust of the palate is for flavour. The lust of ambition is for gratification. Man's greatest age is one hundred years. A medium old age is eighty years. The lowest estimate is sixty years. Take away from this the hours of sickness, disease, death, mourning, sorrow, and trouble, and there will not remain more than four or five days a month upon which a man may open his mouth to laugh. Heaven and Earth are everlasting. Sooner or later every man has to die. That which thus has a limit, as compared with that which is everlasting, is a mere flash, like the passage of some swift steed seen through a crack. And those who cannot gratify their ambition and live through their allotted span, are men who have not attained to TAO.

"Ch'iu! all your teachings are nothing to me. Begone! Go home! Say no more! Your doctrine is a random jargon, full of falsity and deceit. It can never preserve the original purity of man. Why discuss it further?"

Confucius made two obeisances and hurriedly took his leave. On mounting his chariot, he three times missed hold of the reins. His eyes were so dazed that he could see nothing. His face was ashy pale. With down-cast head he grasped the bar of his chariot, unable to find vent for his feelings.

Arriving outside the eastern gate of Lu, he met Liu Hsia Chi, who said, "I have not seen you for some days. From the look of your equipage I should say you had been travelling. I guess now you have been to see Chê."

Confucius looked up to heaven, and replied with a sigh, "I have."

"And did he not rebuff you," asked Liu Hsia Chi, "as I said he would?"

"He did," said Confucius. "I am a man who has cauterized himself without being ill. I hurried away to smooth the tiger's head and comb out his beard. And I very nearly got into the tiger's mouth."

Tzŭ Chang asked Man Kou Tê, saying, "Why do you not practise virtue? Otherwise, it is impossible to inspire confidence. And without confidence, no place. And without place, no wealth. Thus, with a view to reputation or to wealth, duty towards one's neighbour is the true key.

If you were to discard all thoughts of reputation and wealth and attend to the cultivation of the heart, surely you would not pass one day without practising the higher virtues."

"Those who have no shame," replied Man Kou Tê, "grow rich. Those who inspire confidence make themselves conspicuous.

Reputation and wealth are mostly to be got out of shamelessness and confidence inspired. Thus, with a view to reputation or to wealth, the confidence of others is the true key.

If you were to discard all thoughts of reputation and wealth, surely the virtuous man would then have no scope beyond himself."

"Of old," said Tzŭ Chang, "Chieh and Chou sat upon the Imperial throne, and the whole empire was theirs. Yet if you were now to tell any common thief that his moral qualities resembled theirs, he would resent it as an insult. By such miserable creatures are they despised."

"Confucius and Mih Tzŭ, on the other hand, were poor and simple enough. Yet if you were to tell any Prime Minister of to-day that his moral qualities resembled theirs, he would flush with pride and declare you were paying him too high a compliment. So truly honourable is the man of learning. "Thus, the power of a monarch does not necessarily make him worthy; nor do poverty and a low station necessarily make a man unworthy. The worthy and the unworthy are differentiated by the worthiness and unworthiness of their acts."

"A petty thief," replied Man Kou Tê, "is put in gaol. A great brigand becomes ruler of a State. And among the retainers of the latter, men of virtue will be found.

"Of old, Duke Huan, named Hsiao Poh, slew his elder brother and took his sister-in-law to wife. Yet Kuan Chung became his minister.

"T'ien Ch'êng Tzŭ killed his prince and seized the kingdom. Yet Confucius accepted his pay.

"To condemn a man in words, yet actually to take service under him,— does not this show us practice and precept directly opposed to one another?

"Therefore it was written, 'Who is bad? Who is good? He who succeeds is the head. He who does not succeed is the tail.'"

"But if you do not practise virtue," said Tzŭ Chang, "and make no distinction between kith and kin, assign no duties to the worthy and to the unworthy, no precedence to young and old, how then are the Five Bonds and the Six Ranks to be distinguished?"

"Yao slew his eldest son," answered Man Kou Tê. "Shun banished his mother's brother. Was there kith and kin in that?

"T'ang deposed Chieh. Wu Wang slew Chou. Was that the duty of the worthy towards the unworthy?

"Wang Chi was the legitimate heir, but Chow Kung slew his elder brother. Was that precedence of young and old?

"The false principles of the Confucianists, the universal love of the Mihists,—do these help to distinguish the Five Bonds and the Six Ranks?

"You, Sir, are all for reputation. I am all for wealth. As to which pursuit is not in accordance with principle nor in harmony with right, let us refer to the arbitration of Wu Yoh."

"The mean man," said Wu Yoh, "devotes himself to wealth. The superior man devotes himself to reputation. The moral results are different in each case. But if both would set aside their activities and devote themselves to doing nothing, the results would be the same.

"Wherefore it has been said, 'Be not a mean man. Revert to your natural self. Be not a superior man. Abide by the laws of heaven.'

"As to the straight and the crooked, view them from the standpoint of the infinite.

Gaze around you on all sides, until time withdraws you from the scene.

"As to the right and the wrong, hold fast to your magic circle, and with independent mind walk ever in the way of TAO.

"Do not swerve from the path of virtue; do not bring about your own good deeds,—lest your labour be lost. Do not make for wealth; do not aim at success,—lest you cast away that which links you to God.

"Pi Kan was disembowelled. Tzŭ Hsü had his eyes gouged out.

Such was the fate of loyalty.

"Chih Kung bore witness against his father. Wei Sheng was drowned. Such are the misfortunes of the faithful.

"Pao Chiao dried up where he stood. Shen Tzŭ would not justify himself.

Such are the evils of honesty.

"Confucius did not visit his mother.

K'uang Tzŭ did not visit his father.

Such are the trials which come upon the upright.

"The above instances have been handed down to us from antiquity and are discussed in modern times. They show that men of learning emphasized their precepts by carrying them out in practice; and that consequently they paid the penalty and fell into these calamities."

Discontent asked Complacency, saying, "There is really no one who does not either aim at reputation or make for wealth. If a man is rich, others flock around him. These necessarily take a subordinate position, and consequently pay him court. And it would seem that such subordination and respect constitute a royal road to long life, comfort, and general happiness. How is it then that you. Sir, have no mind for these things? Is it that you are wanting in wit? Or is it that you are physically unable to compete, and therefore go in for being virtuous, though all the time unable to forget?"

"You and your friends," replied Complacency, "regard all men as alike because they happen to be born at the same time and in the same place as yourselves. You look on us as scholars who have separated from humanity and cast off the world, and who have no guiding principle beyond poring over the records of the past and present, or indulging in the logomachy of this and that.

"Were we to lead the mundane lives you do, it would be at the sacrifice of the very conditions of existence. And surely thus we should be wandering far from the royal road to long life, comfort, and general happiness. The discomfort of wretchedness, the comfort of well-being, you do not refer to the body.

The abjectness of terror, the elation of joy, you do not refer to the mind itself. You know that such things are so, but you do not know how they are so. Wherefore, though equalling the Son of Heaven in power, and with all the empire as your personal property, you would not be free from care."

"Wealth," replied Discontent, "is of the greatest service to a man. It enables him to do good, and to exert power, to an extent which the perfect man or the true Sage could never reach. He can borrow the courage and strength of others to make himself formidable. He can employ the wisdom and counsels of others to add clearness to his own deliberations. He can avail himself of the virtue of others and cause it to appear as his own. Without being in possession of a throne, he can wield the authority of a prince.

"Besides, the pleasures of music, beauty, rich food, and power, do not require to be studied before they can be appreciated by the mind; nor does the body need the example of others before it can enjoy them. We need no teacher to tell us what to like or dislike, to follow or to avoid. Such knowledge is instinctive in man. The world may condemn this view, but which of us is free from the taint?"

"The wise man," answered Complacency, "acts for the common weal, in pursuit of which he does not overstep due limits. Wherefore, if there is a sufficiency, he does not strive for more. He has no use for more, and accordingly does not seek it. But if there is not a sufficiency, then he seeks for more. He strives in all directions, yet does not account it greed. If there is a surplus, he declines it. Even though he refused the whole empire, he would not account it honesty. To him, honesty and greed are not conditions into which we are forced by outward circumstances, but characteristics innate in the individual. He may wield the power of the Son of Heaven, but will not employ it for the degradation of others. He may own the whole empire, yet will not use his wealth to take advantage of his fellows. But a calculation of the troubles and the anxieties inseparable therefrom, cause him to reject these as injurious to his nature, not from a desire for reputation.

"When Yao and Shun occupied the throne, there was peace. They did not try to be beneficent rulers. They did not inflict injury by doing good.

"Shan Chuan and Hsü Yu both declined the proffered throne. Theirs was no empty refusal. They would not cause injury to themselves.

"In all these cases, each individual adopted the profitable course in preference to the injurious course. And the world calls them virtuous, whereby they acquire a reputation at which they never aimed."

"It is necessary," argued Discontent, "to cling to reputation. If all pleasures are to be denied to the body and one's energies to be concentrated upon health with a view to the prolongation of life, such life would be itself nothing more than the prolonged illness of a confirmed invalid."

"Happiness," said Complacency, "is to be found in contentment. Too much is always a curse, most of all in wealth.

"The ears of the wealthy man ring with sounds of sweet music. His palate is cloyed with rich meats and wine. In the pursuit of pleasure, business is forgotten. This is confusion.

"He eats and drinks to excess, until his breathing is that of one carrying a heavy load up a hill. This is misery.

"He covets money to surround himself with comforts. He covets power to vanquish rivals. But his quiet hours are darkened by diabetes and dropsy. This is disease.

"Even when, in his desire for wealth, he has piled up an enormous fortune, he still goes on and cannot desist. This is shame.

"Having no use for the money he has collected, he still hugs it to him and cannot bear to part with it. His heart is inflamed, and he ever seeks to add more to the pile. This is unhappiness.

"At home, he dreads the pest of the pilfering thief. Abroad, the danger of bandit and highwayman. So he keeps strict guard within, while never venturing alone without. This is fear.

"These six are the greatest of the world's curses. Yet such a man never bestows a thought upon them, until the hour of misfortune is at hand. Then, with his ambitions gratified, his natural powers exhausted, and nothing but wealth remaining, he would gladly obtain one day's peace, but cannot do so.

"Wherefore, if reputation is not to be enjoyed and wealth is not to be secured, how pitiable it is that men should harass their minds and wear out their bodies in such pursuits!"

CHAPTER XXX. ON SWORDS.

[Spurious.]

OF old, Wên Wang of Chao loved sword-play. Swordsmen thronged his halls, to the number of three thousand and more. Day and night they had bouts before the prince. In the course of a year, a hundred or so would be killed or wounded. Yet the prince was never satisfied.

Within three years, the State had begun to go to rack and ruin, and other princes to form designs upon it. Thereupon the Heir Apparent, Li, became troubled in mind; and said to the officers of his household, "Whosover shall persuade the prince to do away with these swordsmen, to him I will give a thousand ounces of silver."

To this his officers replied, "Chuang Tzŭ is the man."

Thereupon the Heir Apparent sent messengers to Chuang Tzŭ with a thousand ounces of silver, which he would not accept, but accompanied the messengers back to their master.

"What does your Highness require of me," asked Chuang Tzŭ, "that you should bestow upon me a thousand ounces?"

"I had heard," replied the young prince, "that you were a famous Sage, and I ventured to send this money as a present to your servants.

But as you would not receive it, what more can I say?"

"I understand," answered Chuang Tzŭ, "that your Highness would have me cure the prince of his peculiar weakness. Now suppose that I do not succeed with the prince, and consequently with your Highness, the punishment of death is what I have to expect. What good would the thousand ounces be to me then?"

"On the other hand, if I succeed with the prince, and consequently with your Highness, the whole State of Chao contains nothing I could not have for the asking."

"You must know, however," said the young prince, "that my father will only receive swordsmen."

"Well," replied Chuang Tzŭ, "I am a good swordsman myself."

"Besides which," added the Heir Apparent, "the swordsmen he is accustomed to see have all dishevelled hair hanging over their temples. They wear slouching caps with coarse tangled tassels, and short-tailed coats. They glare with their eyes and talk in a fierce tone. This is what my father likes. But if you go to him dressed in your ordinary scholar's dress, the result is sure to be disastrous."

"I will accustom myself to the dress," replied Chuang Tzŭ; and after practising for three days, he went again to see the young prince, who accompanied him into his father's presence.

The latter drew a sharp sword and awaited Chuang Tzŭ's approach. But Chuang Tzŭ, when he entered the door of the audience chamber, did not hurry forward, neither did he prostrate himself before the prince.

"What have you to say to me," cried the prince, "that you have obtained your introduction through the Heir Apparent?"

"I have heard," replied Chuang Tzŭ, "that your Highness loves swordplay. Therefore I have come to exhibit my skill."

"What can you do in that line?" asked the prince.

"Were I to meet an opponent," said Chuang Tzŭ, "at every ten paces, I could go on for a thousand *li* without being stopped."

"Bravo!" cried the prince. "There is not your match in the empire."

"When I fight," continued Chuang Tzŭ, "I make a show of being weak but push a vigorous attack. The last to start, I am the first to arrive. I should like your Highness to make trial of me."

"Rest awhile," replied the prince. "Stay here and await orders. I will arrange a day for you."

Thereupon the prince spent seven days in trying his swordsmen. Some sixty of them were either killed or wounded, but at length he selected five or six and bade them attend in the audience-chamber with their swords. He then summoned Chuang Tzŭ and said, "Now I will see what your swordsmanship is worth."

"I have been longing for this," replied Chuang Tzŭ.

"Does it matter to you," asked the prince, "of what length your weapon may be?"

"Not at all," replied Chuang Tzŭ. "I have three swords, of which I will ask your Highness to choose one. We will then proceed to the trial."

"Which are your three swords?" enquired the prince.

"There is the sword of the Son of Heaven," said Chuang Tzŭ, "the sword of the Princes, and the sword of the People."

"What is the sword of the Son of Heaven?" asked the prince.

"The stone wall of Yen-ch'i is its point," replied Chuang Tzŭ.

The mountains of Ch'i are its edge. Chin and Wei are its back. Chou and Sung are its hilt. Han and Wei are its sheath. It is enclosed in the four hordes of barbarians, wrapped in the four seasons, surrounded by the great ocean. It is made of the five elements. It is the arbiter of punishment and reward. It operates under the influence of the Yin and the Yang. In spring and summer it is at rest. In autumn and winter it moves abroad. Push it, it does not advance. Raise it, it does not go up. Lower it, it does not go down. Whirl it around, it does not change position. Above, it cleaves the floating clouds; below, it cuts through the density of earth. One flash of this blade, and the princes of the empire submit. Such is the sword of the Son of Heaven."

At this the prince seemed absorbed in his reflections. Then he enquired, saying, "And what is the sword of the Princes?"

"The wise and brave," replied Chuang Tzŭ, "are its point. The incorruptible are its edge. The virtuous are its back. The loyal are its hilt. The heroic are its sheath. You may push this sword too, it will not advance. Raise it, it will not go up. Lower it, it will not go down. Whirl it around, it will not change position. Above, it models itself upon the round heaven, in order to keep in harmony with the sun, moon, and stars. Below, it models itself upon the square earth, in order to keep in harmony with the four seasons. It adapts itself to the wishes of the people, in order to diffuse peace on all sides. One flash of this blade is like a roaring clap of thunder. Between the boundaries of the State there is not left one but who yields and obeys the command of his prince. Such is the sword of the Princes."

"And the sword of the People?" enquired the prince.

"The sword of the People," replied Chuang Tzŭ, "has dishevelled hair hanging over its temples. It wears a slouching cap with coarse tangled tassel, and a short-tailed coat. It glares with its eyes and talks in a fierce tone. When it engages in conflict, above, it cuts off head and neck; below, it smites liver and lungs. Such is the sword of the People. It is like a game-cock. One day, its life is cut short, and it is of no more use to the State.

"Now you, great prince, wield sovereign power, and yet you devote yourself to this sword of the People. I am truly ashamed of it."

Thereupon the prince drew Chuang Tzŭ up on to the dais, and the attendants served food, the king three times assisting with his own hand.

"Be seated, great prince," said Chuang Tzŭ, "and compose your mind. I have said all I have to say on swords."

After this the prince did not quit his palace for three months, while the swordsmen, submitting to the new order of things, died in their own homes.

CHAPTER XXXI. THE OLD FISHERMAN.

[Spurious.]

CONFUCIUS, travelling in the Black Forest, rested awhile at Apricot Altar. His disciples sat down to their books, and he himself played upon the lute and sang.

Half way through the song, an old fisherman stepped out of a boat and advanced towards them. His beard and eyebrows were snowy white. His hair hung loose, and he flapped his long sleeves as he walked over the foreshore. Reaching firm ground, he stood still, and with left hand on his knee and right hand to his ear, listened.

When the song was finished, he beckoned to Tzŭ Kung and Tzŭ Lu, both of whom went to him. Then pointing with his finger, he enquired, saying, "What is that man doing here?"

"He is the Sage of Lu," replied Tzŭ Lu.

"Of what clan?" asked the old man.

"Of the K'ung family," replied Tzŭ Lu.

"And what is his occupation?" said the old man.

"He devotes himself," replied Tzŭ Lu, "to loyalty and truth. He practises charity and duty towards his neighbour. He regulates ceremonies and music.

He distinguishes the relationships of man. He is loyal to his prince above, a reformer of the masses below. Thus he will be of great service to the whole empire. Such is his occupation."

"Is he a ruler of a State?" asked the old man.

"He is not," said Tzŭ Kung.

"A minister?" said the old man.

"No," said Tzŭ Kung.

Then the old man laughed and walked away, saying,

"Charity is charity, yet I fear he will not escape the wear of mind and tear of body which imperil the original purity of man. How far, alas, has he wandered from the true path!"

Tzŭ Kung went back and told Confucius, who, laying aside his lute, arose and said, "This man is a Sage!"

Thereupon he followed the old man down the shore, catching him up just as he was drawing in his boat with his staff. Perceiving Confucius, the old man turned round to receive him, at which Confucius stepped back and prostrated himself twice before advancing.

"What do you want, Sir?" asked the fisherman.

"Just now, venerable Sir," replied Confucius, "you left without finishing your remarks. In my stupidity I cannot make out what you mean. Therefore I have come in the humble hope of hearing any words with which you may deign to help me."

"Well," said the old man, "you are certainly anxious to learn."

At this Confucius prostrated himself twice, and when he got up said, "Yes, I have been a student from my youth upwards until now, the sixty-ninth year of my age. Yet I have never heard the true doctrine, which I am now ready to receive without bias."

"Like species follow like," answered the old man. "Like sounds respond to like.

This is a law of nature. I will now with your leave apply what I know to what you occupy yourself with,—the affairs of men.

"The Son of Heaven, the princes, the ministers, and the people,—if these four fulfil their proper functions, the result is good government. If they quit their proper places, the result is unutterable confusion. When the officials mind their duties and the people their business, neither is injured by the other.

"Barren land, leaky roofs, want of food and clothing, inability to meet taxation, quarrels of wives and concubines, no precedence between young and old,—such are the sorrows of the people.

"Capacity unequal to one's duties, and inability to carry on routine work, absence of clean-handedness, and carelessness among subordinates, lack of distinction and want of preferment,—such are the sorrows of ministers.

"The Court without loyal ministers and the State in rebellion, the artisan unskilful and the tribute unsatisfactory, the periodical levées unattended and the Son of Heaven displeased,—such are the sorrows of the princes.

"The two great principles of nature working inharmoniously, heat and cold coming at irregular seasons so that men and things suffer, the princes rebellious and fighting among themselves so that the people perish, music and ceremonies ill regulated, wealth dissipated, the relationships of man disregarded, the masses sunk in immorality,—such are the sorrows which fall to the share of the Son of Heaven.

"But now you. Sir, occupying neither the more exalted position of ruler nor performing the subordinate functions of minister, nevertheless take upon yourself to regulate music and ceremonies and to distinguish the relationships of man, in order to reform the masses. Are you not travelling out of your own sphere?

"Further, men have eight blemishes, and there are four things which obstruct business. These should be investigated.

"Meddling with matters which do not matter to you, is prying.

"To push one's way in, regardless of neglect, is to be forward.

"To adapt one's thoughts and arrange one's words, is sycophancy.

"To applaud a person, right or wrong, is flattery.

"To love speaking evil of others, is slander.

"To sever friendships and break ties, is mischievousness.

"To praise people falsely with a view to injure them, is malice.

"To give ready assent with a view to worm out the wishes of others, good and bad alike, is to be a hypocrite.

"These eight blemishes cause a man to throw others into confusion and bring injury upon himself. The superior man will not have him for a friend; the enlightened prince will not employ him as his minister.

"To love the conduct of great affairs, and to introduce change into established order with a view to gain reputation,—this is ambition.

"To strive to get all into one's own hands, and to usurp what should be at the disposal of others,—this is greed.

"To know one's faults but not to correct them, to receive admonition but only to plunge deeper,—this is obstinacy.

"To suffer those who are like oneself, but as for those unlike not to credit them with the virtues they really possess —this is bigotry.

"Such are the four things which obstruct business. And only he who can put aside the above eight and abstain from the above four is fit for instruction."

At this Confucius heaved a sigh of distress. Then having twice prostrated himself, he arose and said, "Twice was I driven from Lu. I was tabooed in Wei. My tree was cut down in Sung. I was surrounded by the Ch'êns and the Ts'ais. I know not what my fault is that I should have suffered these four persecutions."

"Dear me!" said the old man in a vexed tone, "How slow of perception you are.

"There was once a man who was so afraid of his shadow and so disliked his own footsteps that he determined to run away from them. But the oftener he raised his feet the more footsteps he made, and though he ran very hard his shadow never left him. From this he inferred that he went too slowly, and ran as hard as he could without resting, the consequence being that his strength broke down and he died. He was not aware that by going into the shade he would have got rid of his shadow, and that by keeping still he would have put an end to his footsteps. Fool that he was!

"Now you occupy yourself with charity and duty to one's neighbour. You examine into the distinction of like and unlike, the changes of motion and rest, the canons of giving and receiving, the emotions of love and hate, and the restraint of joy and anger. Yet you cannot avoid the calamities you speak of.

"Reverently care for your body. Carefully preserve your natural purity. Leave externals to others. Then you will not be involved. But as it is, instead of improving yourself you are trying to improve other people. Surely this is dealing with the external."

"Then may I enquire," said Confucius in a tone of distress, "what is the original purity?"

"Our original purity," replied the fisherman, "is the perfection of truth unalloyed. Without this, we cannot influence others. Hence, those who weep to order, though they mourn, do not grieve. Those who assume anger, though violent, do not inspire awe. Those who affect friendship, though they smile, are not in unison."

"Real mourning grieves in silence. Real anger awes without expression. Real friendship is unison without the aid of smiles. Our emotions are dependent upon the original purity within; and accordingly we hold the latter in esteem.

"If applied to human affairs, then in serving our parents we are filial, in serving our prince we are loyal, in the banquet hour we are merry, in the hour of mourning we are sad.

"The object of loyalty is successful service; of a banquet, mirth; of mourning, grief; of serving parents, gratifying their wishes. If the service is accomplished, it matters not that no trace remain.

If parents be gratified, it matters not how. If a banquet results in mirth, the accessories are of no importance. If there be real grief in mourning, it matters not what ceremonies may be employed.

"Ceremonial is the invention of man. Our original purity is given to us from God. It is as it is, and cannot be changed.

Wherefore the true Sage models himself upon God, and holds his original purity in esteem. He is independent of human exigencies. Fools, however, reverse this. They cannot model themselves upon God, and have to fall back on man. They do not hold original purity in esteem. Consequently they are ever suffering the vicissitudes of mortality, and never reaching the goal. Alas! you, Sir, were early steeped in deceit, and are late in hearing the great doctrine."

Confucius, having again prostrated himself twice, arose and said, "It has been a godsend to meet you, Sir, to-day. Pray allow me to follow you as your servant, that I may benefit by your teaching. I venture to ask where you live that I may enter upon my duties and learn the great doctrine."

"I have heard," replied the old man, "that if a man is a fit companion, one may travel with him into the uttermost depths of TAO. But that if he is not a fit companion, and does not know TAO, one must avoid his company, that no harm may befall. Excuse me, I must leave you." Thereupon he pushed off his boat, and disappeared among the reeds.

"Yen Yüan then brought up the chariot, and Tzŭ Lu offered the hand-cord to Confucius. But the latter paid no attention. He waited until the ripples on the water had smoothed down and the sound of the punt-pole had died away, before he ventured to get up.

Tzŭ Lu, who was at the side of the chariot, enquired saying, "Master, I have been in your service now for a long time, yet never did I see you treat any man like this. In the presence of a ruler of ten thousand or a thousand chariots, I have never seen you treated other than with great respect, while you yourself would wear a haughty air. Yet before this old fisherman, leaning on his punt-pole, you cringe and bow and prostrate yourself twice before answering. Is not this too much? The disciples do not know what to make of it. Why this behaviour to an old fisherman?"

"Yu!" cried Confucius, resting on the bar of the chariot; "it is difficult to make anything of you. You have long studied ceremonies and duty to your neighbour, yet you have not succeeded in getting rid of the old evil nature. Come here, and I will tell you.

"To meet an elder without respect is want of ceremony. To see a Sage and not to honour him, is not to be in charity with man. Unless you are in charity with man, you cannot humble yourself before a fellow-creature. And unless you can honestly do this, you can never attain to that state of original purity; but the body will constantly suffer. Alas! there is no greater evil than not to be in charity with man. Yet in such a plight, O Yu, are you.

"Further. TAO is the source of all creation. Men have it, and live. They lose it, and die. Affairs in antagonism thereto, fail; in accordance therewith, succeed. Therefore, wherever TAO abides, there is the reverence of the true Sage. And as this old fisherman may be said to possess TAO, could I venture not to respect him?"

CHAPTER XXXII. Lieh Tzŭ.

Argument:

—Outward manifestation of inward grace—Its dangers—Self-esteem —Its errors—Inscrutability of TAO—Artificiality of Confucius— Tests of virtue—Chuang Tzŭ declines office—His death.

W HEN Lieh Tzŭ went to Ch'i, half way there he turned round and came back. Falling in with Poh Hun Wu Jen, the latter said, "How is it you are so soon back again?"

"I was afraid," replied Lieh Tzŭ.

"Afraid of what?" asked Poh Hun Wu Jen.

"Out of ten restaurants at which I ate," said Lieh Tzŭ, "five would take no payment."

"And what is there to be afraid of in that?" enquired Poh Hun Wu Jen.

"The truth within not being duly assimilated," replied Lieh Tzŭ, "a certain brightness is visible externally. And to conquer men's hearts by force of the external is to induce in oneself a disregard for authority and age which is the precursor of trouble.

"A restaurant keeper is one who lives by retailing soup. When his returns are counted up, his profit is but small, and his influence is next to nothing. But if such a man could act thus, how much more the ruler of a large State? His bodily powers worn out in the duties of his position, his mental powers exhausted by details of administration, he would entrust me with the government and stimulate me by reward. That is what I was afraid of."

"Your inner lights are good," replied Poh Hun Wu Jen; "but if you remain stationary at this point, the world will still gather around you."

Shortly afterwards Poh Hun Wu Jen went to visit Lieh Tzŭ, and lo! his court-yard was filled with boots.

Poh Hun Wu Jen stood there awhile, facing the north, his cheek all wrinkled by resting it on his staff. Then, without a word, he departed.

Upon this being announced to Lieh Tzŭ, he seized his shoes and ran out barefoot.

When he reached the outer gate, he called aloud, "Master! now that you have come, will you not give me medicine?"

"It is all over!" cried Poh Hun Wu Jen. "I told you that the world would gather around you. It is not that you can make people gather around you. You cannot prevent them from doing so. Of what use would my instruction be? Exerting influence thus unduly over others, you are by them influenced in turn. You disturb your natural constitution, and are of no further account.

None of your companions

Warn you of this.

Their paltry talk

Is but poison to a man.

They are not awake, not alive to the situation.

How should one of these help you?

"The shrewd grow weary, the wise grieve. Those who are without abilities have no ambitions. With full bellies they roam happily about, like drifting boats, not caring whither they are bound."

There was a man of the Chêng State, named Huan. He pursued his studies at a place called Ch'iu-shih. After three years only, he had graduated as a Confucianist; and like a river which fertilises its banks to a distance of nine *li*, so did his good influence reach into three families.

He caused his younger brother to graduate as a Mihist. But inasmuch as in the question of Confucianism *versus* Mihism, the father took the side of the Mihist, at the end of ten years Huan committed suicide.

Then the father dreamed that Huan appeared to him and said, "It was I who caused your son to become a Mihist.

Why give all the credit to him who is but as the fruit of an autumn pine?"

Verily God does not reward man for what he does, but for what he is. And it was in this sense that the younger brother was caused to become a Mihist.

Whereas a man who should regard his distinctive abilities as of his own making, without reference to his parents, would be like the man of Ch'i who dug a well and then wanted to keep others away from it.

Hence the saying that the men of to-day are all Huans.

Wherefore it follows that men of true virtue are unconscious of its possession. How much more then the man of TAO? This is what the ancients called escaping the vengeance of God.

The true Sage rests in that which gives rest, and not in that which does not give rest. The world rests in that which does not give rest, and not in that which does give rest.

Chuang Tzŭ said, "To know TAO is easy. The difficulty lies in the elimination of speech. To know TAO without speech appertains to the natural. To know TAO with speech appertains to the artificial. The men of old were natural, not artificial.

"Chu P'ing Man spent a large patrimony in learning under Chih Li I how to kill dragons. By the end of three years he was perfect, but there was no direction in which he could show his skill.

"The true Sage regards certainties as uncertainties; therefore he is never up in arms. Men in general regard uncertainties as certainties; therefore they are constantly up in arms. To accustom oneself to arms causes one to fly to arms on every provocation; and to trust to arms is to perish.

"The intelligence of the mean man does not rise beyond bribes and letters of recommendation. His mind is beclouded with trivialities. Yet he would penetrate the mystery of TAO and of creation, and rise to participation in the ONE. The result is that he is confounded by time and space; and that trammelled by objective existences, he fails to reach apprehension of that age before anything was.

"But the perfect man,—he carries his mind back to the period before the beginning. Content to rest in the oblivion of nowhere, passing away like flowing water, he is merged in the clear depths of the infinite.

"Alas! man's knowledge reaches to the hair on a hair, but not to eternal peace."

A man of the Sung State, named Ts'ao Shang, acted as political agent for the prince of Sung at the court of the Ch'in State. When he went thither, he had a few carriages; but the prince of Ch'in was so pleased with him that he added one hundred more.

On his return to Sung, he visited Chuang Tzŭ and said, "As for living in poverty in a dirty hovel, earning a scanty subsistence by making sandals, with shrivelled face and yellow ears,—this I could not do. Interviewing a powerful ruler, with a retinue of a hundred carriages,—that is my forte."

"When the prince of Ch'in is sick," replied Chuang Tzŭ, "and he summons his physician to open a boil or cleanse an ulcer, the latter gets one carriage. The man who licks his piles gets five. The more degrading the work, the greater the number of carriages given. You, Sir, must have been attending to his piles to get so many carriages. Begone with you!"

Duke Ai of Lu asked Yen Ho, saying, "Were I to make Confucius a pillar of my realm, would the State be profited thereby?"

"It would be most perilous!" replied Yen Ho. "Confucius is a man of outward show and of specious words. He mistakes the branch for the root.

He seeks to impress the people by an overbearing demeanour, the hollowness of which he does not perceive.

If he suits you, and you entrust him with the welfare of the State, it will only be by mistake that he will succeed.

"To cause the people to leave the true and study the false does not so much affect the people of to-day as those of coming generations. Wherefore it is better not to have Confucius.

"The difficulty of governing lies in the inability to practise self-effacement. Man does not govern as God does.

"Merchants and traders are altogether out of the pale. Or if chance ever brings them within it, their rights are never freely admitted.

"External punishments are inflicted by metal and wood. Internal punishments are inflicted by anxiety and remorse. Fools who incur external punishment are treated with metal or wood. Those who incur internal punishment are devoured by the conflict of emotions. It is only the pure and perfect man who can succeed in avoiding both."

Confucius said, "The heart of man is more dangerous than mountains and rivers, more difficult to understand than Heaven itself. Heaven has its periods of spring, summer, autumn, winter, daytime and night. Man has an impenetrable exterior, and his motives are inscrutable. Thus some men appear to be retiring when they are really forward. Others have abilities, yet appear to be worthless. Others are compliant, yet gain their ends. Others take a firm stand, yet yield the point. Others go slow, yet advance quickly.

"Those who fly to duty towards their neighbour as though thirsting after it, drop it as though something hot. Thus the loyalty of the superior man is tested by employing him at a distance, his respectfulness by employing him near at hand. His ability, by troublesome missions. His knowledge, by unexpected questions. His trustworthiness, by specification of time limits. His integrity by entrusting him with money. His fidelity, by dangerous tasks. His decorum, by filling him with wine. His morality, by placing him in disreputable surroundings. Under the application of these nine tests, the inferior man stands revealed.

"Chêng K'ao Fu, on receiving his first appointment, bowed his head. On receiving his second appointment, he hunched his back. On receiving his third appointment, he fell upon his face, walking away at the side of the path.

Who would not try to be like him?

"Yet ordinary men, on their first appointment, become selfimportant. On their second, they give themselves airs in their chariots. On their third, they call their own fathers by their personal names. Which of them can be compared with Hsü Yu of old?

"There is nothing more fatal than intentional virtue, when the mind looks outwards. For by thus looking outwards, the power of introspection is destroyed.

"There are five sources of injury to virtue. Of these, that which aims at virtue is the chief. What is it to aim at virtue? Why a man who aims at virtue practises what he approves and condemns what he does not practise.

"There are eight causes of failure, three certain elements of success. There are six sources of strength and weakness.

"Beauty, a long beard, size, height, robustness, grace, courage, daring,—these eight, in which men surpass their fellows, are therefore passports to failure.

"Modesty, compliance, humility,—these three are sure roads to success.

"Wisdom manifests itself in the external. Courage makes itself many enemies. Charity and duty towards one's neighbour incur many reproaches.

"To him who can penetrate the mystery of life, all things are revealed. He who can estimate wisdom at its true value, is wise. He who comprehends the Greater Destiny, becomes himself part of it. He who comprehends the Lesser Destiny, resigns himself to the inevitable."

A man who had been to see the prince of Sung and had been presented with ten chariots, was putting on airs in the presence of Chuang Tzŭ.

"At Ho-Shang," said the latter, "there was a poor man who supported his family by plaiting rushes. One day his son dived into the river and got a pearl worth a thousand ounces of silver. The father bade him fetch a stone and smash it to pieces, explaining that he could only have got such a pearl very deep down from under the nose of the dragon, which must have been asleep. And he said he was afraid that when the dragon waked, the boy would have a poor chance.

"Now the State of Sung is deeper than a deep river, and the prince of Sung is fiercer than a dragon. To get these chariots, you must have caught him asleep. And when he wakes, you will be ground to powder."

Some prince having invited Chuang Tzŭ to enter his service, Chuang Tzŭ said in reply to the envoy, "Sir, have you ever noticed a sacrificial ox? It is bedecked with ribbons and fares sumptuously. But when it comes to be slaughtered for the temple, would it not gladly exchange places with some neglected calf?"

When Chuang Tzŭ was about to die, his disciples expressed a wish to give him a splendid funeral. But Chuang Tzŭ said, "With Heaven and Earth for my coffin and shell; with the sun, moon, and stars as my burial regalia; and with all creation to escort me to the grave,—are not my funeral paraphernalia ready to hand?"

"We fear," argued the disciples, "lest the carrion kite should eat the body of our Master"; to which Chuang Tzŭ replied, "Above ground I shall be food for kites; below I shall be food for mole-crickets and ants. Why rob one to feed the other?

"If you adopt, as absolute, a standard of evenness which is so only relatively, your results will not be absolutely even. If you adopt, as absolute, a criterion of right which is so only relatively, your results will not be absolutely right. Those who trust to their senses become slaves to objective existences. Those alone who are guided by their intuitions find the true standard. So far are the senses less reliable than the intuitions. Yet fools trust to their senses to know what is good for mankind, with alas! but external results."

CHAPTER XXXIII. THE EMPIRE.

[Summary by early editors.]

SYSTEMS of government are many. Each man thinks his own perfect. Where then does what the ancients called the system of TAO come in? There is nowhere where it does not come in.

It may be asked whence our spirituality, whence our intellectuality. The true Sage is born; the prince is made. Yet all proceed from an original ONE.

He who does not separate from the Source is one with God. He who does not separate from the essence is a spiritual man. He who does not separate from the reality is a perfect man. He who makes God the source, and Tĕ the root, and TAO the portal, passively falling in with the modifications of his environment,—he is the true Sage.

He who practises charity as a kindness, duty to one's neighbour as a principle, ceremony as a convenience, music as a pacificator, and thus becomes compassionate and charitable,—he is a superior man.

He who regulates his conduct by law, who regards fame as an external adjunct, who verifies his hypotheses, who bases his judgment upon proof,— such men rank one, two, three, four, etc. It is thus that officials rank. In a strict sense of duty, in making food and raiment of paramount importance, in caring for and nourishing the old, the weak, the orphan, and the widow, they all exemplify the principle of true government.

Thus far-reaching was the extension of TAO among the ancients.

The companion of the gods, the purifier of the universe, it nourishes all creation, it unites the empire, it benefits the masses. Illuminating the fundamental, it is bound up with the accessory, reaching to all points of the compass and to the opposite extremes of magnitude. There is indeed nowhere where it is not!

How it enlightened the polity of past ages is evidenced in the records which historians have preserved to us. Its presence in the Canons of *Poetry*, *History*, *Rites*, and *Music*, has been made clear by many scholars of Chou and Lu. It informs the Canon of *Poetry* with its vigour, the Canon of *History* with its usefulness, the Canon of *Rites* with its adaptability, the Canon of *Music* with its harmonising influence, the Canon of *Changes* with its mysterious Principles, and the *Spring and Autumn* with its discriminations. Spread over the whole world, it is focussed in the Middle Kingdom, and the learning of all schools renders constant homage to its power.

But when the world is disorganised, true Sages do not manifest themselves, TAO ceases to exist as ONE, and the world becomes cognisant of the idiosyncrasies of the individual. These are like the senses of hearing, sight, smell, and taste,—not common to each organ. Or like the skill of various artisans,—each excellent of its kind and each useful in its turn, but not equally at the command of all.

Consequently, when a mere specialist comes forward and dogmatises on the beauty of the universe the principles which underlie all creation, the position occupied by the ancients in reference to the beauty of the universe, and the limits of the supernatural,—it follows that the TAO of inner wisdom and of outer strength is obscured and prevented from asserting itself Every one alas! regards the course he prefers as the infallible course. The various schools diverge never to meet again; and posterity is debarred from viewing the original purity of the universe and the grandeur of the ancients. For the system of TAO is scattered in fragments over the face of the earth.

Not to covet posthumous fame, nor to aim at dazzling the world, nor to pose as a benefactor of mankind, but to be a strict self-disciplinarian while lenient to the faults of others, —herein lay the TAO of the ancients.

Mih Tzŭ and Ch'in Hua Li became enthusiastic followers of TAO, but they pushed the system too far, carrying their practice to excess. The former wrote an essay *Against Music*, and another which he entitled *Economy*.

There was to be no singing in life, no mourning after death. He taught universal love and beneficence towards one's fellow men, without contentions, without censure of others. He loved learning, but not in order to become different from others. Yet his views were not those of the ancient Sages, whose music and rites he set aside.

The Yellow Emperor gave us the *Hsien-ch'ih*. Yao gave us the *Ta-chang*. Shun, the *Ta-shao*. Yü, the *Ta-hsia*. T'ang, the *Ta-hu*. Wên Wang, the *P'i-yung*. Wu Wang and Chou Kung added the *Wu*.

The mourning ceremonial of old was according to the estate of each, and determined in proportion to rank. Thus, the body of the Son of Heaven was enclosed in a seven-fold coffin. That of a feudal prince, in a five-fold coffin. That of a minister, in a three-fold coffin. That of a private individual, in a two-fold coffin. But now Mih Tzŭ would have no singing in life, no mourning after death, and a single coffin of only three inches in thickness as the rule for all alike!

Such doctrines do not illustrate his theory of universal love; neither does his practice of them establish the fact of his own personal self-respect. They may not suffice to destroy his system altogether; though it is unreasonable to prohibit singing, and weeping, and rejoicing in due season.

He would have men toil through life and hold death in contempt. But this teaching is altogether too unattractive. It would land mankind in sorrow and lamentation. It would be next to impossible as a practical system, and cannot, I fear, be regarded as the TAO of the true Sage. It would be diametrically opposed to human passions, and as such would not be tolerated by the world. Mih Tzŭ himself might be able to carry it out; but not the rest of the world. And when one separates from the rest of the world, his chances of developing an ideal State become small indeed.

Mih Tzŭ argued in favour of his system as follows:—Of old, the great Yu drained off the flood of waters, and caused rivers and streams to flow through the nine divisions of the empire and the parts adjacent thereto,— three hundred great rivers, three thousand branches, and streams without number. With his own hands he plied the bucket and dredger, in order to reduce confusion to uniformity, until his calves and shins had no hair left upon them. The wind bathed him, the rain combed him; but he marked out the nations of the world, and was in very truth a Sage. And because he thus sacrificed himself to the commonwealth, ages of Mihists to come would also wear short serge jackets and straw sandals, and toil day and night without stopping, making self-mortification their end and aim, and say to themselves, "If we cannot do this, we do not follow the TAO of Yü, and are unworthy to be called Mihists."

The disciples of Hsiang Li Ch'in, the followers of the five princes, Mihists of the south, such as K'u Huo, Chi Ch'ih, and Têng Ling,—all these studied the canon of Mih Tzŭ, but their disagreements and agreements were not identical. They called each other schismatics, and quarrelled over the "hard and white," the "like and unlike," and argued over questions of "odd and even." Chü Tzŭ was their Sage, and they wanted to canonise him as a saint, that they might carry on his doctrines into after ages. Even now these differences are not settled.

Thus we see that Mih Tzŭ and Ch'in Hua Li, while right in theory, were wrong in practice. They would merely have taught mankind to vie with each other in working the hair off their calves and shins. The evil of that system would have predominated over the good. Nevertheless, Mih Tzŭ was undoubtedly a well-meaning man. In spite of failure, with all its withering influences, he stuck to his text. He may be called a man of genius.

Not to be involved in the mundane, not to indulge in the specious, not to be overreaching with the individual, nor antagonistic to the public; but to desire the tranquillity of the world in general with a view to the prolongation of life, to seek no more than sufficient for the requirements of oneself and others, and by such a course to purify the heart, —herein lay the TAO of the ancients.

Sung Hsing and Yin Wên became enthusiastic followers of TAO. They adopted a cap, shaped like the Hua Mountain, as a badge. They bore themselves with kindly discrimination towards all things. They spoke of the passive qualities of the heart as though they had been active; and declared that whosoever could bring joy among mankind and peace within the girdle of ocean should be made ruler over them.

They suffered obloquy without noticing the insult. They preserved the people from strife. They prohibited aggression and caused arms to lie unused. They saved their generation from wars, and carried their system over the whole empire, to the delight of the high and to the improvement of the lowly. Though the world would have none of them, yet they struggled on and would not give way. Hence it was said that when high and low became tired of seeing them, they intruded themselves by force. In spite of all this, they did too much for others, and too little for themselves.

"Give us," said they, "but five pints of rice, and it will be enough." The master could not thus eat his fill; but the disciples, although starving, did not forget the world's claims.

Day and night they toiled on, saying, "Must we necessarily live? Shall we ape the so-called saviours of mankind?"

"The superior man," they say, "is not a faultfinder. He does not appropriate the credit of others. He looks on one who does no good to the world as a worthless fellow. He regards prohibition of aggressive actions and causing arms to lie unused, as external; the diminution and restraint of our passions, as internal. In all matters, great or small, subtle or gross, such is the point to which he attains."

To be public-spirited and belong to no party, in one's dealings not to be all for self, to move without being bound to a given course, to take things as they come, to have no remorse for the past, no anxiety for the future, to have no partialities, but to be on good terms with all,—herein lay the TAO of the ancients.

P'êng Mêng, T'ien P'ien, and Shên Tao, became enthusiastic followers of TAO. Their criterion was the identity of all things. "The sky," said they, "can cover but cannot support us. The earth can support but cannot cover us. TAO can embrace all things but cannot deal with particulars."

They knew that in creation all things had their possibilities and their impossibilities. Therefore they said, "Selection excludes universality. Training will not reach in all directions. But TAO is comprehensive."

Consequently, Shên Tao discarded all knowledge and selfinterest and became a fatalist.

Passivity was his guiding principle. "For," said he, "we can only know that we know nothing, and a little knowledge is a dangerous thing.

"Take any worthless fellow who laughs at mankind for holding virtue in esteem, any unprincipled vagabond who reviles the great Sages of the world, and subject him to torture. In his agony he will sacrifice positive and negative alike. If he can but get free, he will trouble no more about knowledge and forethought. Past and future will cease to exist for him, in his then neutral condition.

"Move when pushed, come when dragged. Be like a whirling gale, like a feather in the wind, like a mill-stone going round. The mill-stone as an existence is perfectly harmless. In motion or at rest it does no more than is required, and cannot therefore incur blame.

"Why? Because it is simply an inanimate thing. It has no anxieties about itself. It is never entangled in the trammels of knowledge. In motion or at rest it is always governed by fixed laws, and therefore it never becomes open to praise. Hence it has been said, 'Be as though an inanimate thing, and there will be no use for Sages.'

"For a clod cannot be without TAO,"—at which some fullblooded young buck covered the argument with ridicule by crying out, "Shên Tao's TAO is not for the living, but for the dead!"

It was the same with T'ien P'ien. He studied under P'êng Mêng; with the result that he learnt nothing.

P'êng Meng's tutor said, "Those of old who knew TAO, reached the point where positive and negative ceased to exist. That was all."

Now the bent of these men is one of opposition, which it is difficult to discuss. They act in every way differently from other people, but cannot escape the imputation of purpose.

What they call Tao is not TAO; and what they predicate affirmatively cannot escape being negative. The fact is that P'êng Mêng, T'ien P'ien, and Shên Tao, did not know TAO. Nevertheless they all had a certain acquaintance with it.

To make the root the essential, to regard objective existences as accidental, to look upon accumulation as deficiency, and to meekly accept the dispositions of Providence,—herein lay the TAO of the ancients.

Kuan Yin and Lao Tzŭ became enthusiastic followers of TAO.

They based their system upon nothingness, with ONE as their criterion. Their outward expression was gentleness and humility. Their inward belief was in unreality and avoidance of injury to all things.

347

Kuan Yin said, "Adopt no absolute position. Let externals take care of themselves. In motion, be like water. At rest, like a mirror.

Respond, like the echo.

Be subtle, as though non-existent. Be still, as though pure. Regard uniformity as peace. Look on gain as loss. Do not precede others. Follow them."

Lao Tzŭ said, "He who conscious of being strong, is content to be weak,—he shall be a cynosure of men.

"He who conscious of purity, puts up with disgrace,—he shall be the cynosure of mankind.

"He who when others strive to be first, contents himself with the lowest place, is said to accept the contumely of the world.

"He who when others strive for the substantial, contents himself with the unsubstantial, stores up nothing and therefore has abundance. There he is in the midst of his abundance which comes to him without effort on his part. He does nothing, and laughs at the artifices of others.

"He who when others strive for happiness is content with security, is said to aim at avoiding evil.

"He who makes depth of fundamental importance and moderation his rule of life, is said to crush that which is hard within him and temper that which is sharp.

"To be in liberal sympathy with all creation, and not to be aggressive towards one's fellow-men,—this may be called perfection."

O Kuan Yin! O Lao Tzŭ! verily ye were the true Sages of old.

Silence, formlessness, change, impermanence, now life, now death, heaven and earth blended in one, the soul departing, gone no one knows where: suddenly, no one knows whither, as all things go in turn, never to come back again;—herein lay the TAO of the ancients.

Chuang Tzŭ became an enthusiastic follower of TAO. In strange terms, in bold words, in far-reaching language, he gave free play to his thoughts, without following any particular school or committing himself to any particular line.

He looked on the world as so sunk in corruption that it was impossible to speak gravely. Therefore he employed "goblet words" which apply in various directions; he based his statements upon weighty authority in order to inspire confidence; and he put words in other people's mouths in order to secure breadth.

In accord with the spirit of the universe, he was at peace with all creation. He judged not the rights and wrongs of mankind, and thus lived quietly in his generation. Although his book is an extraordinary production, it is plausible and harmless enough. Although the style is most irregular, it is at the same time ingenious and attractive.

As a thinker, he is endlessly suggestive. Above, he roams with God. Below, he consorts with those who are beyond the pale of life and death, who deny a beginning and an end. In relation to the root, he speaks on a grand and extensive scale. In relation to TAO, he establishes a harmony between man and the higher powers. Nevertheless, he yields to the modifications of existence and responds to the exigencies of environment. His arguments are inexhaustible, and never illogical. He is far-reaching, mysterious, and not to be fully explored.

Hui Tzŭ was a man of many ideas. His works would fill five carts. But his doctrines are paradoxical, and his terms are used ambiguously.

He calls infinite greatness, beyond which there is nothing, the Greater One. He calls infinite smallness, within which there is nothing, the Lesser One.

He says that that which is without dimensions measures a thousand *li*.

That heaven and earth are equally low. That mountain and marsh are equally level.

That the sun at noon is the sun setting.

That when an animal is born, it dies.

That the likeness of things partly unlike is called the lesser likeness of unlikes. That the likeness of things altogether unlike is called the greater likeness of unlikes. That southwards there is no limit, and yet there is a limit. That one can reach Yüeh to-day and yet be there before. That joined rings can be separated. That the middle of the world is north of Yen and south of Yüeh.

That he loves all creation equally, just as heaven and earth are impartial to all.

Accordingly, Hui Tzŭ was regarded as a great philosopher and a very subtle dialectician; and became a favourite with the other dialecticians of the day.

He said that there were feathers in an egg.

That a fowl had three feet.

That Ying was the world.

That a dog could be a sheep. That a mare could lay eggs. That a nail has a tail.

That fire is not hot.

That mountains have mouths.

That wheels do not press down the ground.

That the eye does not see.

That the finger does not touch. That the uttermost extreme is not the end. That a tortoise is longer than a snake.

That a carpenter's square is not square.

That compasses will not make a circle.

That a round hole will not surround a square handle. That the shadow of a flying bird does not move. That there is a moment when a swiftly-flying arrow is neither moving nor at rest. That a dog is not a hound.

That a bay horse and a dun cow are three.

That a white dog is black.

That a motherless colt never had a mother.

That if you take a stick a foot long and every day cut it in half, you will never come to the end of it.

And such was the stuff which dialecticians used to argue about with Hui Tzŭ, also without ever getting to the end of it.

Huan T'uan and Kung Sun Lung were of this class. By specious premisses they imposed on people's minds and drove them into false conclusions. But though they won the battle in words, they did not carry conviction into their adversaries' hearts. Theirs were but the snares of the sophist.

Hui Tzŭ daily devoted his intelligence to such pursuits, purposely advancing some preposterous thesis upon which to dispute. That was his characteristic. He had besides a great opinion of his own wisdom, and used to say, "The universe does not hold my peer."

Hui Tzŭ makes a parade of his strength, but is devoid of any sound system. An eccentric fellow in the south, named Huang Liao, asked why the sky did not fall and the earth sink; also, whence came wind, rain, and thunder.

Hui Tzŭ was not backward in replying to these questions, which he answered unhesitatingly. He went into a long discussion on all creation, and talked away without end, though to himself he seemed to be saying very little. He supplemented this with most extraordinary statements, making it his chief object to contradict others, and being desirous of gaining fame by defeating all comers. Thus, he was never popular. Morally, he was weak; physically, he was violent. His was a dark and narrow way.

Looked at from the point of view of the TAO of the universe, the value of Hui Tzŭ may be compared with the efforts of a mosquito or a gadfly. Of what use was he to the world? As a specialist, he might have succeeded. But to let him put himself forward as an exponent of TAO, would have been dangerous indeed.

He would not however be content to be a specialist. He must needs roam insatiably over all creation, though he only succeeded in securing the reputation of a sophist.

Alas for the talents of Hui Tzŭ! He is extravagantly energetic, and yet has no success. He investigates all creation, but does not conclude in TAO. He makes a noise to drown an echo. He is like a man running a race with his own shadow. Alas!

THE END.

Printed in Great Britain
by Amazon

26805048R00205